Our National Wetland Heritage

A Protection Guide

Second Edition

**Jon Kusler, Ph.D.,
and Teresa Opheim**

AN ENVIRONMENTAL LAW INSTITUTE® PUBLICATION

The Environmental Law Institute, *ELR*, the *Environmental Law Reporter*, and *The Environmental
Forum* are registered trademarks of the Environmental Law Institute in Washington, DC

Printed in the United States of America.

ISBN 0-911937-65-X

Cover photograph of Searsport, Maine, by Bill Witt.

All divider page photographs are courtesy of the Library of Congress, with the exception of the photograph
on page 11, which is courtesy of the Old Newbury Historical Society, and the one on page 23, which is
courtesy of the Minnesota Historical Society.

Contents

Preface

This is a guide for local governments, land trusts, conservationists, landowners, teachers, students, and others who are interested in protecting and restoring wetlands through citizen and local government action. Much has been learned about wetlands since the guidebook was first published in 1983, and many excellent books are available about wetlands. Yet this is still the most comprehensive general publication specifically designed to help people take action on the local level.

Citizens and local governments must play an increasingly important wetland protection and restoration role during the next decade. Public funding cuts at the state and federal levels likely will continue, and all levels of government are placing an increased emphasis on coordinating and integrating wetland, floodplain, stormwater management, pollution control, and other water and land use-related programs in a watershed context. Local planning and management of wetlands and related water resources can provide this integration and coordination at the

grassroots level — where it is most effective. Doing so can help protect and restore wetland resources while simultaneously providing greater predictability and reduced regulatory duplication for landowners.

In this new edition, we have added more material on understanding wetlands, restoration, interpretation and education, and more. We hope the guide will inspire you to value wetlands and give you the information you need to conserve them in your own community. Our national wetland heritage can be found in your backyard, your community, and your state. We should pass on this rich legacy to our children and theirs by treating wetlands as the natural treasures they are.

Jon Kusler
Teresa Opheim

Foreword

The first edition of *Our National Wetland Heritage: A Protection Guide* represented a significant contribution to the wetland protection literature. The guide has been cited widely in the technical literature, and it has served as a model for several state wetland protection handbooks. Reprinted six times, it has been an Environmental Law Institute best seller.

This new edition of *Our National Wetland Heritage* comes at a particularly crucial time. The need for effective approaches on the local level that accommodate both wetland protection and economic growth has never been more critical. The new edition contains not only updated material from the original version that has withstood the test of time, but also more information on strategies that have come to the forefront in the last decade, including restoration and incentive programs for landowners.

This guidebook draws upon the expertise of decades. Jon Kusler, Ph.D., the Executive Director of the Association of State Wetland Managers, is a well-respected scientist, lawyer, and writer with nearly 30 years of experience working on wetlands and water resource management matters. Teresa Opheim is the Editor of ELI's *National Wetlands Newsletter* and has edited and written many other publications and articles on environmental

law and policy matters. The Environmental Law Institute not only has provided wetland professionals the popular *National Wetlands Newsletter* since 1978, but it also has conducted extensive research and numerous conferences and seminars on a variety of wetland topics, including mitigation banking and local protection strategies. In recent years, ELI has increased its public information role, helping the U.S. Environmental Protection Agency set up the toll-free National Wetlands Hotline and presenting annually the National Wetland Awards.

A force for improving environmental law and policy since 1969, ELI recognizes that our future environmental protection efforts will succeed only if we use the full range of available talent and protection options. *Our National Wetland Heritage* follows that philosophy by providing information on the wide variety of techniques available to citizens dedicated to improving wetland protection on the local level.

J. William Futrell
President
Environmental Law Institute

Acknowledgements

The Environmental Law Institute (ELI) gratefully acknowledges the financial support of Philip Morris Companies Inc. in this reprinting of *Our National Wetland Heritage: A Protection Guide*. Philip Morris' 40-year support of environmental protection programs and publications reflects the company's extensive role in agriculture and in the protection and conservation of natural resources. This reprinting would not have been possible without Philip Morris' support.

The original guide was based on a technical report prepared with funding from the U.S. Fish and Wildlife Service. ELI thanks Richard Newton, Corbin Harwood, Tim Henderson, Victor Cole, Scott Hausmann, Dr. Joseph Larson, Moira Mcdonald, Jeanne Melanson, Sara Nicholas, Margaret Strand, Philip Tabas, Gene Whitaker, and Dr. Joy Zedler for their

contributions to the first and second editions and for their helpful suggestions. Thanks also to The Nature Conservancy, the Chesapeake Bay Foundation, the Pacific Estuarine Research Laboratory at San Diego State University, the National Wildlife Federation, Ducks Unlimited, the Wetlands America Trust, the National Geographic Society, the Hackensack Meadowlands Development Commission, the Natural Resources Conservation Service, Friends of the Chicago River, and the Land Trust Alliance for their offerings of expertise and materials. At the Environmental Law Institute, Erik Meyers, James McElfish, Jessica Wilkinson, and Vanessa Reeves contributed to the revised guide. Pederson Design of Bloomington, Minnesota, provided the design and layout for the publication.

Why You Should Protect Wetlands

Chapter 1 will help you understand how wetlands are part of our natural and cultural heritage, why they are so important to our national health, and how wetland protection and restoration policies have evolved to help stem the large wetland losses that we have incurred. Use this chapter to gain an understanding of why you — as a citizen, land trust, or local government official — should be part of the efforts nationwide to protect and restore wetlands.

President George Bush, in his 1988 election campaign and later as president, endorsed a policy calling for "no net loss" of our nation's wetlands. In 1990 Congress required that the U.S. Army Corps of Engineers achieve a no net loss goal for future water resources projects. In 1993 President Clinton further endorsed the no net loss goal and called for a long-term gain of wetlands when he issued a comprehensive wetland policy.

These bipartisan pronouncements were extraordinary. Why should American presidents and Congress — plus state legislators, local governments, land trusts, and citizens — be interested in the protection and restoration of wetlands? This guidebook will help explain why and the exciting and varied ways in which Americans are moving to put into practice their beliefs in the value of wetlands.

Our wetland heritage

The United States was at one time blessed with an abundance of 225 million acres of wetland. Salt marshes lined our coasts, swamps bordered our lakes and rivers, and wetlands large and small dotted the countryside across the continent. Wetlands were an intrinsic part of the American frontier.

In ways that we are just beginning to appreciate, wetlands played a critical role in our natural resource and cultural heritage. They were key to the abundance of clean, clear water found throughout the nation. Native Americans used them widely. The Ojibway gathered wild rice from the marshes of Minnesota for countless generations. The Creek settled on and carried out agriculture on the floodplains of southern rivers. The Plains Indians constructed their winter camps below bluffs on rivers, where they were protected from bitter winter storms and had a ready supply of fish, game, fuel, and water.

Early settlers were equally dependent upon wetland resources, including the fish and game and natural crops, such as cranberries, that wetlands supplied. Colonists began building towns in and around the salt marshes of the East Coast and used the upper marshes for livestock grazing and production of salt hay. Inland marshes were used for fishing, waterfowl hunting, and game hunting.

To the west, the Spanish planted a colony among the mud flats and salt marshes of San Diego Bay. In the south, the Cajuns settled in the Louisiana wetlands and developed a distinctive culture defined in large part by the bayous that became their home. The Carolina swamps provided refuge for escaped slaves, who could live a life of freedom in them, and for a famous Revolutionary War general, who hid in them after raids on the British. Even very small wetlands have offered large contributions to our national heritage: Tiny Walden Pond in Massachusetts, for example, inspired the writings of Henry David Thoreau.

A diminished resource

Early settlers used wetlands extensively, but they had little appreciation of the role wetlands played in meeting their needs. Little by little,

"Our village life would stagnate if it were not for the unexplored forests and meadows which surround it. We need the tonic of wildness — to wade sometimes in marshes where the bittern and the meadow-hen lurk...."

— Henry David Thoreau, *Walden* (1854)

A heritage unfolds Selected events affecting wetlands

Before 1492 ~ Native Americans extensively use wetlands for hunting, fishing, shellfishing, and harvesting of natural crops (wild rice, cranberries).

Before 1492

1492 forward

1492 forward ~ European settlers use wetlands for hunting, fishing, shellfishing, harvesting of natural crops. Drainage occurs for agriculture.

1849-1860 ~ Congress enacts Swamp Land Acts, granting 15 states 65 million acres, in order to encourage them to "reclaim the lands for flood control and drainage."

1800s

1890 ~ Congress adopts the Rivers and Harbors Act, which regulates fills in navigable waters of the United States.

1900s

1900-1960 ~ Extensive drainage, filling, damming, and diking of wetlands, harvesting of timber. Half of the wetlands in the United States are lost.

1947 ~ Everglades National Park is created by Congress.

1940s

1968-1975 ~ Most coastal states adopt coastal wetland regulation statutes or include wetland protection as part of broader coastal zone or shoreland zoning statutes. Twelve states adopt freshwater wetland protection statutes. An estimated 3,000-4,000 local governments adopt wetland protection ordinances.

1960s

1963 ~ Massachusetts becomes the first state to adopt a wetland protection statute.

1968 ~ Congress adopts the National Flood Insurance Program, which provides subsidized flood insurance for communities adopting floodplain regulations consistent with national minimum standards.

1972 ~ Congress adopts the Coastal Zone Management Act, including a grant program for states.

1970s

1972 ~ Congress adopts what is now called the Clean Water Act. Included is Section 404 requiring permits from the U.S. Army Corps of Engineers for discharges into "waters of the United States." Courts later interpret this to include wetlands.

1977 ~ President Jimmy Carter adopts a Wetland Protection Order that requires federal agencies to avoid activities in wetlands, if practical.

1985 ~ The U.S. Supreme Court confirms, in *U.S. v. Riverside Bayview Homes,* that the Corps may regulate adjacent wetlands, even where no surface water or hydrological connection exists between the wetland and an adjacent water body.

1980s

1985 ~ Congress adopts "Swampbuster" provisions of the Food Security Act, whereby Congress intends to prevent the conversion of wetlands to croplands by withholding various government subsidies from farmers who drain wetlands.

1988 ~ President George Bush endorses a goal of "no net loss" of wetlands. Federal agencies begin to implement that goal in federal land management and a broad range of other programs.

1990 ~ Congress requires, in amendments to the Water Resources Development Act, that the U.S. Army Corps of Engineers achieve "no net loss" of wetlands in water projects.

1990s

1990 ~ Congress creates the Wetland Reserve Program as part of the Food Security Act reauthorization.

1993 ~ President Bill Clinton issues a wetland policy that endorses the "no net loss" goal and sets forth a broad range of recommendations for better protecting wetlands while also better meeting landowner needs.

1993-1996 ~ Federal agencies undertake a broad range of actions, including formulation of restoration plans for the Kissimmee River and the Everglades in Florida, and rivers in the Northwest. Many local and regional governments begin wetland and watershed planning efforts.

over the next two centuries, salt marshes were diked, drained, and filled. Riverine wetlands were channelized and drained. Isolated freshwater wetlands were drained widely for agriculture. By 1954, drainage, fill, and construction had destroyed almost 50 percent of our nation's wetland heritage. An estimated 45 million acres were lost to commercial development, agriculture, and other uses. More than 17 million wetland acres were destroyed in seven states alone. One researcher has estimated that between 1940 and 1969, more than 25 percent of the nation's remaining salt marshes were destroyed.

By the 1980s, wetland destruction was widespread, and many of the remaining wetlands had been damaged by water pollution, timber cutting, land drainage, and other activities. Few wetlands in the continental United States remained in a pristine state.

With this destruction and damage came unforeseen problems. Waterfowl and wildlife disappeared. Water quality deteriorated. Springs vanished. Floods increased, and damage to property skyrocketed. Construction in partially filled or drained wetlands often was subject to flooding and other natural hazards.

Efforts were made to address these problems at federal, state, and local levels. But often these efforts attempted, unsuccessfully, to address only the effects of wetland drainage — such as flooding — rather than the cause of the problem — wetland loss. State laws were adopted in the early 1900s to restrict hunting and fishing, but these did not bring back the waterfowl and fish that had lost their wetland habitat. The federal government spent more than $80 billion on water pollution control facilities from 1960 to 1989. These efforts did reduce bacterial contamination and toxics, but they addressed only a portion of the pollution problem. The federal government spent more than $12 billion to construct dams, dikes, levees, and channelization projects to reduce flood damages. The projects partially protected many areas from flooding by large flood events, but overall flood losses actually climbed because of increased runoff and increased stormwater flood losses due to destruction of wetlands, fills, grading, and other disturbance of natural drainage and retention areas.

Protection begins

Early on, the importance of wetlands to wildlife, fisheries, and broader ecosystems was recognized by scientists. Beginning early in the twentieth century, the first national and state efforts were made to protect some of the larger wetlands as national parks or wildlife refuges. Everglades National Park was established in 1947 to protect this wetland ecosystem. Other major wetlands that are part of the national refuge system include Klamath Basin (in south-central Oregon and northeastern California), Okefenokee (in southeastern Georgia), and Aransas (on the coast of southeast Texas).

> ❧
>
> **Salt marshes once lined our coasts, swamps bordered our lakes and rivers, and wetlands large and small dotted the countryside across the continent.**

In the 1960s and early 1970s, scientists' recognition of the importance of wetlands to water quality grew, although public recognition of this and a broad range of other heritage values came more slowly. Congress adopted several environmental protection measures during this time, including the National Environmental Policy Act, the Federal Water Pollution Control Act, and the Coastal Zone Management Act. Although wetland protection was not their primary goal, these measures were important in establishing the overall mechanisms to protect wetlands. The most important of these laws for wetland protection was the Federal Water Pollution Control Act, now known as the Clean Water Act. That Act established a comprehensive nationwide pollution control system by regulating pollution sources, including fills and discharges into waters of the United States. In its early regulations, the U.S. Army Corps of Engineers, the administrator of the dredge and fill program, defined its jurisdiction to cover only traditionally navigable waters. However, as a result of a 1975 court decision, *Natural Resources Defense Council v. Callaway*, the Corps revised its regulations to include adjacent wetlands and isolated waters.

During the late 1960s and early 1970s, many states and local governments also adopted environmental protection statutes and regulations, including wetland and floodplain regulations, pollution controls, coastal zone management planning and regulatory efforts, lake protection and shoreland zoning, and scenic and wild river protection regulations. Wetland protection often was a component of lake and river protection and coastal zone management efforts.

Despite the adoption of these laws, destruction of wetlands continued into the 1980s at a slowed but continued pace for a number of reasons. First, there were major contradictions in national, state, and local policy. Federal financial assistance for draining wetlands continued into the 1970s, despite the adoption of wetland protection regulations. Second, many activities, such as the drainage of wetlands for agricultural activities, were not regulated by regulations. Third, regulatory permits were evaluated on a case-by-case basis, with most permits granted and little consideration given to how a variety of wetland uses would cumulatively result in wetland degradation. And fourth, although efforts were made to regulate fills in individual wetlands, little was done to protect the broader watershed that is essential to wetland ecosystems.

The no net loss goal

Continued loss of wetlands combined with complexity and contradictions in wetland policy at all levels of government prompted the Conservation Foundation to convene a National Wetland Forum in 1987. This Forum, which included leaders from states, environmental organizations, development interests, forestry and agricultural interests, academic institutions, and federal agencies, issued a report in 1988. The report contained a broad range of recommendations for better protecting and restoring wetlands while, simultaneously, better meeting landowners' needs. Most notably, the report called for an interim goal of "no overall net loss of the nation's wetland base" and a long-term goal of "increasing the quantity and quality of the nation's wetlands resource base."

Along with the Bush and Clinton Administrations, many states or local governments explicitly or implicitly have endorsed the no net loss goal. Congress and federal agencies have adopted a broad range of other wetland protection measures as well. These strengthened federal and state measures to protect wetlands, including adoption of the no net loss goal, have been enthusiastically endorsed by environmental organizations, wetland scientists, and many federal, state, and local agency staff.

Consensus and criticism

Public awareness of the value of wetlands has grown steadily over the last three decades. However, during this same period, opposition to wetland regulations also has increased, resulting in powerful conflicts in Congress, in state legislatures, and at local levels.

Most people now agree with the need to protect wetlands. But some believe existing federal and state approaches are unfair, duplicative, uncoordinated, and do not provide sufficient predictability and flexibility to landowners. These critics claim that they do not have an adequate voice in the system and that regulations are economically burdensome. They are particularly critical of regulations as they apply to millions of small, freshwater wetlands throughout the landscape that are not adjacent to rivers, streams, lakes, or the ocean. They also are critical of regulations as they affect forested wetlands, which also do not fit some people's traditional concept of wetlands. These wetlands often are valuable from an ecological perspective, but defining their boundaries (delineation) and mapping and managing them is difficult, due to fluctuating water levels.

Looking to the future, better ways must be found to both protect and restore wetlands and satisfy the critics' concerns. Experience at all levels of government over the last two decades suggests that there are practical ways to reconcile the protection and restoration of wetlands (including smaller, isolated ones) with landowners' needs. Improved education is needed so that citizens know why and how wetlands are valuable. Mapping and delineation efforts and technical assistance must be improved, so that wetland boundaries are clear. Increased financial incentives are needed for citizens. Duplication and inconsistencies in federal, state, and local wetland regulations must be reduced, and wetland protection needs to be better coordinated with other techniques, such as advanced land use and watershed planning.

All of these measures require committed participation by you, as a citizen, a member of a land trust, or a local government official.

Causes of wetland losses

❋ Drainage for crop and timber production; mosquito and flood control; commercial, industrial, and other development; other purposes

❋ Dredging and stream channelization for reservoir and navigation channel maintenance, access channels, flood protection, and coastal housing developments

❋ Dispersion of water inflows for irrigation, flood control, and other purposes

❋ Construction of dikes, dams, levees, and seawalls for flood control, irrigation, and storm surge protection

❋ Filling for solid waste disposal; roads; bridges; and commercial, residential, and industrial development

❋ Discharges of materials into waters, including herbicides, pesticides, and other pollutants from industrial plants and agriculture

❋ Grading for road construction, residential, industrial, and commercial development and other purposes

❋ Excessive nutrient loadings from domestic sewage and agricultural runoff

❋ Sediments from dredging, filling, agriculture, and land development

❋ Surface water extraction and groundwater pumping for municipal water supplies and irrigation, reducing water supply to wetlands

❋ Mining or disturbance of wetland soils for sand and gravel, coal, peat, and other minerals

❋ Cutting or other removal of wetland vegetation for agricultural, forestry, land development, and other purposes

Continued protection and restoration of the Everglades, Big Cypress, Great Dismal Swamp, the Mississippi Delta Bayous, and other large and nationally known wetlands is essential. But protection and restoration of smaller, locally significant wetlands throughout the American landscape also are critical. We have the remnants of our national heritage, and these remnants often are in our backyards, where clean water and clean air count the most.

Americans have come to realize over the last three decades that wetlands mean a lot to our communities, to how we work, how we play, and what we value. In the tradition of Lewis and Clark, canoeists paddle the small rivers and creeks near their urban homes. Rafters treasure the riverine wetlands that provide respite from the rapids of the Colorado River, as did the Civil War Major John Wesley Powell more than a hundred years ago. As their ancestors did before them, children delight in the call of the killdeer and the sight of the heron, and duck hunters stir the sediment of marshes in the early morning dawn.

Functions and values

"Wetland functions and values" is a commonly used phrase among wetland experts. "Functions" exist in the absence of society and normally are part of the self-sustaining properties of an ecosystem. "Values" are the goods and services that emanate from functions. A wetland's value indicates how important we decide a wetland's functions are to us. (For example, the removal of dissolved substances is a biogeochemical function that a wetland may perform. The maintenance of water quality is the resulting value.) Wetlands also are subject to a variety of natural hazards, and development in them can cause nuisances and threaten public safety as well as damage private property.

Wetlands are important to you and your community because they have the following functions and values:

Flood conveyance. There are more than 3.2 million miles of rivers, streams, and creeks in the United States. They form a drainage network in every state and every climate throughout the nation. All rivers, creeks, and streams (even those in deserts) are subject to periodic flooding. When floods occur, riverine wetlands and adjacent floodplain lands form natural floodways that convey waters from upstream to downstream points. Fills or structures that are located within floodway areas block flood flows, causing increased flood heights on adjacent and upstream lands and increased downstream velocities.

Barriers to waves and erosion. Coastal wetlands and those inland wetlands adjoining larger lakes and rivers reduce the impact of storm tides and waves before they reach adjoining "upland" areas. Waves instead break on beach and wetland areas, dissipating much of their energy. Wetland vegetation, with its complicated root systems, binds and protects the soil against erosion.

Mangrove forests are particularly resistant. A study of coral islands off the coast of British Honduras (now called Belize) dramatically demonstrated the importance of mangroves. After Hurricane Hattie struck in 1961, with 200 mile-per-hour winds and tides 15 feet above normal, islands covered with natural vegetation suffered little damage and actually accumulated new material left by the storm. However, islands that previously had been cleared of natural vegetation were severely eroded. Since 1830, at least 20 of the cleared and farmed islands of that Central American country have totally disappeared because of the erosive force of tropical storms.

Flood storage. Inland wetlands store water during times of rainfall and flood and slowly release it to downstream areas, lowering flood peaks. To help grasp the importance of wetlands in flood storage, consider this fact: A one-acre wetland will hold 330,000 gallons of water if flooded to a depth of one foot. Storage of rain and flood waters is important to all landowners (even those who live in deserts), since intense rains and snow melt occur throughout the entire nation. Wetlands may be important in temporarily storing water from even modest rains that otherwise would flood basements, parking lots, or roads. They also can be important for larger flood events. When severe floods struck eastern Pennsylvania, sweeping out hundreds of bridges, many bridges were destroyed, but two were left standing below Cranberry Bog, a natural area protected by The Nature Conservancy.

A study by the Massachusetts Water Resources Commission on the Neponsit River indicated that the loss of 10 percent of the wetlands along that river would result in flood stage increases of one and a half feet, and the loss of 50 percent of the wetlands would increase the flood stage by three feet. The Minnesota Department of Natural Resources has computed that it costs $300 to replace each acre-foot of flood water storage lost in that state. (In other words, if development eliminates a one-acre wetland that naturally holds a depth of 12 inches of water during a storm, the replacement cost would be $300.) Based on a 1972 study comparing parts of the Charles River in Massachusetts, the U.S. Army Corps of Engineers determined that the loss of 8,422 acres of wetlands near Boston within the Charles River Basin would have resulted in annual flood damage of more than $17 million. For this reason, the Corps chose to preserve the wetlands instead of constructing extensive flood control facilities.

Erosion and sediment control. Wetlands stabilize the banks and beds of drainage ditches, creeks, small streams, seeps and springs, and oceans, reducing erosion and sedimentation in adjacent waters. When wetlands reduce flood flows and the velocity of flood waters, they reduce erosion and allow flood waters to drop their sediment. Wetland vegetation filters and holds sediment that otherwise would enter lakes, rivers, ponds, and the oceans. Unretarded, sediment may result in rapid filling of lakes and reservoirs, and the destruction of fish habitats.

Pollution prevention and control. Wetlands that are adjacent to coasts, lakes, and rivers intercept sediments, nutrients, and

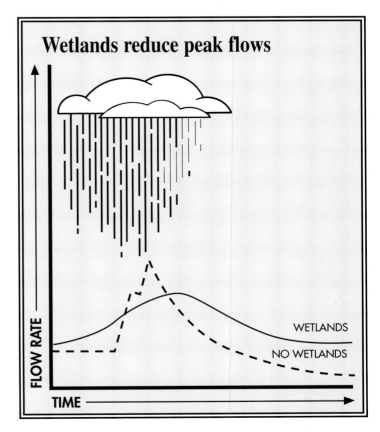

other natural and man-made pollutants and protect water bodies. These wetlands also filter sediment, organic matter, and chemicals from a wide range of pollution sources in flowing streams and lakes, while microorganisms in the wetlands utilize dissolved nutrients and break down organic matter. A study of Tinicum Marsh in Pennsylvania revealed significant reductions in BOD (biochemical oxygen demand), phosphorus, and nitrogen within three to five hours in samples taken from heavily polluted waters flowing through a 512-acre marsh. A study on the effects of a wetland adjacent to Lake Wingra in Wisconsin indicated that 200-300 kilograms per year of phosphorus now entering the lake would have been trapped, had not 300 wetland acres been destroyed by development. A number of investigators now are studying the use of man-made or natural wetlands as tertiary treatment facilities for domestic, industrial, and storm water wastes.

Fish and shellfish production. Salt marshes provide protected nursing areas for the fingerlings of important commercial fishes such as cod, herring, and mackerel. In 1991, the dockside value of fish landed in the United States was $3.3 billion, which served as the basis of a $26.8 billion fishery processing and sales industry. Louisiana's marshes alone produced an annual commercial fish and shellfish harvest of 1.2 billion pounds, worth $244 million, in 1991. Investigators have estimated that 60 percent of the species of commercial importance either pass their entire lives in estuarine environments or require estuaries as nursery grounds. Inland wetlands also are important to freshwater fisheries as spawning grounds for species such as northern pike and, to a lesser extent, walleyes and muskies.

In addition, coastal wetlands are important sources of nutrients for fin and shellfish. The net primary productivity (net plant growth) of salt marshes exceeds that of all but the most intensively cultivated agricultural areas. Estimates of 10 tons per acre per year for cattail have been made. When wetland plants die, bacterial and fungal decomposers transform the tissues into minute fragments of food and vitamin-rich detritus, which are carried into tidal creeks, bays, and offshore waters. Many species of fish and shellfish depend upon this detritus.

Habitat for waterfowl and other wildlife, including rare and endangered species. Both coastal and inland wetlands provide essential breeding, nesting, feeding, and predator escape habitats for many forms of waterfowl, mammals, and reptiles. The land-water interface, including adjacent buffer areas, is among the richest wildlife habitat in the world. This concentration of wildlife is due to the presence of abundant water needed by all life forms, rich and diverse vegetation that serves as the basis for food chains, and cover provided by both wetland and shore vegetation.

Many wildlife species, including ducks, geese, swans, herons, marsh hawks, egrets, muskrats, minks, beavers, otters, and alligators, depend upon wetlands for survival. Other species, such as ospreys, marsh birds, song birds, pheasants, grouse, bobcats, raccoons, and minks, use wetlands for nesting, resting, or feeding areas.

The habitat value of a wetland depends upon the following factors: the diversity and arrangement of vegetation; the amount of open water; the relationship of the wetland to topographic features, lakes, streams, and other wetlands; the size of the wetland and surrounding habitat; water chemistry; and the permanence of the wetland.

Almost 35 percent of all rare and endangered animal species are either located in wetland areas or are dependent upon them, although wetlands only constitute about 5 percent of the nation's lands. In addition, many endangered plant species also require wetland habitat. A few examples of wetland-dependent endangered species include the least tern, brown pelican, and whooping crane.

Recreation. Twenty million Americans enjoy recreational fishing. Many sport and commercial fishes are dependent upon wetlands as sources for food or spawning. More than two million Americans hunt waterfowl, which depend on wetlands for feeding, breeding, and resting. All together, more than half of all U.S. adults — 98 million people — hunt, fish, birdwatch, or photograph wildlife. These activities, which all rely on healthy wetlands, added an estimated $59.5 million to the national economy in 1991.

Water supply. With the growth of urban centers and dwindling water supplies, wetlands increasingly are important as a source of groundwater and surface water. A study of wetlands in Massachusetts indicates that at least 60 Massachusetts cities and towns have municipal water production wells in or very near wetlands and that the number of wetlands underlaid by productive groundwater supplies is large. Wetlands also store and purify surface waters that may be extracted at downstream points.

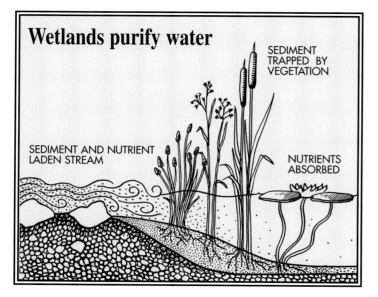

Wetlands purify water

SEDIMENT TRAPPED BY VEGETATION

SEDIMENT AND NUTRIENT LADEN STREAM

NUTRIENTS ABSORBED

Wetland functions

Wetlands function	How wetlands perform function	Factors determining the importance of function	Threats
Flood conveyance	Some wetlands (particularly those immediately adjacent to rivers and streams) serve as floodway areas by conveying flood flows from upstream to downstream points.	Stream characteristics, wetland topography, and size, vegetation, location of wetland in relationship to river or stream, existing encroachment on floodplain (such as dikes, dams, and levees)	If flood flows are blocked by fills, dikes, or other structures, increased flood heights and velocities result, causing damage to adjacent upstream and downstream areas.
Wave barriers	Wetland vegetation, with massive root and rhizome systems, binds and protects soil.	Location of wetland adjacent to coastal waters, lakes, and rivers; wave intensity; type of vegetation; and soil type	Removal of vegetation increases erosion and reduces capacity to moderate wave intensity.
Flood storage	Some wetlands store and slowly release flood waters.	Wetland area relative to watershed, wetland position within watershed, surrounding topography, soil infiltration capacity in watershed, wetland size and depth, stream size and characteristics, outlets (size, depth), vegetation type, substrate type	Fill or dredging of wetlands reduces their flood storage capacity.
Sediment control	Wetland vegetation binds soil particles and retards the movement of sediment in slowly flowing water.	Depth and extent of wetland, wetland vegetation (including type, condition, density, growth patterns), soil texture type and structure, normal and peak flows, wetland location relative to sediment of vegetated buffer	Destruction of wetland topographic contours or vegetation decreases wetland capacity to filter surface runoff and act as sediment traps. This increases water turbidity and siltation of downstream reservoirs, storm drains, and storm channels.
Pollution control	Wetlands act as settling ponds and remove excess nutrients and other pollutants by filtering and causing chemical breakdown of pollutants.	Type and size of wetland, wetland vegetation (including type, condition, density, growth patterns), source and type of pollutants, water course, size, water volume, streamflow rate, microorganisms	Destruction of wetland contours or vegetation decreases natural pollution capability, resulting in lowered water quality for downstream lakes, streams, and other waters.
Fish and wildlife habitat	Wetlands provide water, food, and nesting and resting areas. Coastal wetlands contribute detritus needed by fish and shellfish in nearby estuarine and marine waters.	Wetland type and size, dominant wetland vegetation and diversity of life forms, location of wetland within watershed, surrounding habitat type, juxtaposition of wetlands, water chemistry, water quality, water depth, existing uses	Fills, dredging, damming, and other alterations destroy and damage flora and fauna and decrease productivity. Dam construction is an impediment to fish movement.
Recreation (water-based)	Wetlands provide wildlife and water for recreational uses.	Wetland vegetation, wildlife, water quality, accessibility to users, size, relative scarcity, facilities provided, surrounding land forms, vegetation, land use, degree of disturbance, availability of similar wetlands, distribution	Fill, dredging, or other interference with wetlands will cause loss of area for boating, swimming, bird watching, hunting, and fishing.
Water supply (surface)	Some wetlands store flood waters, reducing the timing and amount of surface runoff. They also filter pollutants. Some serve as sources of domestic water supply.	Precipitation, watershed runoff characteristics, wetland type and size, outlet characteristics, location of wetland in relationship to other water bodies	Fills or dredging cause accelerated runoff and increase pollution.
Aquifer recharge	Some wetlands store water and release it slowly to groundwater deposits. Many other wetlands are discharge areas for a portion or all of the year.	Location of wetland relative to water table, fluctuations in water table, geology (including type and depth and permeability), size of wetland depth. Aquifer storage capacity, groundwater flow, runoff retention measures	Fills or drainage may destroy wetland aquifer recharge capability, thereby reducing base flows to streams and groundwater supplies for domestic, commercial, or other uses.

Source: David Lavine et al., Evaluation of Inland Wetland and Water Course Functions, *Connecticut Inland Wetland Project (1974) (modified)*

Values and hazards

Values

Isolated wetlands

1. Habitat for both upland and wetland species of wildlife
2. Flood water retention
3. Sediment and nutrient retention
4. Scenic beauty

Lake margin wetlands

1. See values for isolated wetlands, above
2. Removal of sediment and nutrients from inflowing waters
3. Fish spawning area

Riverine wetlands

1. See values for isolated wetlands, above
2. Sediment control, stabilization of river banks
3. Flood conveyance

Estuarine and coastal wetlands

1. See values for isolated wetlands, above
2. Fish and shellfish habitat and spawning areas
3. Nutrient source for marine fisheries
4. Protection from erosion and storm surges

Barrier island

1. Habitat for dune-associated plant and animal species
2. Scenic beauty

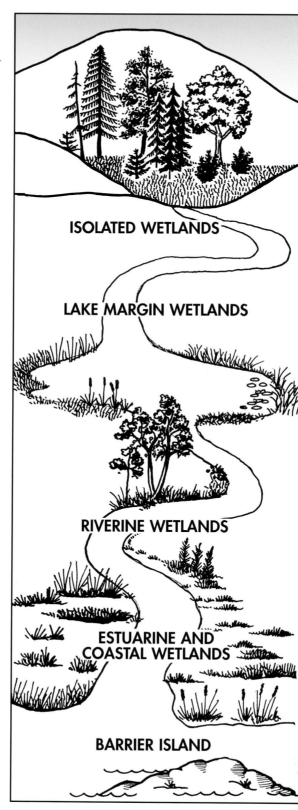

ISOLATED WETLANDS

LAKE MARGIN WETLANDS

RIVERINE WETLANDS

ESTUARINE AND COASTAL WETLANDS

BARRIER ISLAND

Hazards

Isolated wetlands

1. Flooding and drainage problems for roads and buildings due, in some instances, to widely fluctuating surface water and groundwater levels
2. Serious limitations for on-site waste disposal
3. Limited structural-bearing capacity of soils for roads and buildings due to high content of organic materials

Lake margin wetlands

1. See hazards for isolated wetlands, above

Riverine wetlands

1. See hazards for isolated wetlands, above
2. Flood conveyance areas subject to deep inundation and high velocity flows
3. Sometimes erosion areas

Estuarine and coastal wetlands

1. See hazards for riverine wetlands, above
2. Often severe flood hazard due to tidal action, riverine flooding, storm surges, and wave action
3. Sometimes severe erosion area in major flood due to wave action

Barrier island

1. Often high energy wind and wave zone
2. Often severe erosion problem

Food production. Because of their high natural productivity, both tidal and inland wetlands have unrealized food production potential for harvesting of natural crops. As population grows, this capability may become of international significance. In the past, coastal marshes were extensively harvested for salt hay. While this practice has declined, some harvesting continues both for feed and for use as mulch since salt hay does not contain the weed seeds that plague inland hay. Research indicates that cattails hold enormous potential for production of protein. One researcher suggests that cattails may yield up to 150 tons per acre and produce 35 tons of cattail flour. Coastal aquaculture, such as propagation of oysters, also has considerable potential.

Historic, archaeological values. Old settlements of Native peoples are located in coastal and inland wetlands, which served as sources of fish and shellfish. Wetlands such as the Everglades in Florida and the Concord Marshes in Massachusetts bear important historical associations as wildlife and hunting areas, battlegrounds, and as sites of early settlements.

Education and research. Both tidal and coastal marshes provide educational opportunities for nature observation and scientific study. Examples include the National Estuarine Research Reserves, the Orono Bog used by the University of Maine, wetlands at the University of Wisconsin Arboretum, and the Mamacoke Island Marshes of the Connecticut Arboretum, used by Connecticut College.

Open space and aesthetic values. Both tidal and inland wetlands are areas of great diversity and beauty and provide open space for recreational and visual enjoyment. Visual values depend upon wetland type, size, landform, contrast, and diversity, as well as associated water body size and type, surrounding land use, and other factors.

Timber production. Forested wetlands are an important source of timber, despite the physical problems of timber removal. The value of standing timber in southern wetland forests has been estimated at $8 billion.

Natural hazards

Activities in wetlands may be subject to natural hazards, and they may increase hazards on other lands:

Flood hazards. The importance of wetlands in conveying flood flows, storing flood waters, and acting as storm barriers was noted above. Activities in wetlands may increase flood and erosion damages on other lands, and be themselves subject to flooding and other natural hazards.

Flood hazard maps prepared by the National Flood Insurance Program reveal that many coastal, estuarine, riverine, and lake fringe wetlands are subject to serious flooding due to

> ❧
> **Duplication and inconsistencies in federal, state, and local wetland regulations must be reduced, and wetland protection needs to be better coordinated with other techniques, such as advanced land use and watershed planning.**

deep and frequent inundation by floods, storm surges, and high tides. Coastal wetlands are particularly subject to severe hazards. During extreme flood events, such areas may be flooded to heights of 10 to 15 feet or more and be buffeted by large waves.

Coastal flood problems grow more serious as the world sea level slowly rises. In some instances, coastal land actually sinks due to compaction of peat, loss of water from aquifers, or tectonic adjustments of the earth's crust. Sea level is rising at the rate of about three inches a century on a worldwide basis, due to the melting of glaciers. The combined effect of sea level increase and sinking of land areas is particularly serious in areas such as the Louisiana coast and Galveston, Texas.

The filling of coastal wetlands or the construction of minor sea walls may increase flood problems. Filling often steepens the gradient of beach, causing waves to break destructively upon the newly created lands. In extreme flood events, sea walls may tear free and add to the enormous force of incoming storm waves and high-velocity flood flows.

The filling of inland wetlands also increases riverine flood problems. Fills and development within these areas block the passage of flood waters, thereby increasing flood heights and velocities on other lands. The significance of wetland flood conveyance and storage differs, depending upon the type of stream and its flood characteristics, watershed characteristics, the location of the wetland in the stream, the configuration and width of the floodway, and alternative flood storage areas. Wetlands located along small, steep gradient streams in hilly and mountainous regions often are small and subject to high velocity and short flooding. In contrast, wetlands located along large, low-gradient rivers such as the Mississippi often are large and subject to low velocity and longer flooding. Even here, however, development near the stream channel may cumulatively block flood flows and destroy flood storage, increasing flood heights in downstream areas.

Ephemeral wetlands, which exist only in the spring or times of heavy rainfall, also are subject to flooding. Buildings located in ephemeral wetlands may be subject to basement flooding and drainage problems as well as inundation. Efforts to reduce flooding through construction of ditches or installation of drain tiles with outlets to downstream waters increase runoff and decrease groundwater recharge.

Erosion. Development in coastal mangrove forests and other coastal wetland vegetation often is subject to severe flood erosion and wind damage and may increase damage to backlying lands. Coastal and inland wetlands bind the soil and reduce water velocities. Eroded material is trapped in wetland vegetation, protecting adjacent lakes and streams.

Hazards due to lack of soil support. Because of the high organic and water content of soils in coastal and inland wetlands, dwellings, other structures, roads, and bridges built in wetlands often have structural support problems. Organic and waterlogged soils slowly compact under pressure, resulting in differential settling of construction. In some instances, this may cause flooding, and, more often, cracks and shifts in building foundations and walls.

Hazards due to limitations for on-site waste disposal. Septic tanks and solid absorption systems operate poorly in the high groundwater and organic soils found in wetlands. The plumbing and sanitary codes of many states require that the bottom of the soil absorption system be at least four feet above high groundwater. Failure of a septic tank system may result in surface discharges of raw sewage, causing health hazards, odors, and pollution of nearby waters.

At the end of the 20th century, considerable progress has been made in the United States in adopting wetland protection and restoration policies at federal, state, and local levels. However, development continues at a rapid pace in this country, and all of our creativity is needed to secure a future of financial well being as well as wetland and other natural resources wealth.

For those working on the local level, there is much to do. Landowners often are unaware of wetland protection and restoration techniques. There are serious gaps in federal and state programs and limitations upon funding and staff. Many communities, if they do have a local protection strategy at all, need to rethink and refine it to fit with modern-day needs.

Only with local action can long-term protection of our wetland heritage occur. On the local level, people know which protection and restoration tools will work best in their communities. On the local level, the friendships and acquaintances exist to build lasting coalitions.

Endnotes

The Conservation Foundation, *Protecting America's Wetlands: An Action Agenda* (1988).

L. Cowardin et al., *Classification of Wetlands and Deepwater Habitats of the United States* (U.S. Fish and Wildlife Service, 1979). FWS/OBS-79-31.

T. Dahl, *Wetlands Losses in the United States 1780s to 1980s* (U.S. Fish and Wildlife Service, 1990).

W. Mitch and J. Gosselink, *Wetlands,* second edition (Von Nostrand Reinhold, 1993).

National Research Council, *Restoration of Aquatic Ecosystems* (National Academy Press, 1992).

W. Niering, *Wetlands: The Audubon Society Nature Guides* (Alfred A. Knopf, 1985).

W. Niering, *Wetlands of North America* (Thomasson-Grant, 1991).

R. Tiner, Jr., *Wetlands of the United States: Current Status and Recent Trends* (U.S. Fish and Wildlife Service, National Wetlands Inventory, 1984).

1600s: Massachusetts

The Marsh as the Commons

Portions of the narrow barrier island of sand dune and marsh that today is Plum Island in Massachusetts was included in a land grant of 1621–22 and was treated for the first 150 years of colonial times as a resource. Open pastureland was limited, and marshes of the island, which extends from the Merrimack River to the Ipswich River, were offered for grazing the colonists' livestock. The salt hay from the marshes also was used for bedding and mulching and as insulation to bank against the foundations of houses.

Early on, the island contained three settlements: Newbury, Rowley, and Ipswich, each of which jostled with each other to lay claim to the island's resources. There was no fencing on the island, and much contention developed. Ipswich complained that the horses and cattle placed on the island by Newbury residents to forage during the winter months were destroying the vegetation and " . . . would be the ruin and utter destruction of the whole island. . . ." Even in colonial times, there was concern about erosion, and the selectmen tried through regulations to prevent the destruction of the dunes lest the shifting sands overrun the valuable salt meadows.

— from Plum Island: The Way It Was, by Nancy V. Weare (Newburyport Press: 1993)

Understanding the Resource

To protect and restore wetlands effectively, you must understand them. Chapter 2 explains what wetlands are and discusses their various types, how they have been formed, and some of their critical characteristics. Use the chapter to help you design your protection and restoration efforts and to ascertain whether those efforts are consistent with the scientific principles discussed here.

Wetlands are transitional areas between uplands and aquatic areas such as lakes, rivers, estuaries, and oceans. They are subject to permanent or temporary flooding (inundation) or saturation that changes the character of the vegetation and soils.

Wetlands vary drastically in size, location, hydrologic conditions, and physical, chemical, and biological processes and characteristics. The salt marshes of New Jersey are wetlands, as are the playas of Texas and the vernal pools of California. Some wetlands are dry for much of the year; others have had standing water for a thousand years. Wetlands can be small, isolated depressions that contain stable hydrology and the same soil type and vegetation. They also can be large complexes, with a range of soils, hydrology, and vegetation.

Different definitions of "wetland" have been adopted at federal, state, and local levels, depending on the context and the management objectives. Three of the most common definitions applied at the federal level appear in the box on page 15. These three include the U.S. Fish and Wildlife Service's definition, which is used in the National Wetland Classification System and for the National Wetland Inventory; the definition used for the federal regulatory system, the Section 404 program; and the definition used by the U.S. Department of Agriculture in its program to encourage wetland

conservation (the Swampbuster program). (Where a farmer needs both a wetland determination from the Section 404 and Swampbuster programs, federal agencies have agreed that the Department of Agriculture's wetland definition will be used on agricultural lands to avoid duplication.)

The three definitions cover quite similar areas on the ground, but there are differences. The Fish and Wildlife Service definition encompasses the most aquatic area, because it includes lands submerged up to two meters. On the other hand, the Swampbuster definition in some instances encompasses more infrequently flooded land because it emphasizes soils.

A recent National Academy of Sciences study concerning wetland definition suggested a fourth definition for wetlands, which emphasizes the essential common feature of all wetland definitions — wetness and the characteristics that follow from such wetness:

A wetland is an ecosystem that depends on constant or recurrent, shallow inundation or saturation at or near the surface of the substrate. The minimum essential characteristics of a wetland are recurrent, sustained inundation or saturation at or near the surface and the presence of physical, chemical, and biological features reflective of recurrent, sustained inundation or saturation. Common diagnostic features of wetlands are hydric soils and hydrophytic vegetation. These features will be present except where specific physicochemical, biotic, or anthropogenic factors have removed them or prevented their development.

Over a period of years, federal and state agencies have developed a variety of delineation manuals to help them apply these wetland definitions in their programs. These manuals differ somewhat but all use a combination of water, substrate (soils), and vegetation to characterize wetlands. The manual presently used by most federal agencies is the 1987 U.S. Army Corps of Engineers' *Manual for the Delineation of Jurisdictional Wetlands.*

Origins

Wetlands can best be understood in terms of the hydrologic cycle and their hydrologic settings. In the hydrological cycle, water continuously moves from the sea to the atmosphere to the land and then back to the sea again.

At coastal locations, the water in wetlands comes principally from the sea through daily tidal action, storm surges, seiches, and wave action. Sea water may travel some distance inland along surface water and in groundwater systems. In estuarine environments, the water comes both from the sea and inland sources. Some inland wetlands are connected closely with lakes and streams, and many others are isolated or partially isolated from surface drainage and fed by groundwater discharge. Precipitation also contributes water to inland wetlands.

Wetlands are formed in five main ways:

Glaciers. By melting, scraping, scooping, scouring, and depositing soil, glaciers created many of the wetlands located in the northern tier of the United States 9-12,000 years ago. Glaciers created wetlands in several ways: As they receded, they left chunks of ice, which melted and created pits and depressions in glacial moraines, till, and outwash. Lakes and wetlands were formed where the depressions intersected the groundwater table or where fine clay and organics sealed their bottoms and runoff waters collected. The majority of the smaller wetlands in states where glaciers passed through — including Alaska, Maine, Michigan, Minnesota, New York, North Dakota, Washington, and Wisconsin — were formed in this way.

In addition, glaciers dammed rivers, often creating glacial lakes, sometimes thousands of square miles in area. Once the ice retreated, the lakes were partially drained, which resulted in extensive low-lying areas with peat deposits. Many of the mid-sized to largest wetlands in the glaciated states were formed this way.

In some places, glaciers scooped out and scoured river valleys and soft bedrock deposits, creating, in some instances, large, deep lakes such as the Great Lakes and New York's Finger Lakes and, in others, shallow depressions and wetland areas, including many wetlands on the Canadian Shield.

Rising and falling sea levels. Coastal and estuarine fringe wetlands (which are defined below) form wherever the ocean inundates a gently sloping beach of sand, gravel, silt, or other particulate matter. Wetlands are largest where they are protected from wave action by a harbor, barrier island, or reef, although they also form in some open coastal locations such as the Gulf of

> **Some wetlands are dry for much of the year; others have had standing water for a thousand years.**

Mexico. For example, wetlands are common along the mouths of rivers and streams, and the low-elevation topography along the Atlantic and Gulf coasts. Wetland vegetation traps sand and other sediment, gradually building the wetland to a higher elevation than the adjacent open water. The deposit of organic matter and the formation of peat add to this process. Rising and falling sea levels (which are due to the formation and subsequent melting of glaciers near the poles) result in the gradual inland and shoreward migration of coastal and estuarine wetlands.

Erosion and deposition by rivers. Floodplain wetlands, such as those along the Mississippi River, are formed when streams downcut into bedrock and soil and alluvium are deposited on adjacent lands during floods. Major wetlands are found along mature streams with low gradients and large sediment loadings. These wetlands periodically are flushed and scoured by major floods.

Other natural processes. Wetlands form in other ways as well. For example, wetlands in the Sandhills of Nebraska were formed by wind action. Reelfoot Lake in Tennessee was formed by the sudden sinking of the earth due to earthquakes. Similarly, San Francisco Bay was formed by movement along the San Andreas fault. Beaver dams play a major role in forming smaller inland wetlands in the forested areas of the nation. Over the years, trapping greatly reduced beaver populations, but regulations have resulted in major increases in populations — and beaver dams — in recent years.

Human activities. Human beings have created many wetlands. Major man-made wetlands include wetlands at the margins of reservoirs and farm ponds; wetlands created by water stabilization measures on lakes; vegetation-lined pits and depressions created by gravel pits and mines; poor drainage areas caused by roads, irrigation systems, levees, fills, and buildings; and wetlands created intentionally by the government and conservation groups.

The characteristics of man-made wetlands often are different from those of natural wetlands, and many do not offer the same benefits as natural wetlands because they are subject to high rates of sedimentation and pollution.

Wetland types

The diverse wetland types that exist in the United States are known by many names locally, including swamps, marshes, bogs, vernal pools, seeps, fens, prairie potholes, and kettleholes. Wetlands have been described in a variety of more precise ways for scientific and planning purposes, based upon the sources of water, vegetation, soils, and other characteristics. The best known scientific classification system is found in the National Wetland Classification System, which forms the basis for the National Wetland Inventory. Major wetland types under this classification are marine, estuarine, riverine, lacustrine, and palustrine. See the box on page 19 for definitions of these wetland types.

The hydrogeomorphic (HGM) approach, which is under development to assess how wetlands function, classifies wetlands according to hydrologic setting and the flow of waters. The HGM classification system is worth learning, because it likely will be used widely in the near future:

Riverine fringe wetlands occur in valleys adjacent to stream channels. These wetlands are formed by erosional and depositional processes. The source of water can be precipitation, overbank flow from adjacent stream channels, groundwater, or a combination of these sources. The bottomland hardwoods of the lower Mississippi River alluvial valley (as far north as southern Illinois and western Kentucky) are examples of riverine wetlands.

Estuarine fringe wetlands occur in brackish-saline coastal settings. Their dominant water source is the tides. Estuarine fringe wetlands are created by rising and falling sea levels. Estuarine fringe wetlands are found, for example, in the Chesapeake Bay, San Francisco Bay, and along the Gulf Coast.

Lacustrine fringe wetlands occur in association with freshwater lakes. Many of these lakes and wetlands were created by glaciers. As with estuarine fringe wetlands, the adjacent body of water serves as the dominant source of water and controls the water table and the hydrology in the wetland. Water moves horizontally and in two directions in the wetland. The marshes around the Great Lakes and those adjacent to Flathead Lake in Montana are examples of lacustrine fringe wetlands.

Depressional wetlands have a closed contour shape at an elevation lower than the surrounding landscape. Most depressional wetlands in the northern United States have been created

What is a wetland? Some definitions

The term "wetland" has a variety of definitions, depending upon the context in which the definition is used. Here are the three principal wetland definitions used on the national level:

Regulatory definitions

Regulatory definitions do not necessarily encompass all wetlands, as they are written to take into account laws or policies. Two main regulatory definitions are used in the federal wetland protection system: The U.S. Army Corps of Engineers uses one definition to implement provisions of the Clean Water Act; the Department of Agriculture's Natural Resources Conservation Service (NRCS) uses a different definition to implement the Swampbuster provisions of the Food Security Act. The Corps definition references the importance of inundation and saturation — hydrologic conditions — as the prime determinant of wetland status. The NRCS definition emphasizes the importance of hydric soil as a critical indicator of wetland status. (Please note that several federal agencies have agreed that the NRCS definition will be used on agricultural lands for determining the extent of wetlands under both the Section 404 and the Swampbuster programs.)

From the U.S. Army Corps of Engineers:

Wetlands are "those areas that are inundated or saturated by surface or ground water at a frequency and duration sufficient to support, and that under normal circumstances do support, a prevalence of vegetation typically adapted for life in saturated soil conditions. Wetlands generally include swamps, marshes, bogs, and similar areas."

(42 *Federal Register* 37125-26, 37128-29, July 19, 1977)

From the Natural Resources Conservation Service:

"The term 'wetland,' except when such term is part of the term 'converted wetland,' means land that —
(A) has a predominance of hydric soils;
(B) is inundated or saturated by surface or groundwater at a frequency and duration sufficient to support a prevalence of hydrophytic vegetation typically adapted for life in saturated soil conditions; and
(C) under normal circumstances does support a prevalence of such vegetation.
"For purposes of this Act and any other Act, this term shall not include lands in Alaska identified as having high potential for agricultural development which have a predominance of permafrost soils."
(Federal Agricultural Improvement Reform Act of 1996, Section 1201(a)(18))

Assessment definition

The Department of Interior's U.S. Fish and Wildlife Service (FWS) has developed a definition that serves as the basis for the national assessment and mapping of wetlands. The FWS definition is not directly a regulatory one, but it does represent the perspective of the Fish and Wildlife Service, which interacts constantly with the regulatory agencies. The FWS definition uses the three factors for wetland identification — soils, vegetation, and hydrology.

"Wetlands are lands transitional between terrestrial and aquatic systems where the water table is usually at or near the surface or the land is covered by shallow water. For purposes of this classification wetlands must have one or more of the following three attributes: (1) at least periodically, the land supports predominantly hydrophytes; (2) the substrate is predominantly undrained hydric soil; and (3) the substrate is nonsoil and is saturated with water or covered by shallow water at some time during the growing season of each year."
(Cowardin et al., *Classification of Wetlands and Deepwater Habitats of the United States*, 1979)

Hydrology and wetland health

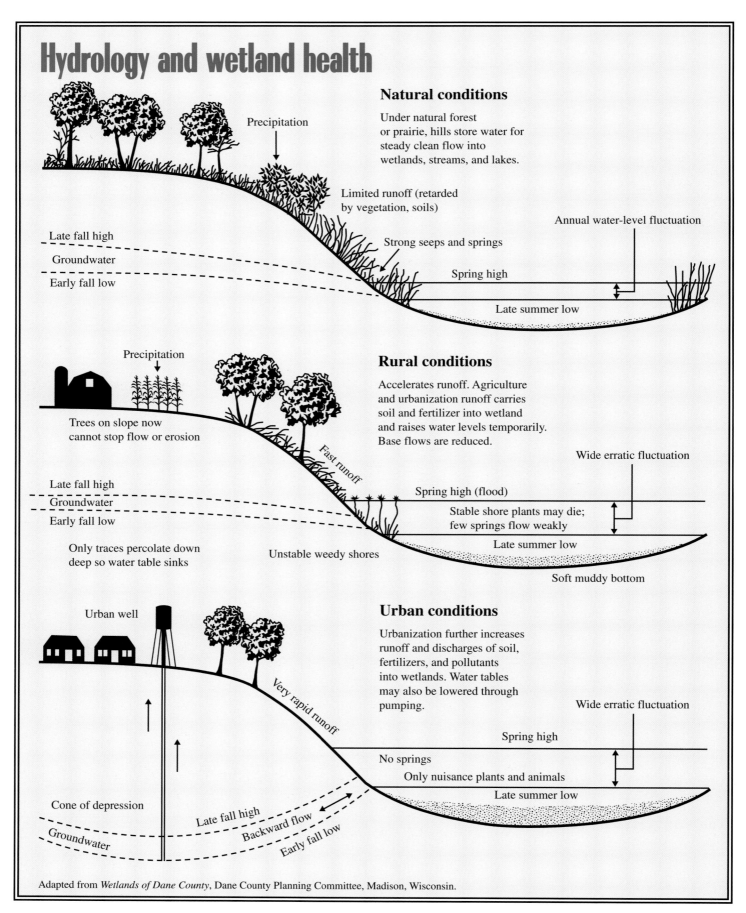

Natural conditions

Under natural forest or prairie, hills store water for steady clean flow into wetlands, streams, and lakes.

Precipitation

Limited runoff (retarded by vegetation, soils)

Strong seeps and springs

Annual water-level fluctuation

Late fall high

Groundwater

Early fall low

Spring high

Late summer low

Rural conditions

Accelerates runoff. Agriculture and urbanization runoff carries soil and fertilizer into wetland and raises water levels temporarily. Base flows are reduced.

Precipitation

Trees on slope now cannot stop flow or erosion

Fast runoff

Late fall high

Groundwater

Early fall low

Only traces percolate down deep so water table sinks

Unstable weedy shores

Wide erratic fluctuation

Spring high (flood)

Stable shore plants may die; few springs flow weakly

Late summer low

Soft muddy bottom

Urban conditions

Urbanization further increases runoff and discharges of soil, fertilizers, and pollutants into wetlands. Water tables may also be lowered through pumping.

Urban well

Very rapid runoff

Cone of depression

Groundwater

Late fall high

Backward flow

Early fall low

Wide erratic fluctuation

Spring high

No springs

Only nuisance plants and animals

Late summer low

Adapted from *Wetlands of Dane County*, Dane County Planning Committee, Madison, Wisconsin.

P77876

Shorelines and wetland health

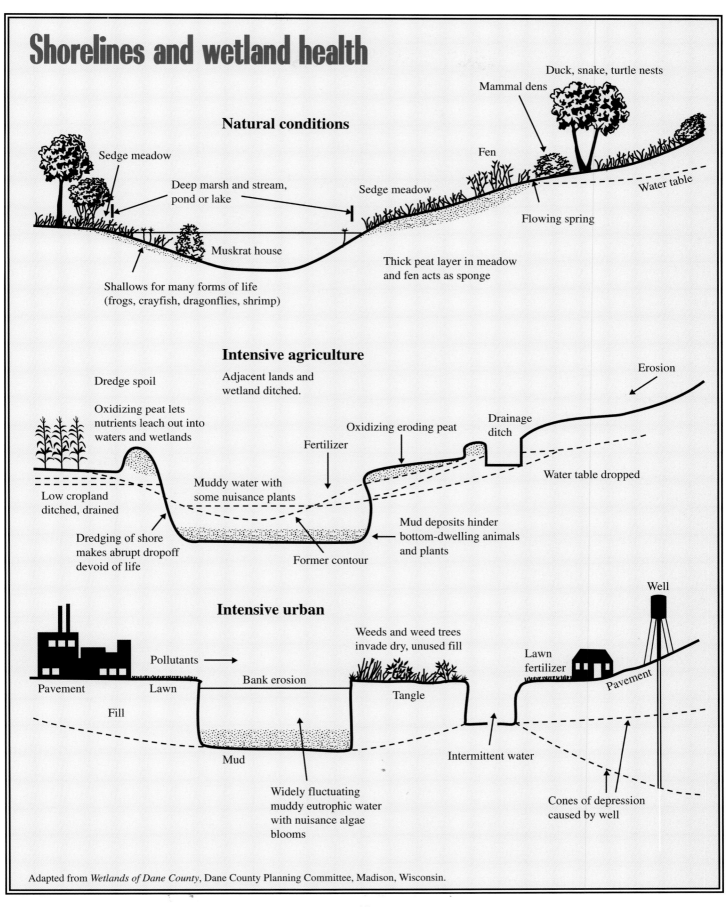

Adapted from *Wetlands of Dane County*, Dane County Planning Committee, Madison, Wisconsin.

by glaciers, although some were created by wind and other processes. In this type of wetland, surface and shallow subsurface water from the surrounding watershed moves toward the lowest elevation in the depression from at least three directions. The source of water may be precipitation, surface water moving over land or in confined channels, groundwater, or a combination of the three. The prairie pothole marshes of the Dakotas, Minnesota, and Iowa are depressional wetlands, as are California's vernal pools.

Slope wetlands occur on hill or valley slopes, and the primary source of water is throughflow of surface water or groundwater discharging at the surface to create shallow surface and subsurface flows. Slope wetlands often occur at the headwaters of streams, the margins where floodplains and uplands meet, and where low-permeability layers of bedrock are exposed. They differ from riverine wetlands because they do not have defined water channels. The fens of northern Minnesota, Canada, and Alaska, and avalanche chutes in the Western United States are slope wetlands.

Mineral soil flats are wetlands that occur in areas that are relatively flat, but they also can occur on slopes. The dominant source of water is precipitation, and the water is transported vertically through the wetland. The wet pine flatwoods of North Carolina are mineral soil flats as are the playas of Texas and Oklahoma.

Organic soil flats are similar to mineral soil flats but with different soil types. They occur in areas that are relatively flat, but they also can occur on slopes. Precipitation is the dominant source of water, and the water is transported vertically through the wetland. Examples of organic soil flats include the peat bogs of the northern and western United States and portions of the Everglades.

How wetlands work

Wetlands are characterized by certain general scientific features or properties. Misunderstandings about these properties can lead to well-meaning but ill-conceived mismanagement of wetland resources. Here are several of those features that are important to understand as wetland definition, delineation, assessment, planning, regulation, and restoration efforts are undertaken:

As partly terrestrial and partly aquatic systems, wetlands contain a broad range of ecological niches. Wetlands encompass an array of shallow water and saturated soil environments that possess some of the characteristics of both terrestrial (land) and aquatic systems. Indeed, because of differences in water depths and fluctuating water levels, portions of wetlands (and, in some instances whole wetlands) resemble true aquatic systems some of the time, terrestrial systems part of the time, and intermediate systems part of the time.

The surface water and groundwater levels of all wetland systems fluctuate due to daily tides, seasonal variations in precipitation and runoff, long-term precipitation cycles, and the activities of humans or other animals.

Over time, this broad assembly of ecological niches (aquatic, terrestrial, and intermediate systems) creates great biological diversity in wetlands. Even a temporary wetland may be very important to the nesting, spawning, breeding, or feeding of a particular plant or animal species. (Rainforests also offer great biodiversity, because they too are made up of diverse ecological niches: the canopy, intermediate, and forest floors.)

Water levels fluctuate in wetlands. Although the magnitude varies, the surface water and groundwater levels of all wetland systems fluctuate due to daily tides, seasonal variations in precipitation and runoff, long-term precipitation cycles, and the activities of humans or other animals, such as the beaver. Some of these wetland fluctuations are very large. For example, in the Northeast, daily tidal fluctuations may be 10 feet or more. Hurricanes and inland storms commonly flood coastal, estuarine, and lower riverine wetlands to depths of five to 15 feet. Water levels in wetlands dependent upon groundwater and snowmelt, such as prairie potholes, often fluctuate four to five feet or more over a period of years.

The water levels of other water bodies, such as lakes, streams, estuaries, and the oceans, also fluctuate. But the consequences and the role of the fluctuations in such aquatic systems are quite different. Lakes, permanent streams, and the oceans are permanently flooded ecosystems occupied primarily by plants and animals able to live in a permanently aquatic environment.

Wetlands are sensitive to changes in water regimes. Because they have shallow waters and vegetation that is sensitive to water depth, wetlands undergo dramatic changes in response to even minor changes in water regimes. Unlike lakes or streams and other water bodies where a change in water levels of one foot usually makes only minor differences in the systems' boundaries, characteristics, and functions, a change of one foot in a wetland can temporarily make it dry or open water. This means that particular vegetation — hydric vegetation — often will grow at one location in a wetland in a wet year, a second location in an intermediate year, and not at all in a dry year. As habitats shift from year to year, their use by various animals also varies dramatically.

At one time, it was believed that many wetlands progressed in an orderly "succession" from open water to marshes to shrubs to forested swamps and, finally, to dry land because of gradual infilling by organic matter and sediments. Indeed, analysis of sediment profiles and pollen samples suggests that such succession does occur in some depressional wetlands. However, many wetlands have moved through continuous cycles of open water, marsh, scrub/forest, and dry land for thousands of years. In some instances, the seeds of plants stay dormant in the soil during dry or wet periods and germinate again only when condi-

Wetlands and deepwater habitats

The five major systems

The best-known classification system is commonly called the Cowardin system, after one of the principal scientists who developed it for the U.S. Department of the Interior. The Cowardin system is used for the national assessment and mapping of wetlands.

Marine	Estuarine	Riverine	Lacustrine	Palustrine
The open ocean overlying the continental shelf and its associated high-energy coastline. Marine habitats are exposed to the waves and currents of the open ocean, and the water regimes are determined primarily by the ebb and flow of oceanic tides.	Deepwater tidal habitats and adjacent tidal wetlands that usually are semi-enclosed by land but have open, partly obstructed, or sporadic access to the open ocean. Ocean water is at least occasionally diluted by freshwater runoff from the land.	Includes all wetlands and deepwater habitats contained within a channel, with two exceptions: 1) wetlands dominated by trees, shrubs, persistent emergents, emergent mosses, or lichens, and 2) habitats with water containing ocean-derived salts in excess of 0.5 percent.	Includes wetlands and deepwater habitats with all of the following characteristics: 1) situated in a topographic depression or a dammed river channel; 2) lacking trees, shrubs, persistent emergents, emergent mosses or lichens with greater than 30 percent areal coverage; and 3) total area exceeds 20 acres.	All nontidal wetlands dominated by trees, shrubs, persistent emergents, emergent mosses or lichens, and all such wetlands that occur in tidal areas where salinity due to ocean-derived salts is below 0.5 percent.

Source: Cowardin et al., Classification of Wetlands and Deepwater Habitats of the United States, U.S. Department of the Interior (1979)

tions are right. In others, plants and animals migrate upslope or downslope as wetness increases and decreases. (This, however, requires sufficient open land adjacent to permit migration.)

Floods, hurricanes, and other catastrophic events often benefit wetlands in the long-term. Floods, hurricanes, and other natural events can irreparably damage wetlands habitats, particularly where there are no adjacent sites for migration of species or seed stock. However, most riverine, coastal, and estuarine and many depressional wetlands are in fact long-lived precisely because of hurricanes, floods, droughts, and fires. For example, the Everglades ecosystem has survived thousands of hurricanes, droughts, and fires. This seemingly anomalous feature of wetlands — short-term damage due to extreme events with long-term benefits — is poorly understood by the public and policy makers.

Hurricanes and high-velocity floods scour sediments and organic matter, removing them from existing wetlands or creating new wetlands at nearby sites. Droughts temporarily destroy hydrophytic vegetation and allow oxidation and compaction of organic soils. Fires burn peat and other organic matter. In fact, fire is considered a valuable management tool for many wetlands, including for The Nature Conservancy's Disney Wilderness Preserve near Orlando, Florida.

Wetlands function in a watershed context. They have close ecological and hydrologic relationships with adjacent lands and with other wetlands and aquatic systems. Many wetland functions and values depend upon a wetland's linkages with other wetlands and adjacent aquatic and terrestrial systems.

For example, lands immediately adjacent to wetlands act as buffers, protecting wetlands from sediments and pollutants. These lands also serve as critical habitat to many of the birds and animals that live in wetlands. As water levels fluctuate seasonally and over the years, wetland plants and animals that cannot tolerate solely aquatic environments must be able to migrate up and down the low gradient slopes. Riverine wetlands along with rivers, lakes, and streams, form natural corridors for migration of fish, birds, mammals, and reptiles. The destruction of a portion of a river corridor may prevent the migration of animals from downstream to upstream points.

Wetlands serve as important fish and shellfish breeding and feeding areas if they are connected with adjacent coastal and estuarine waters and lakes and streams. Fills, dikes, or other measures that isolate wetlands from adjacent wetlands or waters destroy such functions. Construction of a sea wall at the landward boundary of a salt marsh, for example, will prevent inland migration of the marsh when sea level rises. Such diking in fact threatens many coastal wetlands. (In light of these considerations, many states and local governments have adopted wetland buffer requirements of 50-200 feet for filling, grading, use of septic tanks, and other activities.) Dikes may also destroy natural wetland flood control, flood conveyance, and pollution control functions.

How a landscape is used has a great deal to do with the quality of a wetland. Even relatively minor human activities, such as groundwater pumping, often disrupt headwater riverine wetlands, depressional wetlands, and slope wetlands. Land use determines, to a considerable extent, the type and quantity of sediment, nutrients, debris, and pollutants entering wetlands. Greatly increased sediment and nutrient loadings from watersheds that are undergoing urbanization, agricultural development, or clear-cutting can change dramatically plant and animal species and can quickly destroy wetlands. This is particularly true for various isolated, depressional, and lakeshore wetlands that are not periodically cleaned of sediments by storm wave action or high-velocity river flows. Many of the pothole and kettlehole wetlands in the northern tier of states and southern portions of Canadian provinces are at particular risk from excessive sedimentation and nutrients, because they are natural sediment traps and lack any effective flushing mechanisms.

The materials entering a wetland and the relationship between inflows and outflows determine many of the short-term and long-term functions of a wetland. Consider the pollution control function of a naturally occurring wetland along a small lake in an undeveloped watershed. Under natural conditions, the wetland may play a limited role in reducing pollutants because there are few pollutants in the watershed. But the future pollution control role of this wetland ought not to be overlooked should the watershed become urbanized and runoff, sediment, and nutrient loadings greatly increase. Similarly, a wetland along a rural stream may appear to have limited present economic "value" for flood conveyance and flood storage, because there are no houses immediately adjacent to the stream to be damaged by increased flood heights due to filling of the wetland. However, the future flood loss reduction role may be great as buildings are constructed near the stream.

Given all the connections between wetlands and their surrounding landscape, it is no surprise that protecting and restoring wetland systems often depend upon effective watershed and land use planning, planning that will affect water quantity, water levels, and hydroperiod (the period of wetland soil saturation or flooding). This is particularly true for isolated and small wetlands where the principal sources of water are direct precipitation, surface runoff from the surrounding lands, and the groundwater system. Wetlands adjacent to major lakes and streams may be less sensitive to natural changes in the immediate watershed, because they are linked with water levels in the adjacent water bodies. Coastal and estuarine wetlands are even less likely to be artificially altered as long as there is open passage of ocean water, since water levels depend primarily upon relatively constant tides.

A bird's eye view

Wetlands are extraordinarily dynamic and complex systems with thousands of variations in soil type, plant life, animals, functions, and values. We have provided you with some of the basic wetland properties that are essential to the protection and

> **To get to know wetlands on your land and in your community, observations in the field are crucial. Walk the boundaries of some wetlands or get out into them by canoe.**

restoration of these systems. More detailed information is available in many excellent books, including William A. Niering's *Wetlands of North America* and William J. Mitch and James G. Gosselink's *Wetlands*.

To get to know wetlands on your land and in your community, however, observations in the field are crucial. Walk the boundaries of some wetlands or get out into them by canoe or on a boardwalk at a wetland interpretive site. What do you see? Likely there will be an amazing mosaic of trees, shrubs, grasses, sedges, birds, fish, and animals.

To understand the relationship of wetlands to other water bodies — the broader hydrologic regime — will take more. Imagine yourself as a bird soaring several thousand feet over your wetland. Alternatively (and a little more practically), examine a local topographic map or wetland map (available from many states or from the National Wetland Inventory).

Imagine rain falling on the land. Where does it go? Some of it sinks into the soil, but during a rainy period, much of it runs off the surface into depressions, drainage ditches, small streams, and finally larger streams. Wetlands are located in these depressions, at the bottoms of drainage ditches, and along small streams. Wetlands form much of the drainage network.

The wetland vegetation binds the soil and slows the runoff, reducing erosion and subsequent sedimentation in drainage ditches and small streams and along the banks of ponds. The wetland vegetation and soils intercept sediment, nutrients, litter, and other pollutants from upland areas and prevent these pollutants from running into ponds, lakes, or other water bodies and into larger lakes, streams, estuaries, and the oceans.

A bird's eye view will tell you much about your wetland in the broader hydrologic regime, but you must watch the wetland over a season or several seasons to understand its true nature. Place a stick in the soil near the edge of your wetland. Or pick a tree, rock, or other stable feature on the edge of a wetland on other lands. Visit the same spot in the dry season, the wet season, and intermediate times. Observe the amazing changes in water levels, vegetation, and animals. You will begin to understand the dynamic and true nature of wetlands — and why they are both very valuable and challenging to define, delineate, and manage.

Endnotes

Association of State Wetland Managers, *Wetland Hydrology* (1988).

M. Brinson, *A Hydrogeomorphic Classification for Wetlands* (U.S. Army Corps of Engineers, Waterways Experiment Station, 1993). Technical Report WRP-DE-4.

L. Cowardin et al., *Classification of Wetlands and Deepwater Habitats of the United States* (U.S. Fish and Wildlife Service, 1979). FWS/OBS-79-31.

K. Gilman, *Hydrology and Wetland Conservation* (John Wiley & Sons, 1994).

J. Kusler, W. Mitsch, and J. Larson, "Wetlands," *Scientific American* (January 1994).

W. Mitch and J. Gosselink, *Wetlands*, second edition (Von Nostrand Reinhold, 1993).

National Research Council, *Wetlands: Characteristics and Boundaries* (National Academy Press, 1995).

A.W. Stone and A.J. Stone, *Wetlands and Groundwater in the United States* (American Groundwater Trust and Audubon Society of New Hampshire, 1994).

1900s: Minnesota and Wisconsin

The Sacred Harvest

For countless generations, the Ojibway people of northern Minnesota and Wisconsin have been told the story about a time when their people lived on the East Coast of North America. Prophets spoke of a great journey the Ojibway would have to make if they were to survive. The journey would be complete, the prophets said, only when the people reached a land where food grew abundantly in the water. This place would be their home, and the food a gift of the Creator.

The Ojibway migration took many hundreds of years. In the mid–1500s, the Ojibway found northern Minnesota and Wisconsin, one of the few regions in the world with ideal conditions for wild rice to grow naturally. Wild rice — or mahnomin — became a staple of the Ojibway diet. The seeds from wild rice, which is actually a grain that grows on top of a long grass, sprout and anchor their roots into the newly stirred soil of wetlands in late April. Later, during the warm days and cool nights of late August and early September, the plant ripens and its grains are ready to be gathered. Today, mahnomin continues to help the Ojibway survive the region's cold, harsh winters.

— *from* The Sacred Harvest: Ojibway Wild Rice Gathering *by Gordon Regguinti (Lerner Publications Company: 1992)*

What Citizens Can Do

Chapter 3 introduces many of the wetland protection strategies that are available to citizens. Use the chapter to get an overview of your options to effect change as a citizen. Throughout the rest of the book, the strategies are discussed in more detail.

How can you as a private citizen protect and restore wetlands? The opportunities are many, and they include strategies that involve banding together with other groups of citizens, working to effect the outcomes of governmental programs, and simply protecting and restoring wetlands on your own land. You can educate yourself and others about the importance of wetlands, the opportunities for using wetlands in non-harmful ways, and activities that should be avoided because they injure or destroy wetlands. You can campaign for protective guidelines and policies concerning use of government-owned wetlands. You can show private landowners how to protect their wetlands through enlightened land management practices. In addition, you can use and help others use deed restrictions and other protective techniques to ensure future protection, and you can organize into nonprofit organizations or join existing organizations that acquire wetlands and lobby for governmental protection. Also, you can persuade your local government to adopt a no net loss wetland policy by resolution (see Chapter 10).

An enormous array of talent and energy is available in the private sector if you can tap and mobilize it for wetland protection. A local advertising agent may be willing to put together an attractive citizens guidebook on wetlands. An art teacher might illustrate the book. A high school science teacher may help identify common plant and animal species found on private wetlands. Local lawyers might informally explain to wetland owners some of the tax advantages for charitable donation of wetlands to conservation organizations. Together, these talents can be extremely effective.

Some options for working together and techniques for protecting and restoring wetlands include the following:

Citizens action groups

Private citizens often can best protect wetlands by banding together in informal or formal citizens action groups. Many of these groups have been started over the last decade. Some call themselves "friends of" a particular wetland or river, such as the Friends of Ding Darling Wildlife Refuge in Florida or Friends of Creux Meadows in Wisconsin. Some operate with letterhead and formal organization; others are more informal bird clubs, hiking groups, or fishing camps. Whatever the name and structure, what is important is a commitment to joint action — a commitment, for example, to meet with wetland landowners to discuss protection and restoration, construct duck nesting boxes, create a wetland boardwalk, or lobby a local conservation commission to adopt a wetland ordinance.

One citizens group success story is that of Sanibel, an island off the southwest coast of Florida. A 12,500-acre crescent filled with beaches, estuaries, mangrove swamps, tidal flats, a freshwater river, and many plant and animal species, Sanibel was relatively undeveloped until 1963, when construction of a three-mile causeway connected the island with the mainland. Development skyrocketed in the early 1970s; the value of building permits issued for Sanibel during one week of 1973 exceeded the value of all of those issued in 1972.

In 1973, the Sanibel-Captiva Conservation Foundation, a citizens organization, mounted a

"With 75 percent of the nation's remaining wetlands in the lower 48 states located on privately owned property, cooperation with the private sector in implementation of wetlands protection and restoration is crucial."

— White House Office on Environmental Policy, *Protecting America's Wetlands: A Fair, Flexible, and Effective Approach* (1993)

major campaign against the haphazard construction of condominiums that destroyed the mangrove swamps, taxed the freshwater system, and preempted public access to the beaches. Citizens groups raised a $20,000 warchest, formed a Sanibel Home Rule Study Group, hired a professional planning consultant, and held public meetings to organize support. On November 5, 1974, Sanibel's residents voted to free themselves from the control of the county government and to incorporate the island as the City of Sanibel, with the power to establish a city council and adopt a master plan and zoning ordinances that would preserve the island's fragile environment. Separate incorporation was necessary because the county would not adopt adequate zoning to control development. Much of the job of fund-raising and organization fell upon retired citizens living on Sanibel who had free time, a dedication to the island, and enormous administrative and creative talents from their years of experience as businessmen and women, lawyers, artists, and scientists.

Sanibel's citizens prepared a comprehensive land use plan with the assistance of consulting firms. Citizens committees carried out much of the data-gathering for the effort. The plan, adopted in 1976, established low-density zoning for coastal and inland wetland areas and performance standards for development to minimize impacts on natural systems. The plan does not prevent further development of Sanibel, but it does limit total population and reduce the impact of development in the fragile wetland areas.

Land trusts

Over the last several decades, citizens — nearly 900,000 of them — have banded together to form or join the nearly 1,100 land trusts that exist now in the United States. These land trusts provide protection for more than four million acres of land through deed restrictions, conservation easements, acquisition, land exchanges, and other approaches. Most of the land trusts have as one of their goals the protection of wetlands, and some focus primarily on wetlands. Land use planning, lobbying on conservation issues, environmental education, and technical assistance also are common activities. The Land Trust Alliance in Washington, D.C., has published a number of extremely useful guidebooks to help citizens form land trusts, negotiate conservation easements, and otherwise protect lands. (The endnotes to this chapter include some of the Alliance's publications.)

Environmental organizations

A private citizen may protect and restore wetlands, including gaining tax benefits (if you are a landowner), by working with environmental organizations.

Thousands of state and local citizens organizations play wetland protection roles. These include conservation commissions in the New England states, duck and wildlife clubs throughout the nation, historic preservation groups, and private foundations established to administer trusts and estates. For example, town conservation commissions in New Jersey, New York, and Connecticut are protecting wetlands by gathering

---

Tips for landowners

To maximize wetland benefits and reduce costs to you:

❋ **Avoid wetlands in filling, grading, drainage, and other activities that will damage or destroy your wetlands.** Locate activities on upland sites to the extent possible. This will help you avoid problems with natural hazards (such as flooding and structural bearing capacity), protect the benefits of natural wetland values to you and others, and avoid the high costs of permitting when wetlands must be altered.

❋ **Protect your wetland's natural wetland benefits, such as flood storage, flood conveyance, water quality protection, groundwater recharge, and waterfowl and fish habitat.**

❋ **Enhance natural wetland benefits and values.** Stock wetlands with fish (to improve fishing). Put in nesting boxes for waterfowl and other birds, and locate observation trails along your wetlands (bird watching for you and your family). Create "ecotone buffers" for wildlife, and remedy pollution problems.

❋ **Seek real estate tax reductions for wetlands on your property.** Enroll in open space assessment programs, adopt deed restrictions, or grant conservation easements for your property.

❋ **Seek technical and financial assistance for protecting and restoring wetlands.** Sources of possible assistance include the U.S. Fish and Wildlife Service, the Natural Resources Conservation Service, state fish and wildlife agencies, local land trusts, and conservation organizations such as The Nature Conservancy.

❋ **Gain income tax benefits by donating easements or fee interests in your wetlands.** You may be able to gain substantial tax savings from donations to your local government, land trusts, and conservation organizations.

---

data, conducting workshops, and commenting on proposed development and acquisition activities. Duck clubs in California and other western states are principal actors in acquiring and protecting wetlands. Private foundations such as the Ford Foundation and the Rockefeller Foundation have funded the preparation of wetland protection guidebooks for use by local governmental officials in Connecticut and Massachusetts.

Wetland regulatory programs

Well-informed individuals can contribute to successful public wetland regulatory programs in a variety of ways, including by organizing support for these programs, suggesting provisions for wetland legislation, closely supervising agency actions, and keeping a sharp lookout for violations and potential public and private threats to wetlands.

Federal programs. On the federal level, the statute with the most direct impact on wetland protection is *Section 404 of the Clean Water Act.* (See Chapter 8 for a more extended discussion of federal programs.) Section 404 requires the U.S. Army Corps of Engineers to evaluate permit applications for the discharge of dredged or fill material into waters of the United States, including wetlands. Under the Clean Water Act, the U.S. Environmental Protection Agency may approve state programs operating in place of the Corps for a portion of the waters affected by Section 404.

A public hearing or meeting where citizens are given an opportunity to comment is required for most federal and state Section 404 permit applications. Citizens who are directly affected by issuance of permits can request public hearings. (To stay apprised of permit applications, write to the Corps' District Engineer, EPA, or the state wetland protection agency and request that your name be placed on a mailing list for notification of proposed permits affecting wetlands.) At public hearings or meetings, be prepared to present facts that demonstrate the adverse impacts of proposed activities on wetlands. If federal projects are involved, you might work to monitor whether environmental impact statements are completed before permits are issued.

Individual permits are not required for some dredge or fill activities, either because the impact on the environment is presumed to be minimal or because a general permit for all such activities already has been issued. Even in these situations, however, citizens should notify the Corps of Engineers or the appropriate state agency of dredge and fill activities that may require special attention. Citizens also act as watchdogs for the government agencies by reporting activities undertaken without a proper permit or violations of permit conditions.

An additional avenue for citizen action is the *National Environmental Policy Act (NEPA)*. NEPA requires preparation and review of an environmental impact statement before any major federal action is undertaken that will significantly affect the quality of the environment. Major federal actions include those undertaken directly by federal agencies and those funded, licensed, or approved by federal agencies. If, for example, the Federal Highway Administration funds the extension of a state highway through a wetland, that action may be deemed a major federal action and will require an environmental impact statement before the highway is constructed. It is at this juncture that citizens can influence the decision-making process.

Under NEPA, citizens must be given an opportunity to comment on draft environmental impact statements, and their comments must be seriously considered by the federal agency in the preparation of the final environmental impact statement. Although NEPA does not require that activities with adverse environmental impacts be abandoned, the importance of citizen involvement in highlighting the detrimental side effects of a proposed activity cannot be overemphasized. Even if a project is not halted as a result of a negative review, it may be significantly modified to alleviate the potential harm. For example, an

agency may substitute a bridge on pilings that allows the free flow of water in wetlands for a proposed solid fill structure. If citizens believe that an environmental impact statement fails to include necessary information, or that statutory requirements for preparing the EIS were not followed, they may be able to bring suit challenging the adequacy of the statement.

Although NEPA is a federal statute, many states have adopted state environmental policy acts or regulations patterned after NEPA. Thus, state actions also may be subject to environmental impact statement requirements, including the opportunity for citizen participation and the possibility of citizens suits if requirements of the state act are not met.

A third important federal statute providing citizen input to wetland use is the *Coastal Zone Management Act of 1972*, which makes federal funds available to the states for comprehensive coastal land and water management plans. The coastal zone is defined by the act to include salt marshes, wetlands, beaches, and intertidal areas. In addition, administrative regulations adopted pursuant to the act list coastal wetlands as areas of "particular" concern. All of the states eligible for funding under the Coastal Zone Management Act have applied for program development grants.

The Coastal Zone Management Act requires that citizens play a large role in both the development and implementation

---

Jerry McCollum, Madison, Georgia:
Protecting swamplands from urban expansion

The Alcovy River, a tributary of the Altamaha River in Georgia, runs through numerous high-quality swamps, including ancient tupelo gum swamps. The river also lies east of expanding Atlanta, and industrial and residential development is creeping toward it. Jerry McCollum, who heads the Georgia Wildlife Federation, recognized the threats the Alcovy was facing, so in 1993 he began a campaign to protect the valuable habitat that the river provides.

McCollum recruited volunteers and approached other conservation groups, industries, and river landowners, and together they developed a greenway along the Alcovy. Working with The Conservation Fund and others, McCollum helped sign up more than 30 landowners into a landowner registry, and he encouraged them to sign conservation easements. In addition, McCollum has used the river as a center for child and adult education. Now the techniques McCollum used to protect the Alcovy River will be used throughout Georgia, as he and others are planning to implement River Care 2000, a statewide initiative to protect Georgia's 70,000 miles of river and associated wetlands.

When disputes arise

Citizens can have a major impact on wetland decisions with a minor expenditure of resources by assembling information, getting it to the right officials, and maintaining a watchful eye over the regulatory process. However, disputes do arise, and citizens suits may be available when other avenues have failed. Citizens suits are expensive and should be used as a measure of last resort.

There are several legal obstacles to private lawsuits. First, citizens must be able to show that a legally protected right is, or may be, involved. Second, they must demonstrate that they have sufficient stake in the matter to qualify to bring the lawsuit. These concepts are known as "justiciability" and "standing to sue."

There are several ways for a citizen or citizens group to show that an activity that threatens a wetland violates a legally protected right. (Anyone contemplating a suit should consult a lawyer.) Suits may be brought under *statutes expressly authorizing citizens suits.* In some instances, a statute creates a right (such as to enjoy pollution-free waters) and specifically authorizes private suits to enforce that right. For example, the Clean Water Act contains a section authorizing citizens suits against individuals or government agencies that violate water quality standards adopted under the Act, including suits against federal and state permits for the disposal of dredge or fill material into waters of the United States and adjacent wetlands. Several states also authorize citizens suits to protect the environment.

In addition, suits may sometimes be brought under *statutes not expressly authorizing citizens suits.* If the statutes define a legally protected right to protect the environment and citizens can show that they have sufficient stake in the right and the activity that they wish to challenge — in particular that they are directly and substantially injured by the activity — a lawsuit generally will be allowed. For example, assume that a citizen believes that an environmental impact statement (EIS) required by the National Environmental Policy Act (NEPA) before federal funding of a highway through a wetland is inadequate because it does not consider alternative locations for the highway. Assume also that the citizen owns and has long hunted on part of the wetland where the proposed highway will run. Because the citizen has a financial and recreational stake in the site considered for the highway and because NEPA establishes a clear duty to prepare an adequate EIS, the citizen would qualify to bring a lawsuit challenging the failure of the EIS to consider alternative locations.

Some interests commonly are recognized as subject to court protection, even though there are no explicit statutes defining or safeguarding them. For example, the *public trust doctrine* holds that there are certain public rights in water and related land resources that the government must protect in the public interest and cannot give away, sell, or damage, except under special conditions. The doctrine can be used in some instances as the basis for a citizen's lawsuit to restrain governmental or private actions that would damage or destroy wetlands.

There are several *common law theories* for citizens' challenge to potentially destructive wetland activities, even where there is no statutory authority protecting their interests. Common law suits usually are available, however, only where activities directly harm a citizen's land through water pollution, increased runoff, or flood flows. In these circumstances, the citizen can argue that the activity constitutes a nuisance, results in trespass on his land, or violates his rights to use the water and adjacent land.

Another basis for a citizens suit designed to protect wetlands is an *action for violation of a contract.* A citizen can charge violation of the terms of a conservation restriction, easement, or covenant to which the citizen is a party or has a direct interest. Unlike nuisance, trespass, public trust actions, or suits pursuant to a statutory right, this kind of lawsuit does not depend on a publicly created regulation or publicly recognized right. Rather, it stems solely from an agreement between private parties to undertake or refrain from certain activities. Courts will entertain lawsuits to enforce such agreements; however, state laws differ on the validity and enforceability of deed restrictions, covenants, and easements, particularly where innocent purchasers are involved.

One final approach for citizen action in court is through *intervention* in legal proceedings that have been initiated by public bodies or other citizens to protect wetlands. Intervention involves the filing of a brief or joinder in the suit as an interested party. Intervention provides an avenue for citizens to present information concerning factual matters, law, and public policy. In one case, for example, the Environmental Defense Fund and other environmental groups were allowed to intervene in a court case involving the Corps of Engineers' denial of a permit to develop a residential housing complex on the wetlands of Marco Island, Florida.

Winning a lawsuit is just part of the strategy; to make a lawsuit worthwhile, citizens must be able to obtain a remedy from the court that aids wetland protection. Courts may require that the offending parties abide by procedures outlined in the statutes, such as preparation of environmental impact statements. Where suits are based on statutes expressly authorizing suits, the permissible remedy usually is defined by the statute. If no statute is involved, the legal issue in dispute (such as a broken covenant) and the overall circumstances will determine available remedies. Remedies include money damages where the citizen can show actual damage to a private interest. The court also may enjoin the offending activity and order that the land be restored to its original condition. Where a law has been violated, the court may impose a fine on the offending party and, in some instances, share the fine with the private litigant who brought the suit.

of state coastal zone management plans. Because the grant of federal money under the act is a major federal action, an environmental impact statement must be prepared for each state management program that is submitted for federal approval. This provides another access point for citizen comment and recommendation.

State programs. At the state level, many statutes directly or indirectly affect the use of wetlands. (See Chapter 9.) Familiarize yourself with the provisions of your state statutes and ensure that their requirements are met, both by individuals subject to the regulations and agencies responsible for carrying them out. For example, where a statute requires a public hearing on a prepared plan or permit application, citizens may attend such hearings and state their positions. Citizens also can comment on environmental impact statements prepared in connection with the issuance of permits. Early citizen inputs in planning and application processes are most effective in influencing agency decisions.

If a state has not adopted a wetland statute, you can, of course, lobby for legislation.

Local programs. Private citizens often play their strongest role in lobbying for and helping to implement local government wetland planning, regulatory, and other management efforts. (See Chapters 4-7, 10, and 11.) Individually or as part of coalitions and groups, you can work with planning boards and local governments to map, plan, and adopt regulations for wetlands. Once regulations are adopted, you can play roles similar to those for the federal Section 404 program and for state programs. You also can help local governments with public education efforts, monitoring, and enforcement.

Protection and restoration on your land

You as a private landowner may own a portion of a wetland, a whole wetland, or many wetlands. Your wetland may be in a predominantly natural condition, or it may be partly drained, filled, or dredged. How can you protect it? Why should you minimize additional damage to your wetland? Should you work to enhance or restore it?

There are many reasons for protecting, enhancing, or restoring wetlands. You will avoid natural hazards, such as flooding and structural bearing capacity problems, and wetland regulatory permitting requirements. As the thousands of landowners who have done so will attest, enhancement and restoration increases wildlife, fisheries, scenic beauty, pollution control, and other functions. (See Chapters 5 and 11 for more on restoration.)

To best protect wetlands on your property, locate development, roads, and other activities on upland sites and avoid filling, grading, or other activities in or immediately adjacent to a

wetland. It is important to protect not only the wetland but to maintain a vegetated buffer of 50-100 feet around the wetland to reduce sediment and pollution and to increase wildlife values. Many species of wildlife that utilize wetlands need adjacent buffer habitat.

To protect wetlands, you need to protect wetland water supply. This means you shouldn't divert natural streams and other watercourses providing water to wetlands. Also, don't dewater a wetland through excessive groundwater pumping.

Technical assistance and financial grants in aid, including the Partners for Wildlife and Wetland Reserve programs, are available from the U.S. Fish and Wildlife Service and the Natural Resources Conservation Service to help landowners protect and restore wetlands. The 1996 Farm Bill not only endorses the Department of Agriculture's existing technical and financial assistance programs but offers some new options as well, including the Environmental Quality Incentives Program (EQIP) and a flood risk reduction program.

In addition, technical and financial assistance may be available from state agencies and environmental organizations, including local land trusts. A variety of techniques, such as deed restrictions and easements, discussed below, are available to help you restore and enhance wetlands while reducing property taxes and gaining income tax advantages.

Even if you don't actively work to protect your wetlands, carefully consider the consequences of making alterations to them. Reduce the impacts of your activity. Filling or draining your wetland often will result in a loss of what you find valuable, such as the opportunity to view wildlife, hunt waterfowl, fish, and enjoy the wetland's scenic beauty. Filling or draining a wetland may result in increased nutrients, sediment, or other pollution for a pond or reservoir on your property, and may reduce your groundwater supply. Filling or draining may increase flooding on other portions of your properties or on neighboring lands. This can result in considerable friction in the neighborhood — and even expensive lawsuits.

Filling a wetland to create a road, parking lot, or building may create bumps, potholes, and unstable foundations. Basements constructed in filled wetlands often flood due to the continued high groundwater levels that filling doesn't correct. Septic tank/soil absorption systems placed in filled wetlands may fail to operate due to the high groundwater.

Draining, dredging, filling, or otherwise altering a wetland typically will subject a landowner to a variety of time-consuming and expensive federal, state, and local regulations and permitting requirements, including wetland regulations, floodplain regulations, regulations pertaining to the use of public waters, and pollution regulations. (These are discussed in Chapters 4-10.)

> Citizens — nearly 900,000 of them — have banded together to form or join the nearly 1,100 land trusts that exist now in the United States. Most of the land trusts have as one of their goals the protection of wetlands.

Deed restrictions, covenants, and easements

Through deed restrictions, covenants, and easements, private landowners may protect wetlands on their own lands even after their death or sale of the land. The federal and state governments offer tax advantages to encourage the use of these devices. In addition, groups such as The Nature Conservancy help by providing model language for conservation agreements, by becoming a party to preservation agreements, and by acting as a recipient of easements. Here we'll describe deed restrictions, covenants, and easements, and examine their potential for protecting wetlands. (See Appendix C for actual examples.)

As the name implies, *deed restrictions* are clauses placed in deeds restricting the future use of land. When property containing wetlands is sold, donated, or willed, deed restrictions can prohibit uses or activities by the new owners that would destroy, damage, or modify wetlands. Deed restrictions may qualify a landowner for real estate tax breaks, because lands may no longer be developable.

When land is donated or devised to a government agency or charitable organization, the donor may include a reverter clause that provides that if the land is not managed and used as specified in the deed, the property must be returned to the original owner or his or her heirs. Alternately, the reverter clause may require that the land revert to a third party such as the Audubon Society or any other conservation group capable of maintaining the land according to the terms of the restrictions.

Covenants can be used in some situations where deed restrictions, including reverter clauses, are not legally enforceable. A covenant is a contract between a landowner and another party stating that the landowner will use or refrain from using his or her land in an agreed-upon manner. Covenants, like deed restrictions, can require, for example, that landowners refrain from activities that will damage wetlands. The documents containing the covenants can give the individuals acquiring the covenant, their heirs, or any third party the right to enforce the covenants. However, covenants, like deed restrictions, are not enforceable in all states, particularly against subsequent purchasers without notice of the covenants.

Instead of purchasing lands and attaching restrictive covenants to deeds, citizens groups may pay wetland owners to attach covenants to their deeds. The covenants can bind the present owners and all future owners to maintain the wetlands in their natural state, with the citizens group holding rights of enforcement. Once placed in deeds, covenants become deed restrictions.

Conservation easements can be used to transfer certain rights and privileges concerning the use of wetlands to specified individuals or bodies without transferring the title to the land. They have been broadly used to protect wetlands in the Wetlands Reserve Program.

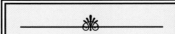

You can contribute to successful public wetland programs by closely supervising agency actions and keeping a sharp lookout for violations and potential threats to wetlands.

Easements are known as "affirmative easements" if they allow the party acquiring the easement to perform affirmative acts on a property (such as gain access to wetlands) and "negative easements" if they require that landowners refrain from certain activities. In addition, easements are distinguished according to whether or not they benefit an adjoining piece of land and are therefore "appurtenant" or exist merely as an agreement between landowners and are "in gross." For example, an easement by which a landowner agrees not to conduct agricultural activities on a slope adjacent to his neighbor's wetland would be a "negative appurtenant" easement. Such an agreement that doesn't involve an adjacent land would be "in gross."

In some states, easements in gross cannot be enforced against anyone other than the original parties to the easement agreement. Because of the uncertainty in many states regarding enforcement of easements, California, Connecticut, Maryland, Massachusetts, and New Hampshire have passed legislation that explicitly recognizes the legality of "conservation" easements and binds all subsequent owners of the property to the terms of the easements for their duration. Of course, if an easement is granted only for a term of years, owners of the property subsequent to expiration of the easement would not be subject to its terms.

A party to a conservation easement has the right to seek enforcement of the agreement. Whether or not others have a right of enforcement depends on state law. In Massachusetts, for example, where conservation easements (known as conservation restrictions) must, in many instances, be approved by a government body, the state attorney general and municipalities can sue to enforce a conservation easement. Massachusetts also has a "Citizen Right of Action Law," whereby any 10 people domiciled in the Commonwealth can sue to enforce conservation restrictions.

There is very little uniformity among the states regarding requirements, validity, enforceability, and tax implications of deed restrictions, covenants, and conservation easements. Anyone contemplating the use of one of these techniques should consult a lawyer concerning the law of the jurisdiction.

Without your work and that of other private citizens and landowners, we will not succeed in realizing our national goal of a long-term gain in wetland resources. As the varied techniques layed out above show, there are many possibilities for contributing to wetland protection. All that is needed is a little savvy on which techniques best serve the needs of your community's people and wetlands — and diligent work to make sure those techniques are implemented.

A little imagination, a lot of expertise

For some excellent examples of how a broad range of innovative techniques can be utilized to protect wetlands and other habitats, look no further than The Nature Conservancy. The Conservancy, headquartered in Arlington, Virginia, repeatedly has demonstrated that a little imagination and a lot of tax expertise can go a long way. (For information on how to contact TNC and other organizations working for wetland protection, see Appendix B.)

The Nature Conservancy has protected approximately 9.5 million acres of land and participated in approximately 17,500 conservation transactions. The organization's success in land protection stems from its wealth of transactional experience, a large revolving land acquisition fund, a well-established line of credit with institutional lenders, and an ability to act quickly and flexibly when natural areas are threatened. In approximately two-thirds of its projects, the Conservancy retains a conservation interest in the acquired land. In the remainder, the land is transferred for management to a cooperative conservation partner organization, which may include the federal government, a state, a university, or a local land trust.

The tax benefits of charitable contributions of conservation land are an important incentive for landowners to protect their lands. Indeed, some form of charitable contribution tax benefits have been involved in nearly 50 percent of the conservation transactions undertaken by the Conservancy over the last 10 years.

Donations may involve outright donation, donation with retention of life estate, gift of a conservation easement, or purchase of the land at less than fair market value as a bargain sale. Each of these methods has different tax consequences for the landowner. The Conservancy counsels landowners on which methods may be most beneficial, yet the Conservancy advises landowners to retain their own attorneys to do the sophisticated analysis necessary to determine the tax consequences of donating or selling land to a nonprofit charitable organization.

Several examples illustrate the Conservancy's savvy (names of individuals and organizations involved in the donations have been deleted by request of the Conservancy):

Donation from a private organization. In one case, a private sporting club donated to the Conservancy 25,000 acres containing important marshes and wetlands on the South Carolina coast. The gift, valued at $20 million, was one of the most valuable donations of land ever made to a private conservation organization in the United States. The Nature Conservancy did not retain ownership of the land, but transferred most of the property to the State of South Carolina for creation of a wildlife management area.

Donation from private individuals. The Conservancy had been in discussions for many years with conservation-minded landowners about the possibility of a gift of their land, which would constitute a critical addition to an ecologically important Northern Atlantic white cedar swamp located in Maine. Recently, the landowners were persuaded that, as a result of changes in the tax laws, a gift would be an attractive alternative from a financial perspective. The gift, of approximately 365 acres, was completed and brought to nearly 1,000 the acres of protected land at the bog. The landowner was able to use the charitable contribution deduction from this gift to offset other income from taxes, thereby providing an attractive financial return.

Donation from a private corporation. A Fortune 500 forest products company donated 350 acres of critical wetlands located in northern New Hampshire. The wetlands provided habitat for a number of rare plants and a stand of virgin old growth spruce fir forest. In addition, the site is the headwaters of the Connecticut River. The donation was motivated not only by the tax benefits that would come from the gift but also by the favorable publicity for the company that resulted from the transaction.

Bargain sale by a private individual. One of The Nature Conservancy's most often used acquisition techniques involves what is called a "bargain sale." Using this technique, The Nature Conservancy usually is able to show a landowner how he or she could benefit from a below-market value sale of the land to the Conservancy. In a bargain sale, the seller sells the land for less than full market value and takes advantage of a federal income tax charitable deduction equal to the difference between the full market value and the actual selling price. In this way, the seller also enjoys a reduction in the federal capital gains tax. In a hypothetical case, for example, assume the landowner had bought the property for only $10,000. If he had sold it for $100,000, the fair market value on the open market, he could have expected a net return after taxes of about $60,480. This contrasts with a net return after taxes of approximately $61,020 that he could obtain pursuant to a bargain sale for $85,000 to The Nature Conservancy, assuming current capital gains and ordinary income tax rates.

Assembling land with different owners. Perhaps the most celebrated land acquisition of The Nature Conservancy has been the acquisition of 13 Virginia barrier islands that form a part of a 60-mile chain of 18 uninhabited islands with pristine marshes. Most of the islands were acquired through bargain sales, with some landowners retaining use rights for up to 20 years.

Endnotes

R. Brooks et al., *Wetlands and Wildlife* (Pennsylvania State University, 1993).

Environmental Concern, *WOW — The Wonders of Wetlands* (1995).

J. Goldman-Carter, *A Citizens' Guide to Protecting Wetlands* (National Wildlife Federation, 1989).

J. Kusler and M. Kentulla, *Wetland Creation and Restoration: The Status of the Science* (Island Press, 1990).

Land Trust Alliance, *Doing Deals: A Guide to Buying Land for Conservation* (1995).

Land Trust Alliance, *1995 National Directory of Land Trusts* (1995).

Land Trust Alliance, *Starting a Land Trust* (1990).

Land Trust Alliance, *The Conservation Easement Handbook* (1996).

Land Trust Alliance, *The Conservation Easement Stewardship Guide* (1991).

Land Trust Alliance, *The Federal Tax Law of Conservation Easements* (1990).

Land Trust Alliance, *Preserving Family Lands* (1992).

B. Lynn, *Discover Wetlands: A Curriculum Guide* (Washington Department of Ecology, 1988).

G. Whitaker, *Wetlands Assistance Guide template* (National Wetlands Conservation Alliance, updated regularly).

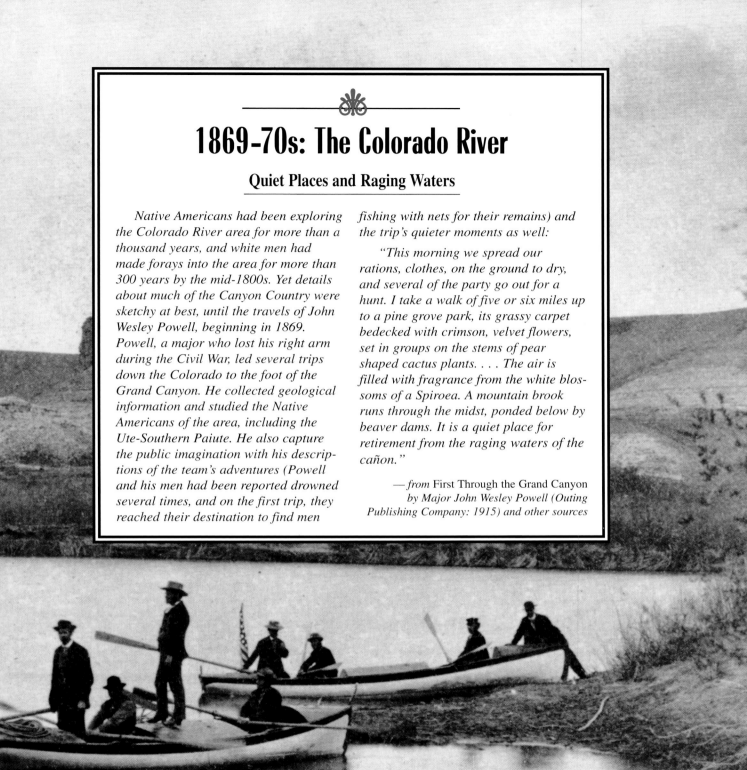

1869-70s: The Colorado River

Quiet Places and Raging Waters

Native Americans had been exploring the Colorado River area for more than a thousand years, and white men had made forays into the area for more than 300 years by the mid-1800s. Yet details about much of the Canyon Country were sketchy at best, until the travels of John Wesley Powell, beginning in 1869. Powell, a major who lost his right arm during the Civil War, led several trips down the Colorado to the foot of the Grand Canyon. He collected geological information and studied the Native Americans of the area, including the Ute-Southern Paiute. He also capture the public imagination with his descriptions of the team's adventures (Powell and his men had been reported drowned several times, and on the first trip, they reached their destination to find men fishing with nets for their remains) and the trip's quieter moments as well:

"This morning we spread our rations, clothes, on the ground to dry, and several of the party go out for a hunt. I take a walk of five or six miles up to a pine grove park, its grassy carpet bedecked with crimson, velvet flowers, set in groups on the stems of pear shaped cactus plants. . . . The air is filled with fragrance from the white blossoms of a Spiroea. A mountain brook runs through the midst, ponded below by beaver dams. It is a quiet place for retirement from the raging waters of the cañon."

— *from* First Through the Grand Canyon *by Major John Wesley Powell (Outing Publishing Company: 1915) and other sources*

What Local Governments Can Do

Chapter 4 introduces many of the techniques available to local governments to protect and restore wetlands. Use the chapter to get an overview of the options available to you as a local official or citizen working with your community's government. Throughout the rest of the book, the strategies are discussed in more detail.

Since state coastal and inland wetland protection statutes were promulgated in the late 1960s and early 1970s, thousands of local governments have adopted and implemented wetland protection efforts. We have learned a lot about which approaches work.

The two most essential components of effective local wetland protection and restoration programs are strong citizen support and the adoption of a clear community wetland protection and restoration policy. That policy is necessary to guide land use planning, water planning, public works projects, zoning, subdivision control, and other government activities.

Local government wetland protection and restoration programs reflect the imagination, talents, knowledge, and enthusiasm of interested citizens and local government officials. Without strong citizen support, chances are slim that governments will adopt wetland protection regulations, acquisition efforts, or tax incentives; or if adopted, that the programs will be tough enough to withstand challenges to them.

Once public programs are adopted, citizens need to provide information for evaluation of development permits and to monitor development in wetlands, since agencies often do not have the human or financial resources to monitor all wetlands. When an agency approves an application for a destructive activity, the decision often is as much the result of citizen apathy as agency policy.

Available options

Local governments implement a broad range of programs which — if properly carried out — will help protect and restore wetlands. (See the table on page 37.) Some of these principal protection options are layed out here, and then discussed throughout the rest of this guidebook.

Adoption of an overall policy to incorporate wetland protection and restoration into government decision making. Community adoption of a simple policy calling for no net loss and a long-term net gain of wetlands can guide all government programs.

Wetland education. Education is needed not only for wetland landowners and other citizens, but for public works departments, community leaders, and interest groups. Crucial topics include wetland values and hazards, threats posed to wetlands by various types of development, and the relationship of wetland protection to broader water and land use goals.

Encouragement and support for private wetland protection efforts by individual landowners or conservation groups. Local governments can encourage private wetland protection efforts through education, tax incentives, mapping, technical assistance, and, in some instances, cost sharing.

Tight monitoring and enforcement of federal, state, and local land and water regulations that directly or indirectly affect the use of wetlands. For example, a community can monitor developments requiring U.S. Army Corps of Engineers permits, report violations to the Corps, and participate in hearings on proposed permits. This approach can improve existing federal regulation without adopting additional new local regulations. (See Chapter 8.)

Donald Reed, Waukesha, Wisconsin:
Using environmental corridors for wetland protection

To effectively manage wetlands in a rapidly urbanizing area, you must plan — but also focus on real-world implementation as well. Donald Reed, a biologist with the Southeast Wisconsin Regional Planning Commission, has done both. Beginning in the mid-1970s, he worked to identify "environmental corridors" in the seven counties of southeast Wisconsin that include Milwaukee and its suburbs. Environmental corridors are linear areas on the landscape that contain concentrations of high-value wetlands, floodplains, shorelines, and other areas critical for groundwater recharge, maintenance of surface water, habitat, and other functions.

A commitment to preserve those corridors was included in the region's land use plan, so Reed went to work with a variety of other agencies to implement the plan through public ownership, state and local shoreland wetland zoning, floodplain zoning, federal wetland regulations, and state utility extension policies. Because of the work by Reed and others, by 1985 about 350 square miles, or about 75 percent of all primary environmental corridor lands in the region, were fully or partially protected. Wetlands comprise about 210 square miles of this total.

Local governments can help administer and enforce a variety of state pollution controls, state sanitary codes prohibiting septic tanks in high groundwater areas, floodplain and floodway regulations, state subdivision regulations, state dredge and fill acts, and state wetland regulations. Communities may also influence federal and state projects proposed for wetland areas by reviewing and commenting on environmental impact statements when these statements are required.

Adoption of environmental impact statement requirements for public and private projects. Adopting these requirements will ensure that developers consider impacts of and alternatives to proposed developments. (See Chapter 7.)

Wetlands and watershed planning. Adopting wetlands and watershed planning efforts not only will help protect and restore wetlands but will help achieve a broad range of other water- and flood-related objectives. (See the discussion below.)

Interim or long-term regulations. Local governments can adopt zoning, subdivision controls, building codes, and special wetland regulations for wetland areas to serve local management and protection goals. Goals may differ, depending upon the circumstances and community preferences, but minimal

goals often include floodway protection and prevention of pollution. (Broader issues and standards are discussed in Chapters 5 and 6.)

Acquisition of fee or partial interest in specific wetlands. Rarely are sufficient funds available to purchase all wetlands. Therefore, local acquisition efforts generally are directed to areas with development threat or special values, such as sites of rare and endangered species. (See Chapter 11.)

Restoration of damaged wetland areas. Local rehabilitation or restoration of wetland areas can reduce erosion on denuded areas, recreate flood storage capability, restore and enhance wildlife habitat, and serve other objectives. (See Chapter 11.)

In addition, *real estate tax incentives for wetlands* can be adopted and *wetland interpretive sites created.* (See Chapter 11.)

Keep in mind that without a well-thought out plan that includes protection and restoration goals and implementation standards, many of these programs could hinder your efforts and may even help destroy wetlands. Key issues in adopting and implementing local government regulatory programs are addressed in Chapters 5, 6, 7, and 10. See also the model wetland protection ordinances contained in Appendix D.

Managing the watershed

When local governments began to adopt wetland protection efforts in the late 1960s, their efforts were quite simple, usually involving mapping of wetland areas and the adoption of wetland conservation zones prohibiting most wetland fills and drainage. This approach continues to be applied, particularly in rural communities with few wetlands and much developable land.

Over a period of years, however, local governments have realized that regulatory approaches need to be supplemented with nonregulatory techniques to achieve particular goals, and local regulations need to be coordinated with federal and state regulations as well. Local wetland regulations also need to be coordinated with local floodplain, stormwater management, water supply, nonpoint source pollution control, tree cutting, coastal zone management, and other regulations. In addition, local regulations need to be coordinated with public works policies (for roads, sewers, and water) and real estate taxation policies.

To formulate overall policies to guide these efforts, some communities have undertaken broader wetland planning or have integrated wetlands into various types of watershed planning. These planning and management efforts have been called by a variety of names, including advanced identification, special area management plans, wetlands and watershed management, environmental corridor management, or multi-objective river corridor management. They vary in scope and objectives, but all involve wetland planning and policy setting in a broader water regime or land use context.

Adoption of an overall wetland policy, such as the no net loss goal that has been adopted by Boulder, Colorado, can guide the individual elements of a broad wetland planning and policy-setting effort. More specific policies then can be formulated and

Selected public wetland protection techniques

Approaches	Advantages	Limitations
Education (such as films, manuals, workshops, conferences)	1. Politically attractive, because it encourages private protection of wetlands 2. Maximizes landowner options	1. Some landowners not responsive 2. Time consuming
Environmental impact statement requirements	1. Requires careful consideration of short- and long-term costs and benefits in decision making 2. Exposes projects to public review	1. Impact review does not protect wetlands unless impact requirements are combined with regulations 2. May be costly and time consuming
Public or private acquisition in fee or easements, through gift, purchase, devise	1. Permanently protects wetland from private development 2. Reduces flood losses 3. Permits scientific and educational use of wetland 4. Permits hunting and other recreational uses 5. No constitutional problem of uncompensated "taking" 6. Federal grants may be available 7. Particularly attractive in urban areas	1. Costly 2. Political opposition may arise to large-scale land acquisition 3. Creates public land management requirements
Land use regulations	1. Protects health and safety from flooding, erosion, pollution 2. Prevents nuisances and fraud 3. Protects wildlife, aesthetic, and other values 4. Low cost to government 5. Can be put into place quickly	1. Must not violate state and federal constitutional provisions 2. May not be adequately enforced 3. Cannot protect all wetlands 4. Generally does not apply to governmental uses 5. Limited application to existing uses
Water level maintenance, impoundment, pumping, other management techniques	1. Stabilizes wetland water levels 2. Increases wetland area 3. Improves wildlife habitat 4. Compensates for effects of prior damage	1. Costly in some instances 2. Maintenance required 3. May disturb flora and fauna
Conservation restrictions (easement or deed restrictions)	1. Prohibits private development while permitting continued private ownership of lands 2. Low cost to government 3. Voluntary, may be politically acceptable	1. Expressly authorized in only a small number of states 2. Does not generally permit public use of land 3. Real estate tax reductions
Real estate tax incentives	1. Encourages private landowners to hold land in open state 2. Reduces burden of restrictions 3. Encourages voluntary protection	1. Reduces local tax revenues 2. Not authorized in all states 3. May not curb speculation in some instances

adopted for specific wetlands within the community. For example, partially degraded wetlands with high restoration potential can be designated for restoration, wetlands on public lands with particular important education values can be designated as "interpretive" sites, and trails, boardwalks, and other interpretative facilities can be constructed. Components of comprehensive wetlands and watershed management efforts are outlined in the table on page 39. Local wetland regulations continue to play the principal role in implementing such efforts.

The West Eugene plan

West Eugene, Oregon, illustrates such a local planning process. West Eugene began its planning efforts after a natural resource study of the town's industrial area had identified major wetlands in the area and the town already had invested more than $20,000,000 for public facilities such as roads and sewers for the area. In 1989, the city council established four objectives for its planning process:

1) To use the best information available to help the community understand the choices available;

2) To find a balance between protection and development that meets state and federal laws;

3) To provide opportunities for involvement of all interested segments of the community in planning development; and

4) To turn a perceived "wetlands problem" into an opportunity.

With this direction, the city council hired the Lane Council of Governments to be project manager. The Lane Council formed a proactive citizens outreach program, mailed out more than 1,000 questionnaires, and conducted many workshops. Summaries of the workshops were provided to the planning commissions, elected officials, and the public.

As the study began, the U.S. Environmental Protection Agency provided the Lane Council with a grant to conduct an "advanced identification" of wetlands. A relatively detailed wetland evaluation was carried out for a 1,300-acre area. The Lane County geographic data system also was used to help with the analysis. Landowners were given an opportunity to review preliminary information that was gathered.

Based upon the analysis, at a May 1990 citizens workshop, three alternatives were presented to the public for the protection of wetlands. The public was involved with creating "visions and goals" for the wetland systems. Wetlands were categorized with an overall no net loss, long-term gain goal.

Local government programs and watershed management

The following selected local government programs may help protect wetlands if they are properly carried out. They can threaten them if not:

Planning and regulatory

Comprehensive land use plan: Plans usually contain an open space element and may specifically address wetland and floodplain areas.

Zoning: Many communities have adopted special wetland protection districts or overlays. These prohibit most activities in wetlands. Some contain density controls, setbacks from waters, and transferable development rights for wetland areas.

Subdivision controls: These often contain requirements that homes be "clustered" together, requirements that parks and open space be dedicated, and stormwater detention requirements.

Sanitary codes: These usually prohibit septic tanks in high groundwater areas.

Floodplain regulations: These usually prohibit fills or other alterations in floodways or broader floodplains. Some prohibit fills in wetlands and other flood storage areas.

Sediment and erosion control, grading ordinances: Some contain buffer and revegetation removal in or near wetlands.

Tree cutting and other vegetation removal ordinances: Some prohibit or limit vegetation removal in or near wetlands and require restoration.

Environmental impact statement requirements: Most require preparation of environmental impact statements for certain types of projects.

Acquisition

Many communities have acquisition programs for parks, recreation areas, greenways, scientific areas, general open space, and public works projects.

Public works projects

These include projects that involve sewers, water supply, solid waste disposal, highways, airports, dikes, levees, channelization, stormwater detention, pipelines, erosion control (bank stabilization), schools, municipal offices, mosquito control, and marinas.

Public land management

(This may overlap with acquisition and public works projects but involves long-term operation and maintenance.) Parks, greenways, sewers, water supply reservoirs, stormwater facilities, forest lands, and other open lands are included here.

A comprehensive watershed management effort: suggested components

❈ Mapping of stream, lake, wetland, and other aquatic resources.

❈ Mapping of other land uses, including land cover, types, and densities of uses.

❈ Description and analysis of the overall hydrologic regime, including low, medium, and high water levels and hydroperiod. (Even relatively superficial analysis may be useful.)

❈ Preliminary assessment of functions, values, and natural hazards of wetlands.

❈ Public outreach and dialogue, including feedback mechanisms to the planning process.

❈ Establishment of water resource and land management goals (pollution control, floodplain management, stormwater management, water supply, etc.) Included should be adoption of a no net loss of wetlands goal.

❈ Designation of potential restoration sites, including potential sites for mitigation banks (if considered desirable).

❈ Establishment of specific standards for particular activities, including activities in wetlands, buffer areas, and broader watershed areas.

❈ Formulation of regulatory and nonregulatory implementation strategies.

❈ Implementation, including supplemental data gathering and analysis through case-by-case permitting.

❈ Applying adaptive management, which involves adjusting the plan as new information becomes available.

Keys to success in this effort were: 1) clear goals and vision; 2) good wetland and other information; 3) an extensive landowners and public involvement process; 4) involvement of all critical players; 5) an integrated approach to wetlands, stormwater, and floodplain management and other resources; 6) good public relations; 7) multiple funding sources; and 8) a lot of hard work.

Over the next decade, local governments will need to play an increasingly strong role in protecting and restoring wetlands, as federal and state budgets and staffing will be cut back to balance budgets. Local governments will need to coordinate with the federal and state efforts to reduce duplication and make the best use of available financial and staff resources. Increasingly, local governments will need to place wetlands in a broader land and watershed management context and to supplement regulations with a broad range of nonregulatory approaches.

Endnotes

Association of State Wetland Managers, *Wetlands and Watershed Management: A Guidebook for Local Governments* (1997).

S. Crane, J. Goldman-Carter, H. Sherk, and M. Senatore, *Wetlands Conservation: Tools for State and Local Action* (World Wildlife Fund, 1995).

T. Henderson, W. Smith, and D. Burke, *Non-Tidal Wetlands Protection: A Handbook for Maryland Local Governments* (Maryland Department of Natural Resources, 1983).

Pennsylvania Department of Environmental Resources, *Wetlands Protection: A Handbook for Local Officials* (1990).

C. Thurow, W. Toner, and D. Erley, *Performance Controls for Sensitive Lands* (American Society of Planning Officials, 1975).

The ultimate plan, adopted in 1992, was more than a wetland plan. It became a multi-objective water resources plan, including natural resources study and management, stormwater quality and conveyance management, floodplain management, recreation, education and interpretation, open space, research, and economic development.

The plan now is being implemented. It helped the city garner $2.97 million in federal grants to buy selected wetlands. More than $1 million in extra funds were obtained for stream restoration and construction of a bike path, and an interpretative center has been created. The city has developed a coordinated local permit procedure and applied for a "local programmatic permit" from the U.S. Army Corps of Engineers.

— The heritage continued —

Bruce Morrison

Lost Island, a wetland in Northwest Iowa. People will treasure and protect only what they understand, which is why education about the value of wetlands is so important. In many areas, such as Boulder, Colorado, and the eastern shore of Maryland, community events are held to celebrate local wetland resources. This wetland in the prairie pothole region is the site of an annual spring wetlands festival, where children and adults gather for demonstrations, canoe trips, hikes, and visits to the nearby wetland interpretation center.

American wetland resources and management today

NEBRASKAland Magazine/Nebraska Game and Parks Commission

A Sandhill crane spreads its wings at Nebraska's Platte River, which each spring provides a "staging ground" for these birds as they migrate from their Southern wintering grounds to northern climes. Sandhill cranes are among the wide variety of waterfowl that find critical habitat in central Nebraska, an area used intensively for agriculture. A variety of initiatives help protect wetlands in the region, including the North American Wetlands Conservation Act, which provides matching grants to private and public agencies to carry out wetland acquisition, restoration, and enhancement projects. The Act was passed in 1989 in part to support the North American Waterfowl Management Plan, an international blueprint for the long-term protection of migratory bird habitat in North America.

A shoreline at Point Lobos, near Carmel, California. Coastal wetlands in the lower 48 states cover more than 26 million acres. Most states give high priority to protecting the wetlands that line their coasts, and federal programs are available to help with those efforts. For example, utilized by many coastal communities is the Coastal Zone Management Program, which provides federal matching grants for the development of protection programs. These programs provide excellent wetland protection opportunities for those working on the local level, as most states have emphasized local and regional rather than state implementation of coastal zone policies.

Baltimore Gas and Electric Company

Patuxent National Wildlife Refuge, near Laurel, Maryland. Mitigation is a crucial part of our federal wetland regulatory program. Under Section 404 of the Clean Water Act, a permit is required for the discharge of dredge and fill materials into the "waters of the United States." If the permit applicant shows that there are no "practicable alternatives" to locating the project in a wetland and that the project's impacts have been minimized, federal guidelines provide that compensation for unavoidable impacts must be provided through activities to restore or create other wetlands. At this site, Baltimore Gas and Electric Company built a 25-acre wetland to mitigate for the federally protected wetlands that were affected by the company's development projects around Washington, D.C.

Virginia Carter

Efforts to preserve, efforts to restore

A bog at the federally owned Apostle Islands National Lakeshore in Wisconsin. Acquisition has been a major strategy in our wetland protection efforts. On the national level, the federal government has preserved a variety of wetlands through the national wildlife refuge system and other programs; many of these sites have citizens groups that support them. Acquisition is a wetland protection option on the state and local levels as well. Acquiring a wetland has several advantages. For example, it can ensure permanent protection of the wetland, whereas regulations are much more susceptible to changing political climates. Despite these advantages, however, the purchase of wetlands can be expensive, particularly in coastal and urbanizing areas, and it can be time-consuming and politically unpopular, especially if done by condemnation. Purchase often cannot buffer the area from adverse developments nearby.

A county forest preserve 30 miles north of Chicago. Restoration work not only is key to turning the tide on our national wetland loss rates, it is an excellent method for getting people committed to wetlands protection. One urban restoration example is the Prairie Wolf Slough project, which will result in the restoration and enhancement of a 42-acre wetland, prairie, and savanna complex on the banks of the Middle Fork of the North Branch of the Chicago River. Citizens groups are playing a leadership role in the project, along with federal, state, regional, and local governments. Recruiting and training adult and student volunteers and establishing environmental education programs have been important elements in the project, as has the solicitation of in-kind services and financial help from businesses and civic organizations. In this picture, members of the Lake County Forest Preserve District's Youth Conservation Corps construct an elevated wooden walkway at the site.

Ted Walker/The Nature Conservancy

Because of a lack of adequate hydrology and other reasons, many on-site mitigation projects have not been successful in replacing wetland functions and values. In Florida, a new approach to on-site mitigation is being tried. At the Disney Wilderness Preserve near Orlando, The Nature Conservancy, The Walt Disney Company, and five regulatory agencies have created a large, *off-site* mitigation project dedicated to restoring and preserving wetlands and other natural communities as an intact ecosystem. The Preserve is located on the Walker Ranch, an 8,500-acre working ranch and natural area 15 miles southeast of existing Disney property. Under the arrangement worked out by the parties, The Walt Disney Company will be able to complete its 20-year development plan without engaging in traditional on-site mitigation for all project aspects. In return, the company purchased the Ranch and provided the funds to restore wetlands and manage them in perpetuity as a reserve.

A restoration site in Snohomish County, Washington. Tens of thousands of wetland restoration and creation projects have been carried out over the last three decades by agencies at the federal, state, and local levels and by the private sector. These projects range in size from a 60,000-acre wetland restoration now under way for an area north of the Everglades, to private projects of a few tenths of an acre on urban residential lots. This wetland was built by the county next to a natural bog that was deteriorating because of nonpoint source pollution coming from nearby rapidly urbanizing areas. The new wetland captures and treats the urban runoff, thereby protecting the bog's water quality and stabilizing its water level fluctuations.

Klaus Richter

Wetlands both urban and rural

Innovative approaches are needed throughout the nation to reconcile wetland protection with economic growth. The Hackensack Meadowlands region in northeast New Jersey, less than 10 miles from New York City, has large expanses of wetlands and enormous development pressure for both upland and wetland sites. The wetlands here are well known as the site of haphazard development, massive solid and hazardous waste dumping — and an innovative planning process that is designed to restore and protect the area's wetland resources. The region's Special Area Management Plan is being developed by a group of agencies to address wetlands enhancement, mitigation banking, streamlined permit processes, and public/private partnerships for improvements that previously were funded almost entirely by the government. According to one of the planners: "The urban estuary of the Meadowlands that was assaulted for many years cannot fully turn around on its own."

Hackensack Meadowlands Development Commission

Although regulation has been the linchpin of our federal wetland protection efforts, in recent years incentive programs have played an increasingly important role, particularly on rural lands such as this ranch in the North Platte Valley of Nebraska. One incentive program is the Wetland Reserve Program, which offers landowners an opportunity to receive payments for restoring and protecting wetlands on their property. Another option for landowners is the Conservation Reserve Program. Under CRP, landowners are given annual rental payments in return for placing environmentally sensitive cropland into an easement and implementing a conservation plan for the land.

With the loss of more than half of the wetlands in the lower 48 states and the shift of population to urban areas, where wetland losses have been much greater, the need for wetland interpretation and education opportunities for city dwellers is more critical than ever. One of the largest urban wetland interpretation sites in the nation is Huntley Meadows in Alexandria, Virginia. The facility, which includes an interpretation center, extensive boardwalks, observation towers, and many educational and interpretive programs, is an oasis for the metropolitan Washington, D.C., area. More than 200,000 visitors a year stop at this site with open freshwater marsh, scrub, and forested wetlands that also serves as a major natural flood storage area.

Challenges scientific and political

Poorly understood by the public and policy makers is a seemingly anomalous feature of wetlands: Short-term damage due to extreme events can have long-term benefits. In fact, many wetlands — including the Florida Everglades ecosystem — are long-lived precisely because they have been subjected to hurricanes, floods, droughts, and fires. Hurricanes and high-velocity floods scour sediments and organic matter, removing them from existing wetlands or creating new wetlands at nearby sites. Droughts temporarily prevent the germination of hydrophytic vegetation and allow oxidation and compaction of organic soils. Fires burn peat, exotic plants, and other organic matter. In fact, fire is considered a valuable management tool for many wetlands, including this one at The Nature Conservancy's Disney Wilderness Preserve near Orlando, Florida.

Walt Thomson/The Nature Conservancy

Commercial fishermen working in Louisiana's Atchafalaya Basin. Louisiana contains 40 percent of the nation's coastal wetlands and a commercial fisheries harvest that is valued at one billion dollars per year. Yet the state's wetlands face a dire future from both an ecological and economic perspective unless the state harnesses significant political resolve to protect the resource. By 2040, Louisiana's shoreline could retreat as much as 33 miles in some areas for a variety of reasons, including the levees that line the length of the Mississippi River. Before the levees were built, as the Mississippi would flood, its water would spread out over the land, depositing the silt and sediment load, which would replenish existing wetlands.

A variety of groups are working to address the problems. On the federal level, a task force of five federal agencies and the State of Louisiana is engaged in comprehensive and long-term planning and projects to restore coastal wetlands. Federal funds are being provided on a matching basis for the construction, implementation, and operation of the projects. On the state level, the Coalition to Restore Coastal Louisiana and others have convinced the state's voters to create a constitutionally protected wetlands restoration fund to be used for state projects and for matching funds required on federal projects.

Greg Guirard

Few wetlands in the lower 48 states are in a pristine state. Water pollution, filling or draining, and the invasion of exotic species such as purple loosestrife, shown here in a wetland in Minnesota, are all implicated. Greatly increased sediment and nutrient loadings from watersheds that are undergoing urbanization, agricultural development, or clear-cutting can change a wetland's mix of plant and animal species dramatically — and can quickly destroy wetlands. The non-native purple loosestrife *(Lythrum salicaria)* is a tall purple-flowered emergent hydrophyte that has spread at an alarming rate throughout the country, aggressively displacing native grasses, sedges, and rushes.

Bill Witt

Protection for public and for private lands

Jon Kusler

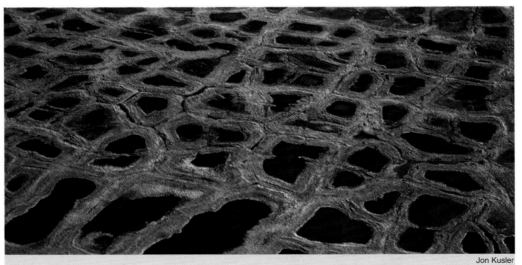

Jon Kusler

These Alaska wetlands were formed by the melting of permafrost. Local involvement is crucial to make sure that programs fit community needs as well as wetland protection. In Alaska, there are approximately 175 million acres of wetlands, comprising approximately 43 percent of the surface area of the state — more wetland acreage than the rest of the United States combined. In 1993 and 1994, a diverse group of Alaska citizens, the U.S. Environmental Protection Agency, and the U.S. Army Corps of Engineers came together to develop the Alaska Wetlands Initiative. The Initiative lists action items to be implemented by the federal agencies, many in coordination with the state, Native peoples, and other participating stakeholders, to ensure wetland protection and appropriate regulatory flexibility to reflect Alaska's unique circumstances.

One-third of the nation's lands are federally owned, such as this wetland site in Rocky Mountain National Park. Wetland protection is required or encouraged on federal lands in a variety of ways that can be influenced by those working on the local level. For example, the National Environmental Policy Act requires that environmental impact statements be prepared for any federal activity with a major impact upon the environment. Under the Act, citizens must be given an opportunity to comment on draft environmental impact statements. In doing so, they can highlight the detrimental side effect of a proposed activity. Even if a project is not halted as a result of a negative review, it may be significantly modified to alleviate potential harm.

During the period ending only in the 1970s, the federal government pursued contradictory wetland policies. In areas of the Midwest such as Kossuth County, Iowa, for example, farmers on some parcels were draining wetlands with monies and technical assistance from the U.S. Department of Agriculture, while nearby farmers — or even the same farmers — were protecting wetlands through easements from the U.S. Fish and Wildlife Service. Today, programs such as "Swampbuster" have become a major part of wetland protection efforts on agricultural lands. Established in the 1985 Farm Bill, Swampbuster discourages the conversion of wetlands to agricultural use by withholding certain federal farm program benefits from farmers who convert or modify wetlands, even those temporary wetlands they are able to crop in most years.

Tim McCabe/Natural Resources Conservation Service

There are more than 3.2 million miles of rivers, streams, and creeks in the United States, which form a drainage network in every state and climate region in the nation, including in the area around Millers River in Massachusetts, pictured here. All of these rivers, streams, and creeks are subject to periodic flooding and need riverine wetlands and adjacent floodplain lands to store flood waters, gradually releasing water downstream. A primary community objective for the control of wetlands is the prevention of harmful activities in these wetlands and floodplains to prevent increase flood heights and velocities and erosion on other lands. Approaches to protect flood-prone uses include tightly controlling fills, buildings, and other obstructions in wetlands that serve as floodway areas and flood storage areas.

Jon Kusler

Protection on a large scale and on a small

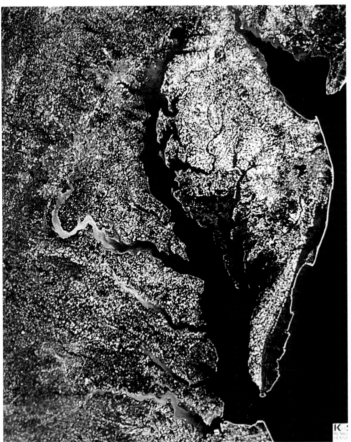

Chesapeake Bay Foundation

Wetlands have close ecological and hydrologic relationships with adjacent lands and with other wetlands and aquatic systems, and a watershed-wide focus is needed to protect them most effectively. Many citizens, land trusts, and local governments are involved in one of the largest of watershed efforts: that for the Chesapeake Bay. The Bay has 150 tributaries draining a watershed of 64,000 square miles in parts of six states (Delaware, Maryland, New York, Pennsylvania, Virginia, and West Virginia) and the District of Columbia. Population in the Bay watershed is 15 million people and will climb by about 3 million by the year 2020. Sprawl development continues to take large amounts of land in the watershed.

For a resource this widespread and challenges that great, individuals, communities, land trusts, environmental groups, and all levels of the government are using a variety of wetland protection techniques, including the adoption of wetland ordinances, monitoring of wetland permitting programs, incentive programs for area landowners, public education programs, and other techniques. All are working toward the policy set in 1988 by the Chesapeake Executive Council, a group of high-ranking officials in the region: "An immediate goal of no net loss with a long-term goal of a 'net resource gain' ... as a means of recovering the values of wetlands already lost over years of inadequate protection."

This composite image, taken by a Landsat satellite, shows a portion of the Bay's watershed, from roughly Baltimore, Maryland, in the north to Norfolk, Virginia, in the south. The marshlands in coastal regions of the Bay are a deep chocolate color, bare fields appear light tan, and the Bay itself is a dark blue/black color. This image shows extensive spring sediment runoff from agricultural lands in rivers such as the Potomac and the James.

A photo mosaic showing marshes adjacent to San Diego Bay—and the extensive urban development of Chula Vista, California. The Bay is the dark green area to the left; the marshes are the orange areas. Also shown are a flood control channel, dredge spoil, constructed islands, highways, and a development. A mixed residential, commercial, and industrial use area such as this presents many management challenges and a stark reminder that how a landscape is used has a great deal to do with the quality of a wetland. Land use determines, to a considerable extent, the type and quantity of sediment, nutrients, debris, and pollutants entering wetlands.

Since 1988, the natural marshes, constructed marshes, and some

upland at this site have been protected as part of the Sweetwater Marsh National Wildlife Refuge, run by the U.S. Fish and Wildlife Service. The coastal wetlands here are managed as a wildlife preserve, and public access is restricted; however, the city of Chula Vista's visitor center near the site is a popular spot for schoolchildren. The wetlands are used by scientists to evaluate how well the natural marshes function compared to the functioning of constructed marshes. Sweetwater Marsh also is the site of an endangered plant reintroduction, which is being undertaken by a company as part of a mitigation project.

Pacific Estuarine Research Laboratory, San Diego State University

Key Issues to Consider

Chapter 5 presents a variety of questions — and some answers — you should consider as you design or revise a wetland protection strategy. Examining these issues will help you devise a program that best fits the needs of your community, thereby making it more likely your efforts will have long-term success.

Although circumstances differ, citizens, land trusts, and local governments face a number of common issues in establishing and implementing wetland and restoration protection programs. These issues include:

• Which wetland definition should be used?

• Is wetland mapping necessary? If so, at what scales and levels of accuracy?

• How can wetlands be delineated on the ground?

• How can protection and management policies be varied for particular wetlands?

• Should wetlands be ranked or classified? If so, how?

• What factors are relevant to selection of protection and restoration implementation techniques?

• What techniques are available for reducing costs of program development and implementation?

• What sources of expertise are available?

• How can legal problems be avoided?

Which wetland definition should be used?

A variety of definitions for "wetlands" are used in the United States for scientific, regulatory, planning, and other purposes. (See Chapter 2.) For an excellent discussion of the various wetland definitions, including the various factors that are relevant to definition of wetlands, see the National Research Council's report *Wetlands: Characteristics and Boundaries.*

Before deciding which wetland definition you should use, first consider the purpose or purposes for the definition. If you wish to help enforce a state or federal wetland regulatory statute or to apply for a permit pursuant to such a statute, use the definition contained in the regulatory statute or regulation. If you wish to adopt local wetland maps using National Wetland Inventory (NWI) maps, use the NWI wetland definition.

If you wish to define wetlands for several purposes simultaneously, such as local regulation and implementation of state and federal regulations, either use several definitions simultaneously or adopt a broad definition that will encompass all of the areas covered by the individual definitions. For example, the NWI definition is quite broad and encompasses areas included by many more specific definitions.

The wetland definition applied in a particular context is important, because it determines the scope of a planning, regulatory, restoration, or other management program.

All wetland definitions use some combination of hydrology, soils, and vegetation to define wetlands. Most wetland definitions include permanently or semi-permanently flooded tidal or coastal areas, including most lake and river fringe wetlands. Differences arise for infrequently flooded or saturated areas with vegetation characteristics of both wetland and upland areas. For example, arguments are made that one frequency of flooding or inundation, such as 14 days, versus another frequency, such as 21 days, should be considered the dividing line between wetland and nonwetland. There also are differences of opinion concerning the time of the year in which flooding or inundation is to be measured, the types of vegetation and soils that characterize a wetland, and the extent to which hydrophytic

"As stewards of these resources, all of us in the public, private, and nonprofit sectors must work together to protect them for the use and benefit of future generations."

— The Conservation Foundation, *Protecting America's Wetlands: An Action Agenda* (1988)

vegetation and hydric soils must be present in all instances.

Generally, local governments must utilize a state wetland definition (or adopt one that is at least as broad as the state's) if they are to implement a state wetland regulatory law. States take several approaches:

Definition based on tidal action. Usually state statutes for coastal wetlands refer to tidal levels. For example, Virginia defines coastal wetlands to include all land "lying between and contiguous to mean water and an elevation above mean low water equal to the factor 1.5 times the mean tide range." Tidal definitions are supplemented with vegetation criteria.

Definition based on inundation by surface waters or flood waters. States define inland wetlands to include areas with standing water and emergent vegetation. All definitions include some areas subject to periodic flooding.

Definition based on vegetation. Vegetation lists for plants capable of growing in wet soils are included in most state statutes. Vegetation lists usually are combined with tidal or flooding criteria.

Tips for delineating wetlands

Easy ones: The boundaries of wetlands with permanent or semipermanent water, sharp topographic gradients (slopes) at their margins, and hydrophytic vegetation often can be delineated quite easily by citizens and local government officials. These wetlands include:

❀ Most coastal and estuarine fringe wetlands. The tide line, which quite closely coincides with the coastal or estuarine wetland boundary, can be identified quite easily in most instances by observing the tide and the vegetation, which changes from easily recognizable salt-tolerant to freshwater species.

❀ Riverine wetlands for moderate- to high-gradient streams with a narrow floodplain. The wetland/upland boundary is narrow due to quick changes in elevation.

❀ Lake fringe wetlands in glaciated regions where most lakes have a topographic "ridge." The wetland/upland boundary also is narrow here due to the topographic ridge.

❀ Other wetlands occupying depressions with sharp topographic gradients.

❀ Permanently or semi-permanently flooded wetlands, such as "swamps," "marshes," and "oxbow wetlands," with standing water, organic soils, and tree and other plant species adapted to aquatic conditions.

More difficult: The boundaries of certain other wetlands are more difficult to delineate, including many altered (by activities of man and natural catastrophes) wetlands, wetlands with gradual topographic gradients at their margins, or wetlands that are less frequently flooded or saturated. Usually the help of a technical expert is needed. Delineation of these wetlands often requires examination of soils, vegetation, hydrologic records, and other less obvious features. These wetlands include:

❀ The "easy ones" (left), if they have been diked, leveed, partially filled, or partially drained.

❀ The "easy ones" (left), after a major flood or hurricane that destroys wetland vegetation and soils.

❀ Many "easy ones" (left) during a major and prolonged drought. Wetland vegetation often disappears.

❀ Seasonally flooded or saturated wetlands, such as tidal/freshwater marshes, wet meadows, and certain shrub and forested wetlands.

❀ Certain seeps, prairie potholes, and other wetlands that depend upon groundwater and are flooded only a portion of the year as groundwater levels fluctuate.

❀ Certain coastal or estuarine wetlands, which grade into freshwater marshes or swamps.

❀ Areas flooded for a single year or several years by unusually high rainfall or snow.

Very difficult: The boundaries of certain other wetlands are even more difficult to delineate and almost always require the help of an expert. Long-term hydrologic indicators (such as land form and flood flow records), soils, historic records, hydrologic monitoring, and other studies may be needed. These wetlands include:

❀ Infrequently or seasonally flooded areas in semi-arid and arid regions, such as certain riparian habitat, playas, wet meadows, and ridge and swale areas (which are found in wet and dry areas in close proximity to oceans and rivers).

❀ Seasonally flooded wetlands (left), which have also been partially drained, filled, diked, etc.

❀ Certain "flats," such as pine flatwood, with little surface flooding and a combination of plant species adopted to both aquatic and non-aquatic environments.

Definition based on soils. In Connecticut, inland wetland areas are defined to include poorly drained, very poorly drained, alluvial, and floodplain soils. Soils are used in other states to supplement vegetation lists.

Some wetland definitions require the presence of hydrophytic vegetation, hydric soils, and wetland hydrology *in all instances*. This means, however, that areas denuded by a flood, hurricane, or fire would be nonwetland for a year or two, wetland again, and then nonwetland after another catastrophic event. This makes little sense and provide landowners with little predictability or certainty.

How can wetlands be delineated?

Wetland delineation involves the application of wetland definition criteria to sites on the ground, including determination whether an area is, in fact, a wetland, and also the boundaries of the wetland. Delineation procedures involve examining plants and soils and various "evidence" of hydrology to determine the boundary between a wetland and upland.

Usually field delineation of wetland boundaries is necessary, even where wetland maps exist, to refine map boundaries. Often boundaries are drawn on a large-scale air photo, and boundaries may be staked on the ground. Wetland delineation can be relatively easy or difficult, depending upon the type of wetland and the circumstances. (See the table on page 54.)

A number of federal wetland delineation manuals have been developed. The best known and most widely used manual is the U.S. Army Corps of Engineers' *1987 Manual for the Delineation of Jurisdictional Wetlands*. This manual is broadly used not only for the federal Section 404 regulatory program but for many other federal agency efforts. Several states, such as Wisconsin, New York, and Michigan, have published their own wetland delineation manuals.

Is mapping needed?

Not all government units with wetland protection programs map wetlands. At the federal level, regulatory maps have not been adopted for the Section 404 program. Instead, the Section 404 program relies upon a written wetland definition, a delineation manual, and the application of the manual in the field. Such an approach is less expensive than mapping and allows delineation to reflect the dynamic nature of wetlands. However, it also creates uncertainty and unpredictability for landowners.

Most local governments with wetland programs have either mapped their wetlands or adopted wetland maps from other sources to help landowners and to comply with state wetland statutes, which often require such mapping.

Several mapping approaches are common. First, communities can adopt existing wetland maps prepared by state agencies.

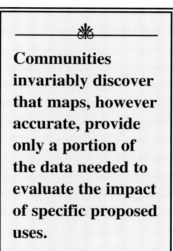

Communities invariably discover that maps, however accurate, provide only a portion of the data needed to evaluate the impact of specific proposed uses.

This has been done in Connecticut, Massachusetts, New York, Virginia, and Wisconsin, where state agencies or universities have undertaken mapping. However, these special state wetland maps are available for only a portion of the country.

Existing state and federal wetland maps usually are at scales of 1:12,000 (1 inch for every 12,000 feet) to 1:24,000, a size that limits their application for local regulatory purposes. Most state and federal inventories have been based on air photo interpretation of vegetation with limited field surveys. Often, communities enlarge existing wetland maps for regulatory purposes. However, scale enlargement does not cure basic inaccuracies.

Second, many communities have adopted federal maps. National Wetland Inventory maps are the most common. But some communities have adopted U.S. Geological Survey (USGS) topographic and planimetric maps, Soil Conservation Service (SCS) soil survey maps, and flood maps prepared by the Federal Emergency Management Agency, the Army Corps of Engineers, and other agencies.

Third, some local governments have prepared new wetland maps through air photo interpretation combined with available wetland data from soil maps, topographic maps, flood maps, existing wetland inventories, field surveys, and other sources. Most efforts emphasize air photo interpretation with limited field sampling.

Usually, enlarged USGS topographic maps, air photos, or town tax maps are used as base maps. Information from other data sources is transferred to the base maps, except in the case of air photos, which may themselves be used as base maps as well as for interpretation of wetland boundaries. Final maps take the form of printed maps, mylar overlays, or air photo reproductions. Wetland maps often are prepared at large scales (1:1,200 to 1:7,200), particularly if they are for urban regulatory purposes. Some examples are listed in the table on page 57 and are illustrated in the figure on page 61.

Several considerations may aid a community in deciding whether to map wetlands and what approach should be taken:

The intended use of wetland maps should be carefully evaluated. For some purposes, wetland maps will need to be supplemented with other types of data. For example, statistical and written data concerning the number of wetlands of a particular type, their values and hazards, uniqueness, ownership, existing uses, and threats from proposed development are important in developing wetland policies, drafting regulatory standards, establishing acquisition priorities, and processing development permits. Only a portion of this information can be gathered through mapping or presented in map form.

Large-scale maps (1:24,000 and larger) usually are needed for wetland regulatory efforts. Maps prepared at small scales often are of little value for regulatory purposes unless they can be enlarged with a satisfactory degree of accuracy, since correlation with ground sites is difficult. But small-scale wetland maps (1:24,000 to 1:100,000) may serve for comprehensive land use planning, public facilities planning, and evaluation of surface water and groundwater flow systems.

Wetland maps must reflect wetland definition criteria and statutory map requirements. New maps are required if statutes or administrative regulations specify particular vegetation or other criteria and existing maps do not incorporate these criteria. Some statutes require preparation of wetland maps, although most are silent as to the need for mapping or map specifics.

Available funds, expertise, and equipment must be considered. Preparation of new, large-scale maps is expensive. Often, existing maps must be used as a matter of economic necessity.

The degree of urbanization and threat to wetland areas influences mapping needs. Depending on the topography of the area, small-scale, less accurate maps may be satisfactory for rural areas with little development pressure. Legal and political challenges to the maps are less common, and individual field inspections may be used to resolve boundary disputes. In contrast, detailed, accurate maps often are needed for urban and urbanizing areas where land values are high and development pressures are severe. Large-scale maps reduce political problems, legal challenges, and the need for field investigations to resolve boundary disputes. However, they also are expensive and cumbersome.

The development standards applied to an area are relevant to map scale and accuracy. In general, large-scale, accurate maps are needed for application of highly restrictive and specific regulations prohibiting private uses. In contrast, small-scale, less accurate maps may be acceptable where more general performance standards are applied, since supplemental data gathering and refinement of boundary lines may be carried out on a case-by-case basis.

Too much emphasis on map scale and accuracy and expensive mapping may interfere with the primary objective of mapping: to provide information for wetland decision making. Communities invariably discover that maps, however accurate, provide only a portion of the data needed to evaluate the impact of specific proposed uses. Even large-scale maps cannot reflect the variability in vegetation, soil types, flood hazards, wildlife, and other parameters that determine the suitability of particular sites for development. Consequently, field investigations must be undertaken to refine wetland boundaries on the ground and to evaluate the impact of each proposed development. For this reason, some communities define wetlands through both maps and written definition criteria (vegetation, soils) that can be applied on the ground through field investigations. Such an approach was upheld by the Wisconsin Supreme Court in the landmark

wetland case *Just v. Marinette County*. There the county adopted USGS topographic maps as basic wetland maps but also provided in an ordinance that, in case of boundary disputes, field surveys would be conducted to determine whether aquatic vegetation referenced in the ordinance actually was found at the site.

Arguments are sometimes made that wetlands should be mapped in urban areas at scales of 1:200 or larger to provide certainty to landowners. However, mapping at this scale is very expensive. In addition, detailed mapping may give rise to the erroneous belief that wetland boundaries can be located with mathematical precision. In fact, boundaries shift somewhat since they reflect a natural transition from water to upland and fluctuating groundwater or surface water levels.

How can protection and restoration policies reflect differences in wetlands?

All wetlands are not of equal value, nor are their natural hazards of equal seriousness. Your community may want to apply special policies to particular types of wetland or areas within a wetland. For example, particularly tight protection policies may be applied to wetlands serving as habitat for a rare or endangered species or as a flood conveyance area (floodway) for rivers or streams. Less restrictive policies may be applied to other wetlands.

States and communities have applied three approaches to reflect differences between wetlands in regulation, planning, and other management:

A regulatory agency or board may undertake case-by-case evaluation of permits and reflect differences in applying criteria and in the attachment of conditions to permits. Most differences between wetland functions and values and other characteristics are assessed on a case-by-case basis as wetland permit applications are submitted to a regulatory agency or site planning occurs on a specific property. For example, permits for activities in lower salt marsh areas may be denied, while permits for activities in high marsh areas may be approved with special conditions. Permits may be denied for activities in the center of wetlands but may be allowed at the margins.

A legislative body or regulatory board may adopt specific written regulations or maps that distinguish wetlands by type, size, and other criteria. In some instances, localities apply protection policies to a particular type or size of wetland but not to others by providing written descriptions of categories or types of wetlands. For example, many states regulate only coastal wetlands. New York regulates only those inland wetlands that are more than 12 acres.

Similarly, many local governments only regulate "mapped" wetlands. Wetland maps are prepared from air photos

> **All wetlands are not of equal value, nor are their natural hazards of equal seriousness. Your community may want to apply special policies to particular types of wetland or areas within a wetland.**

Some principal wetland data sources

Data source	Information displayed	Suggested uses
Topographic maps (7' and 15') (U.S. Geological Survey)	Topographic contours, major roads, railroads, utility lines, contours, water bodies, houses, town names, county and town boundaries, vegetated and nonvegetated wetlands. Scale: 1" = 2,000' or 1" = 24,000'	1. Enlarged for use as wetland base map 2. Interim wetland map 3. Watershed boundaries 4. Source of topographic information
Soil survey maps (Natural Resources Conservation Service)	Soil types Scale: 1" = 2,000', 1" = 1,320', or 4" = 1 mile	1. Interim wetland map 2. Determination of soil suitability for on-site waste disposal 3. Determination of soil structural bearing capacity
State wetland maps	Varied wetland vegetation boundaries Scale: 1" = 24,000' to 1" = 1,200'	1. Interim wetland regulation maps 2. Permanent wetland maps (depends on scale)
Flood hazard boundary maps (U.S. Geological Survey, Federal Emergency Management Agency)	Flood-prone areas Scale: Approx. 1" = 2,000'	1. Interim mapping of wetlands 2. Assess flood hazard potential at wetland sites
Floodplain information reports (U.S. Army Corps of Engineers)	Standard project floodplain, 100-year flood evaluation wetland boundaries on some maps Scale: Range from 1" = 500' to 1" = 1,000'	1. Assess flood hazard potential at wetland sites
Hydrologic investigations atlas: hydrology and water resources (U.S. Geological Survey)	Each map differs and may contain wells, test holes, bedrock, groundwater quality information Scale: 1" = 2,000' or 1" = 24,000'	1. Determine groundwater flow systems 2. Determine aquifer recharge areas
Wetland inventory maps (U.S. Fish and Wildlife Service)	A wide variety of information pertaining to vegetation, water regime, and other parameters Scale: 1" = 24,000' or 1" = 100,000'	1. Regulatory mapping 2. Aid in processing permits 3. Acquisition 4. Siting
Subdivision maps	Dimensions of property, size, and location of house, width of easements. Wetland and floodplain boundaries (some circumstances) Scale: 1" = 40' to 1" = 60'	1. Determine precise wetland boundaries (some instances) 2. Evaluate individual developments
Air photos (Agricultural Stabilization and Conservation Service, now the Farm Service Agency)	Existing uses, vegetation, water resources, roads (black and white stereoscope) Scale: 1" = 24,000'	1. Define wetland boundaries based upon vegetation 2. Use as base maps 3. Evaluate individual proposed uses
Air photos (orthophoto quadrangles) (U.S. Geological Survey)	Existing uses, vegetation, water resources, roads (not stereoscope) Scale: 1" = 24,000'	1. Define wetland boundaries based upon vegetation 2. Are particularly useful as base maps 3. Evaluate individual proposed uses
Surficial geology (U.S. Geological Survey)	Everything on USGS topographic maps plus geologic deposits, bedrock fill sites Scale: 1" = 2,000' or 1" = 24,000'	1. Determine groundwater flow 2. Determine bedrock characteristics
Town, city, county, borough zoning maps	Each municipality has its own map information. Information can include roads, property lines, zoning districts, wetland boundaries, floodplain boundaries. Scale: Range from 1" = 500' to 1" = 1,000'	1. Determine existing uses 2. Determine compatibility of proposed wetland uses with zone classifications and adjacent uses 3. Use as wetland base maps
Assessors' maps	Property lines, owners' names, easements, roads, buildings Scale: 1" = 100' or 1" = 200'	1. Determine wetland areas 2. Grant tax incentives to wetland areas

with a resolution permitting identification of wetlands one-quarter to 1 acre but not smaller wetlands. Other local governments only map wetlands in certain areas (such as coastal zones or shoreland areas within 1,000 feet of lakes).

The New York tidal wetlands program has divided coastal marshes into six types or zones with varying suitability for particular uses: coastal fresh marsh, intertidal marsh, high marsh or salt marsh, coastal shoals, bars and flats, and the littoral zone and adjacent areas. Similarly, Virginia has developed guidelines for use of particular vegetative zones in coastal marshes. The Virginia Institute of Marine Science has produced several guidebooks to assist local governments in identifying these zones, understanding the importance of them, and controlling development.

A state legislature or local agency may "classify" wetlands in advance. Some states and local governments have adopted more formal advance "classification" of wetlands. With this approach, wetlands are grouped or classified, and different policies are applied to different wetlands up front. (See the following discussion.)

Are wetlands to be ranked or classified?

Ranking or classification of wetlands for regulatory or other purposes has been proposed by development groups in recent years but has not been widely undertaken for a variety of reasons:

• Any attempt to systematically rate and rank wetlands on a community or regional basis by taking into account a large number of characteristics may require extremely large amounts of natural resource data and, to a lesser extent, cultural data. Data pertaining to site-specific soils, geology, and wildlife, including rare and endangered species, can be generated only through field surveys at considerable expense.

• The classification may become quickly out of date due to changes in watershed hydrology, such as urbanization, which greatly increases flood peaks and sedimentation and reduces water quality. Classification reflecting existing values may also become quickly outdated, depending upon population growth in a region and changing land uses and needs.

• Any effort to rank wetlands according to a numerical scale must deal with situations where a single value is of primary importance (such as when a bald eagle's nest is found). The ranking system must permit special weighing for this characteristic.

• Any effort to rank according to numerical scale must distinguish between complementary and conflicting values. For example, value scores should not be added where a wetland is habitat for rare species and also a potential groundwater extraction site, if these two uses are incompatible.

• Any effort to rank wetlands should be flexible enough to take into account all factors considered important to a particular wetland decision.

Experience with these and other attempts to rank wetlands according to numerical ranking systems suggests that such systems are useful for certain purposes, such as wetland acquisition, but they have severe limitations for regulatory purposes.

Tips for avoiding legal problems

The best overall strategy is to reduce conflicts and resolve problems before regulations are challenged in court. However, also be prepared for court suits if they become necessary. Recommendations for both avoiding legal problems and preparing for court include:

❋ ***Talk with and educate landowners.*** Help them understand how protecting and restoring wetlands will help and benefit them, not just the public. Help them understand how avoiding wetlands can save them money (by reducing flood damage) and avoid costs. Help them understand how they can comply with regulations and achieve their own land use objectives.

❋ ***Map wetlands to help landowners locate wetland boundaries and make maps readily available.*** This will increase certainty and predictability in use of lands.

❋ ***Provide technical assistance and help to landowners in identification of wetlands, assessment of wetlands, and regulatory permitting.*** This will increase certainty and predictability and reduce frustration and economic burdens.

❋ ***Carefully follow all statutory and ordinance procedures with regard to ordinance adoption, public hearings and notices, mapping, and other requirements.*** Many successful court suits are based upon failure to follow proscribed procedures.

❋ ***Be fair and nondiscriminatory in implementing regulations.*** Both landowners and courts are sensitive to what they perceive as unfair or discriminatory treatment.

❋ ***Reduce real estate taxes and special assessments (sewer, water, and levees, for example) for tightly regulated wetland areas.*** This is a common complaint of landowners.

❋ ***Adopt joint permitting procedures with state and federal regulatory agencies so that landowners have (to the extent possible) one-stop shopping.*** Such joint permitting procedures may involve several levels of government and several types of programs (including the federal Section 404, state wetland and floodplain, local wetland, floodplain, and stormwater programs).

❋ ***Adopt large-lot zoning for wetland areas so that there will be buildable areas on each lot.*** This will provide landowners and purchasers with economic uses and help avoid "takings" problems.

❋ ***Adopt transferrable development rights schemes so that wetland owners may sell and transfer a portion of their development credits to other properties.***

❋ ***Acquire fee interests or conservation easements from landowners for particularly sensitive areas or where regulations will prevent all private use of lands.***

❋ ***Work to provide landowners with financial incentives (such as income tax deductions) for donating fee or partial interests in wetlands.***

If a rating system is to be used to determine the desirability of wetlands for development, some effort also should be made to rate upland sites. Efforts to rate only wetlands may give a false impression that wetlands with low ratings should be developed, even though unrated adjacent upland areas may be more desirable development sites.

An extensive and systematic community effort to map, evaluate, and rank wetlands to define specific policies for particular wetlands and subzones within wetlands was carried out for Dane County, Wisconsin, by a team from the University of Wisconsin Arboretum. This team collected information for each wetland from air photos, field surveys, and other sources to evaluate wetland type, dominant vegetation, water quality, wildlife, major geologic features, acreage, upland and wetland use, extent and type of water and soil, vegetation disturbance, and existing problems. Wetland maps were prepared and each wetland was evaluated for present or possible biological value, scientific value, public use, extent of degradation, and extent of immediate or long-term threats. Wetlands were placed in five priority groupings according to their use and biological value. This information was synthesized in *The Wetlands of Dane County*, which provides both an overview of the size, condition, and value of wetlands in that county and proposes specific management and protection policies and techniques.

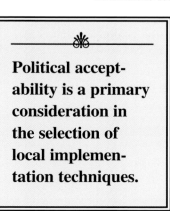

Political acceptability is a primary consideration in the selection of local implementation techniques.

What factors are relevant to the selection of implementation techniques?

Wetland regulations are the most widespread wetland protection implementation technique in use in the United States today, but regulations are subject to many limitations. Public acquisition of wetland areas is sometimes preferable as a means of providing permanent protection and public access. Yet acquisition often is difficult due to escalating land costs and the reluctance of communities to remove land from the tax rolls (although some governmental agencies and nonprofit organizations do pay taxes on publicly owned lands).

The advantages and disadvantages of these and other techniques are summarized in the table on page 37 and are discussed in the chapters that follow. The selection of a particular technique or combination of techniques may depend on several factors:

The scope of local and state regulatory powers. Local units of government and state agencies possess only those powers expressly granted to them through statutes, charters, or, in the case of local governments, home rule provisions. Therefore, the power to adopt particular wetland protection or management techniques varies from one unit of government to another and from state to state. Nevertheless, cities and villages have a wide range of regulatory and land acquisition powers under enabling statutes or home rule provisions in virtually all states.

Political acceptability. Political acceptability is a primary consideration in the selection of acquisition, regulation, rehabilitation, and other local implementation techniques. Legislative acceptance depends on community support. In some instances, new wetland regulations have proven politically unacceptable, and protection must be achieved through nonregulatory approaches. On the other hand, many local legislative bodies are reluctant to fund expensive acquisition efforts and are opposed to condemnation. Here, regulations may be more politically acceptable.

Wetland protection and management goals. Implementation techniques must be related to community and state wetland management goals that often include some or all of the standards suggested in Chapter 6. Particular goals depend on community preferences, political acceptability, wetland characteristics, land ownership, threats, and broader community land and water use plans. Many implementation techniques may serve a wide range of goals. For example, both regulation and acquisition may be used to reduce flood hazards, preserve wetland functions, and reduce water pollution. However, some techniques are needed to achieve specific goals, such as adoption of regulations to control point and nonpoint sources of pollution throughout a watershed and the use of acquisition to permit public use of wetland areas.

Funding. Available funding often is a primary consideration. Public purchase of extensive wetland areas is impossible unless large sums of money are available. Regulations, public education, and environmental impact statement requirements are less expensive.

Available expertise. A community employing planners, biologists, hydrologists, and engineers is better able to adopt and administer sophisticated wetland regulations. One with less expertise may favor outright acquisition.

Rural, urbanizing, and urban conditions. Wetland acquisition often is preferable in urban and urbanizing contexts where land values and taxes are high and public use of land for recreation is needed. In contrast, regulations often are more satisfactory for rural wetlands that face little development pressure.

What techniques are available for reducing costs?

Although state and federal grants-in-aid may be available, typically local wetland programs must be formulated and implemented with little money. Programs often employ a variety of techniques to reduce costs:

• Existing wetland and resource maps are used to avoid the cost of new map preparation. Existing air photos often are applied where new maps are needed. Small-scale mapping may be used initially with refinements through data gathering on a case-by-case basis.

• Regulations and public education techniques are adopted in lieu of expensive public purchase of wetlands.

• Wetland planning, data gathering, regulation, acquisition, and other management efforts are carried out on a priority basis for areas with development threats or special values.

• Interested citizens and conservation organizations are encouraged to play major roles in public education, data gathering, formulation of policies and plans, acquisition and preservation of wetland areas, evaluation of individual developments, monitoring of development, and, in some instances, enforcement efforts.

• Developers may be charged fees and/or be required to prepare environmental impact statements to reduce program costs.

• Wetland programs often share personnel employed by other local programs, including land use planners, municipal engineers, zoning administrators, and sanitary engineers.

How can sources of expertise be tapped?

The lack of hydrological, geological, and biological expertise often is a serious limitation on wetland protection and restoration efforts. This problem is particularly severe for landowners, land trusts, and rural communities.

Communities and agencies often compensate for lack of professional staff by tapping the expertise within the community or other state or federal agencies. Communities often rely on unpaid technical assistance from local science teachers, architects, engineers, birdwatchers, and interested citizens. Communities in some eastern states have appointed local experts to conservation commissions, which map wetlands, adopt regulations, and evaluate individual development permits. Conservation organizations such as The Nature Conservancy and the Audubon Society often provide valuable expertise in wetland protection.

Communities and agencies also rely extensively on sources of outside assistance. Consultants commonly are used to prepare wetland maps or evaluate individual development proposals. University staff and students also may be asked to play major technical assistance roles. For example, University of Massachusetts personnel have mapped wetlands in the entire state and have played a leadership role in state and local wetland protection programs. Similarly, the Connecticut Arboretum and the University of Connecticut have prepared guidebooks, conducted workshops, and evaluated development permits. In many states, university extension personnel have conducted workshops and assisted local legislative bodies in preparing and implementing regulations.

State wetland agencies, geological surveys, planning offices, coastal zone offices, shoreland and floodplain programs, scientific area programs, scenic and wild river programs, water resource agencies, and conservation agencies often play important roles in wetland mapping and program development efforts. For example, the California coastal zone management program is a major source of information for coastal wetland protection in that state; the Washington shoreline program provides a source of

---

❀

Teri Granger, Olympia, Washington:
Preserving wetland functions

Teri Granger knows that it is not enough to simply preserve wetland acreage; we need to make sure that wetlands are able to perform the functions that made them so valuable in the first place. Granger, a state employee, is coordinating an effort for Washington State to develop a scientific approach for quickly measuring how well a specific wetland performs a specific function. She and the other scientists involved in the effort think the Washington State Wetlands Function Assessment Project will become invaluable for effective wetland management decision making in the region.

The work of Granger's team is based on the hydrogeomorphic, or HGM, approach, which is being developed on a national scale (see Chapter 2). Many of the current methods for assessing functions don't provide the information regulators need to make decisions about compensating for losses, and the techniques are not well tailored for Pacific Northwest wetlands, Granger says. The new approach will offer benefits to the regulated community as well, according to Granger, because, if jurisdictions in the state use it consistently, wetland regulatory decisions will become more consistent and predictable.

---

expertise for both coastal and inland wetlands in Washington; and the Florida state planning office has, under the critical area program, developed wetland expertise. Wetland and conservation agencies also provide technical assistance to local communities, including assistance in evaluating individual permits.

Several major federal sources of expertise are available and have been used extensively in some efforts. (See Chapter 11 and Appendix A.) Natural Resources Conservation Service personnel have mapped Connecticut wetlands and provided technical assistance to communities in evaluating the impact of proposed development. Personnel of the U.S. Fish and Wildlife Service also have provided technical expertise, and regional staff from the Federal Emergency Management Agency have provided information concerning the National Flood Insurance Program and floodplain regulations.

How can legal problems be reduced or avoided?

Aside from money and politics, legal restraints are perhaps the greatest factor shaping wetland regulatory programs. The table on page 58 suggests a number of measures for avoiding legal problems.

Communities usually are authorized by enabling statutes, home rule statutes, and constitutional provisions to exercise a

Approaches for mapping wetland areas

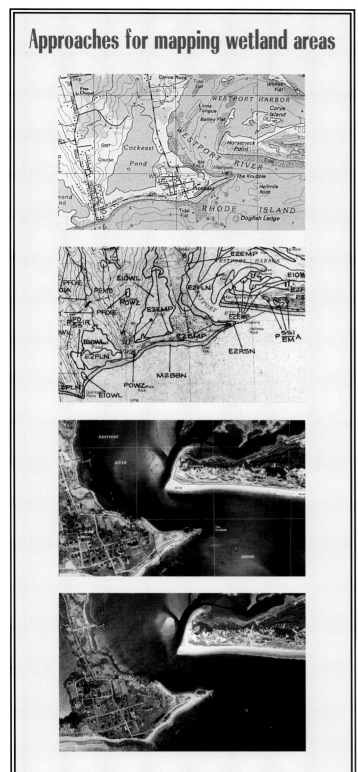

A variety of sources exist for wetland maps. Horseneck Point on the Massachusetts/Rhode Island border is illustrated here (from top to bottom) using a 1) topographic map, 2) a National Wetlands Inventory blueprint, 3) an orthophoto aerial image, and 4) a color infrared aerial photo (shown here in black and white).

wide range of regulatory, acquisition, and other powers. Basic authority usually exists, but specific statutory limitations, such as zoning exemptions pertaining to agricultural uses and state constitutional prohibitions against differential taxation, may present problems. In addition, statutory procedures for regulation, acquisition, and other management approaches must be carefully followed.

Constitutional restraints on regulations often are overestimated. Regulators and administrators should not be intimidated by the possibility that their program will lead to claims that private property has been "taken" without due compensation, or by a perceived need for highly precise boundary maps. Further, there is no need to regulate all wetlands and uses at once.

Regulations must be reasonable and nondiscriminatory. They must balance public and private needs. Community leaders should be more concerned with what is fair and sensible and less about complicated legal requirements that are not as burdensome as popularly believed. Courts are sympathetic to the administrative and budgetary needs of government and do not demand the impossible.

Often legal challenges can be avoided if the programs are carefully designed and implemented. For example, lawsuits can be avoided by educating citizens regarding wetland values and hazards and the need for public control. Public hearings can be held to explain proposed regulation or acquisition plans to citizens and permit them to express themselves in a public forum.

Negotiation is another means of avoiding litigation. Discussions between community leaders and citizens during early stages of project design often can result in project modifications that minimize adverse wetland impacts.

Subtle community pressures often are helpful in avoiding litigation. A strong community wetland protection program, backed by community leaders and broad public support, is a strong deterrent to litigation. Landowners who look to their neighbors for friendship and approval are reluctant to oppose community wishes.

Well conceived and executed community data gathering and planning efforts are another approach to avoid litigation. Court tests are less likely where a community can make a strong factual case for wetland protection. Accurate wetland maps, consistency in application of regulations, data demonstrating the importance of wetland hazards and values, and good record keeping help avoid court suits.

In sum, communities may go overboard in two directions. First, they may be overly concerned with constitutional constraints and thereby be seriously restrained in their protection efforts. Second, they may ignore certain citizens' interests and thereby invite challenge in court. A creative approach may both protect wetlands and reduce objections.

Endnotes

Association of State Wetland Managers, *State Perspectives on Wetland Classification (Categorization) for Regulatory Purposes* (1993).

M. Brinson, *A Hydrogeomorphic Classification for Wetlands* (U.S. Army Corps of Engineers, Waterways Experiment Station, 1993). Technical Report WRP-DE-4.

L. Cowardin et al., *Classification of Wetlands and Deepwater Habitats of the United States* (U.S. Fish and Wildlife Service, 1979). FWS/OBS-79-31.

J. Kusler and M. Kentula, *Wetland Creation and Restoration: The Status of the Science* (Island Press, 1990).

W. Mitch and J. Gosselink, *Wetlands*, second edition (Van Nostrand Reinhold, 1993).

National Research Council, *Restoration of Aquatic Ecosystems* (National Academy Press, 1992).

National Research Council, *Wetlands: Characteristics and Boundaries* (National Academy Press, 1995).

U.S. Army Corps of Engineers, *1987 Wetlands Delineation Manual* (U.S. Army Corps of Engineers, Waterways Experiment Station). Technical Report Y-87-1.

1780s: South Carolina

The Swamp Fox

During the closing years of the American Revolution, a ragged little general named Francis Marion moved like a fox through the swamps of eastern Carolina. Again and again, the British failed to subdue South Carolina because of the warfare waged by Marion and his men. Marion's Brigade would hide in a lair on Snow's Island or Peyre's Plantation by day and emerged stealthily after sunset. They usually struck at midnight, throwing the Tories in a panic. Before day, the Brigade would vanish again behind the morasses of the Peedee or the Santee River.

Marion's was a complex personality, but to Carolina partisans, he was a latter-day Robin Hood, and they told and retold their tales until Marion's exploits and ability to use wetlands to his advantage passed into folklore. Marion was one of the boldest and most dashing figures of the Revolution, as the numerous songs and stories about him proved. As one ditty exclaimed, "The British soldier trembles, when Marion's name is told."

— *from* Swamp Fox: The Life and Campaigns of General Francis Marion, *by Robert D. Bass (Henry Holt and Company: 1959)*

Standards to Guide You

Chapter 6 discusses general standards that are applied at the federal and state levels and in communities' wetland protection programs. Use the chapter to ensure that, as your community develops or updates its wetland protection strategy, it considers the approaches that frequently are used by other communities.

Wetlands vary with respect to dominant vegetation, size, distribution, density, water quality, hazards, and development pressures. Despite these variations, most wetlands share general characteristics with important management implications: They have natural values, and they have natural hazards due to flooding, erosion, and subsidence.

Because of these characteristics, wetlands are undesirable development sites with important hidden costs to landowners and the public. This does not mean that all wetland development will cause problems. However, the high incidence of hazards and values warrants an overall presumption that development should not be located in wetlands if upland alternative sites exist. The "burden of proof" should shift, so that those wishing to undertake activities must show that upland alternatives do not exist and that destruction of wetland functions and natural hazards will not result from wetland activities.

Your community may wish to control wetland uses for a variety of reasons in addition to a desire to protect natural wetland functions and reduce threats from natural hazards. Doing so can minimize community expenses for public services, ensure that wetlands are used for their most appropriate use, and prevent incompatible adjacent land uses. Controlling wetland uses also can result in desirable open space. The real issue is not simply the preservation of wetlands, but the appropriate use of them to advance the safety and general welfare of the community.

Prohibition vs. performance standards

The impact of a particular activity on a wetland varies according to the wetland's characteristics and the type of activity, its design, location, associated uses, and other factors. Wetland regulatory efforts often separate activities into three categories:

• Construction and maintenance of buildings, such as residences, apartments, factories, farmhouses, and commercial establishments. These often are regulated by state and local building codes and zoning ordinances.

• Construction and maintenance of non-building structures, such as roads, bridges, dams, dikes, levees, tunnels, groins, and breakwaters. These sometimes are regulated at the state level through wetland or dredge-and-fill laws, but more often are regulated at the local level through zoning or special codes. Local land use regulations rarely are applied to governmental uses.

• Open space uses not involving building or other construction, such as agriculture, forestry, dredging, solid and liquid waste disposal, drainage, and mosquito control. Dredging and waste disposal are, in some instances, regulated at the state level. Most other open space uses are not regulated.

All three types of activities may have wetland impacts. For this reason, regulatory approaches that control building construction alone are only partially effective.

Because of the variable impact of wetland activities, two principal wetland regulatory approaches are used: (1) a broad exclusion of virtually all uses that might damage wetlands through public acquisition of land or tight regulations, and (2) application of less restrictive

"Humanity is not apart from, but rather must be a vital part of the balanced environmental equation. We should be neither conquerors who control the land, not tourists just passing through."

— Robert M. Thomas,
Florida ranch owner and
1995 National Wetlands
Award nominee (1995)

performance standards and guidelines, incorporating many of the standards discussed below.

There are advantages to complete prohibition of development. First, complete prohibition is necessary in some instances to protect vital wetland functions and to prevent nuisances and severe damage from natural hazards. Practically all uses (even carefully conducted uses) may threaten sensitive plants and animals and reduce wetland educational and scientific values. Second, complete prohibition avoids the problem of cumulative impact when individual uses are permitted on a case-by-case basis. Third, prohibition reduces the data-gathering requirements, since less information is needed if individual uses are not permitted within wetland areas. Fourth, prohibition requires less expertise during administrative phases of a program, since no individual development permits have to be evaluated.

On the other hand, complete prohibition through regulation often is politically difficult and may result in constitutional challenges. Complete prohibition is, in some instances, more appropriately achieved through land acquisition.

The second approach — involving less restrictive performance standards or guidelines — has been applied widely in both state and local regulatory programs. Standards or guidelines may take the form of "performance" standards and apply to a wide range of uses, or they may take the form of more specific standards and apply to particular uses. The standards suggested below and in the table on page 68 are examples of general performance standards that may be applied through a permit procedure.

Performance standards usually employ a combination of quantified and nonquantified criteria aimed at the ultimate impact of uses. Quantified standards may pertain to density of development (lot size), percentage of impermeable surface, water quality standards, and flood protection elevations (such as the 100-year flood). Unquantified standards pertain to wildlife protection, aesthetic values, and other functions and values.

Performance standards have several advantages. First, they reduce wetland protection and management to a relatively discrete and understandable set of principles that may be applied to all types of uses. Second, they permit an examination of the impact of each individual use in terms of its specific design characteristics and the specific values and hazards at a site. Third, they focus data gathering efforts upon specific impacts. Fourth, they often allow a wide number of options in the private use of land, engender less political opposition, and are less vulnerable to constitutional challenges.

Performance standards are, however, subject to several limitations. First, nonquantified performance standards create uncertainty regarding permissible private uses of the land. Second, regulatory agencies often have difficulty in calculating the cumulative impact of private uses. Third, performance standards require considerable time and expertise in administration and enforcement. And fourth, they lead to problems in maintaining a consistent approach.

Although the application of a performance standard approach often is desirable, performance standards may be

---

Three general standards for the use of wetland areas are common cornerstones in wetland management efforts:

1. If there are practical alternatives, development should be located on upland rather than wetland sites.

2. Activities in wetlands should not cause nuisance impacts on other lands (such as flooding, erosion, and water pollution) or be subject to substantial natural hazards.

3. Activities in wetlands should not cause a net loss of wetland function and acreage.

---

combined with more specific standards for particular uses and areas, such as a requirement that residential uses not be located in flood areas.

Standards

Three general standards for the use of wetland areas are broadly applied in wetland management efforts:

1. If there are practical alternatives, development should be located on upland rather than wetland sites.

2. Activities in wetlands should not cause nuisance impacts on other lands (such as flooding, erosion, and water pollution) or be subject to substantial natural hazards.

3. Activities in wetlands should not cause a net loss of wetland function and acreage.

These three overall standards form the cornerstone for wetland planning, regulation, acquisition, and other management efforts. What follows are more specific standards that can serve as the basis for public education, public land use management, comprehensive land use planning, wetland acquisition, zoning ordinances, land use regulation, and the evaluation of proposed developments.

Standard One: Activities in wetlands should not cause damaging increases in flood heights or velocities on other lands or cause other nuisance impacts, such as increased erosion. The activities should not be conducted where they may be seriously damaged by flooding, erosion, or other natural hazards.

A primary community objective for the control of wetland uses is the prevention of nuisances and nuisance-like activities. No landowner has a right to damage other landowners or the public. As noted earlier, certain wetland activities often increase flood heights and velocities and erosion on other lands. Moreover, wetland uses such as residences and commercial uses are themselves subject to flooding and other natural hazards.

The adoption of regulations to reduce flood damages and other natural hazards sometimes has been considered "protecting a man against himself." Nevertheless, the regulations also are justified because they protect subsequent purchasers of property and guests and family of the floodplain occupant. They also help communities avoid substantial expense for flood relief and flood control works.

The statutes of many states require that local units of government adopt floodplain regulations meeting state standards (including California, Kansas, Michigan, Minnesota, New Jersey, New York, Washington, and Wisconsin). In addition, the National Flood Insurance Program requires that local governments adopt floodplain and floodway regulations to qualify for national flood insurance.

Efforts to prevent increased flood heights and velocities on other lands usually emphasize the protection of one essential wetland component: wetland topography. Maintenance of natural contours is needed for the passage of flood flows, flood storage, and the protection of storm barriers. Approaches to prevent increased flood heights and velocities and to protect flood-prone uses include the following:

• Fills, buildings, and other obstructions in wetlands that serve as floodway areas should be tightly controlled. Often floodway areas are defined at state or local levels to include stream channels and overun areas necessary to convey a 100-year flood with no greater than one foot (or so, no lesser figure) of increased flood height. This standard is applied by the Federal Emergency Management Agency in the Flood Insurance Program and by most state floodplain regulatory programs.

• Fills or structures in wetlands serving as flood storage areas should be tightly controlled. Protection of flood storage is not mandated by the National Flood Insurance Program or most state floodplain regulatory programs. However, many communities have adopted such regulations to protect flood storage in the 50- or 100-year floodplain. Such regulations are particularly appropriate for smaller streams in urbanizing areas, where wetlands may play a critical flood storage role.

• Buildings located in wetlands forming part of the 100-year floodplain should be elevated on pilings or other techniques, which will allow the wetland and floodplain to function naturally. Protection to or above the elevation of the 100-year flood is required by state floodplain programs and the National Flood Insurance Program.

• Toxic and hazardous chemicals, wood, and other materials that threaten public safety or cause damage to other lands during flood conditions should not be stored or deposited in wetland areas.

> ❈
>
> **Maintenance of wetland functions requires not only maintaining wetland features but the physical and biological relationships that permit a wetland to perform those functions.**

Standard Two: Wetland activities should not cause water pollution or diminish natural wetland pollution control functions.

Certain activities in wetlands may contribute pollutants to wetlands and downstream areas or alter the capacity of wetlands to assimilate pollutants from other sources. Natural wetland pollution control functions may be destroyed by filling, grading, removing soil, interfering with wetland water supply or circulation, and destroying wetland vegetation.

The prevention of pollution from septic tank and soil absorption systems in high groundwater areas often is a major local and state wetland regulation objective. Faulty septic systems may pollute nearby wells and properties as well as wetland areas.

Approaches to prevent pollution from activities in wetlands or the diminishment of natural wetland pollution control functions include the following:

• Point sources of pollution (such as factories, houses, and commercial establishments) should be regulated through water quality and effluent standards. Point-source pollution controls commonly are adopted at the state level, although some community regulations also have been adopted.

• Plumbing and sanitary codes, and subdivision regulations should be adopted prohibiting septic tank and soil absorption systems in high groundwater areas. These regulations may be adopted at both state and local levels.

• Construction of lagoons, dredging, filling, and disposal of spoil should be regulated within wetland areas. Discharge of dredge or fill materials into the waters of the United States is regulated, in part, by the U.S. Army Corps of Engineers and the U.S. Environmental Protection Agency under the Section 404 program. Dredging in navigable waters is regulated by the Corps of Engineers under Section 10 of the Rivers and Harbors Act. (See Chapters 3 and 8.)

• Storage of chemicals, wood, fuel, and other materials should be regulated in wetland and floodplain areas where the materials may be swept away by flooding. Storage regulations often are included in state and local floodplain regulations.

• Activities that alter wetland contours or vegetation should be regulated, especially where wetlands serve as sediment traps and nutrient filters for lakes, streams, and estuaries.

Standard Three: Buildings, roads, and other structures should not be constructed in areas lacking adequate soil-bearing capacity.

Buildings and other structures located on wetland soils with high water and organic content often settle differentially due to compaction of the soils. This may subject structures to flooding or damaging stresses, and could, in fact, constitute a

Performance standards for protecting wetland functions

General standard	Common activities and processes requiring control	Impact of uncontrolled uses	Application of standard
Prevent filling of wetland by sand, gravel, solid wastes, structures	1. Land fill operations 2. Dredge and spoil disposal 3. Construction of roads, dikes, dams, reservoirs 4. Activities on adjacent land or in the watershed causing sedimentation, such as agricultural operations, timber cutting, road building, urban runoff, mining operations, channelization	1. Destruction of flood storage and flood conveyance capacity 2. Accelerated runoff 3. Destruction of wildlife and vegetative values 4. Reduced groundwater infiltration 5. Destruction of scenic, recreation, education, pollution control functions	1. Prohibit or tightly control filling in all or selected types of wetland areas 2. Prohibit activities that require fills such as dwellings, factories, and roads 3. Establish wetland buffer zones or setbacks for fills and structures to reduce sedimentation from upland sources 4. Regulate grading, top soil removal, and vegetation removal in upland areas
Protect wetland water supply (quantity)	1. Construction of upland stream reservoirs 2. Agricultural and other types of drainage 3. Channelization of streams 4. Pumping of streams, lakes, groundwater supplies 5. Establishment of dikes, levees, sea walls, blocking exchange of tidal flows, flood waters 6. Mosquito control projects	1. Destruction or deterioration of wetland vegetation 2. Reduced aquifer recharge 3. Disturbance or destruction of wildlife species that depend upon wetlands for breeding, feeding, and nutrients 4. Increased salinity (in some instances) resulting in damage to wildlife, vegetation, recreation opportunities	1. Regulate the construction of dams, drainage projects, stream channelization, water extractions 2. Manage reservoirs and flood gates to maintain wetland water supply
Protect wetland soils	1. Dredging, channelization 2. Topsoil removal 3. Construction of reservoirs 4. Mining	1. Disturbance or destruction of vegetation and wildlife habitat 2. Increased water turbidity 3. Decreased recreation, education, wildlife values	1. Regulate dredging, lagooning, mining, wetland soil removal
Maintain free circulation of wetland waters	1. Dikes, dams, levees, seawalls, roads 2. Irrigation projects 3. Fills, grading, buildings	1. Deprived wetland plants and animals of nutrients from flood flows and other sources 2. Prevent the feeding and breeding of aquatic species in wetland areas 3. Buildup of salinity (in some instances)	1. Require that bridges and roads be constructed with minimum impediment to natural drainage 2. Design floodgates and seawalls to maintain tidal action 3. Regulate construction of dikes, levees 4. Require wetland structures to be elevated on pilings
Prevent wetland vegetation from cutting and grading	1. Forestry (some instances) 2. Cranberry cultivation 3. Agriculture 4. Off-road vehicles 5. Filling, grading 6. Soil removal	1. Damage to wildlife habitat 2. Reduced pollution filtering capability 3. Increased water velocities, erosion 4. Destruction of scenic values	1. Control filling, grading, soil removal pollution sources and other activities that destroy the wetland substrate or the water quantity required for specific vegetation

Source: T. Henderson, W. Smith, and D. Burke, Non-Tidal Wetlands Protection: A Handbook for Maryland Local Governments (The Maryland Tidewater Administration, 1983).

threat to public safety, particularly if the structure is a public facility (such as a restaurant or marina).

Approaches to prevent soil-bearing capacity problems include:

• Building codes, zoning, and other regulations should be adopted incorporating performance standards for soil-bearing capacity for buildings, roads, and other structures.

• Performance standards should require use of pilings, hard fill, or other measures to provide adequate foundation support before construction.

• Subdivision regulations should prohibit subdivision of lands with inadequate soil-bearing capacity for intended uses (such as residences).

Standard Four: Wetland activities should not destroy or seriously damage wetland functions and values.

Efforts to protect wetland functions and values must consider the topographic, hydrologic, botanical, and other requirements of each function and the role each plays in maintaining the wetland area. Essential wetland features giving rise to these functions and performance standards needed to protect them are presented in the table on page 68.

Maintenance of wetland functions requires not only maintaining the features but the physical and biological relationships that permit a wetland to perform those functions. For example, if a community or state wishes to maintain a wetland as a fish spawning area, protection measures would be needed to maintain the hydrologic and biological systems.

Standard Five: Wetland activities should be consistent with federal, state, and local land use and water planning and management programs.

Appropriate wetland uses depend upon broader land and water management goals. These goals are determined, in part, by existing uses, existing regulations, adjacent land uses, wetland values and hazards, the impact of proposed uses on wetlands, the need for development, and alternative sites for development. The compatibility of wetland activities with these factors often may be determined without comprehensive community land or water use planning. Nevertheless, such planning can help determine the compatibility of wetland uses with broader social and economic needs, including the demand for new residential, industrial, and commercial development.

Approaches for ensuring compatibility include:

• Wetland activities should comply with all other existing regulations and not cause nuisances to adjacent uses by blocking flood flows, polluting waters, or by causing excessive noise, glare, dust, odors, traffic, or other impacts. Such standards may be incorporated in conservancy, residential, or other zoning for wetlands and adjacent areas that separate incompatible uses (a traditional zoning function). Regulations requiring minimum separation distances between potentially incompatible uses, such as a requirement that solid waste disposal sites not be located

---

Rita Barron, Newton, Massachusetts:
Selling natural flood storage — and wetlands protection

In the late 1960s, when Congress told the U.S. Army Corps of Engineers to do something about flooding from the Charles River, instead of building dams the Corps eventually implemented the Natural Valley Flood Storage Project. Through the project, which the Corps undertook after a good deal of advice from citizens, the agency used a solution that worked with wetland functions instead of destroying them: It acquired fee title or floodplain easements to 9,100 acres of wetland area in order to allow the river to perform naturally when it flooded.

Natural valley flood storage was a new concept to many, and an effective educational effort was needed to pull the project off. For this, the Corps relied on several partners, including Rita Barron, former Executive Director of the Charles River Watershed Association. Barron wrote tabloids to explain natural valley flood storage to landowners and the public. She set up meetings with her association's members who lived along the river, and she organized public information sessions about the Corps' proposal. She went to the media to secure favorable publicity, and even testified before Congress about this project that, several years later, remains a model wetland protection effort.

---

within 1,000 feet of existing residences, are another technique for promoting compatibility of uses. Performance standards for wetland and adjacent uses provide another alternative to ensure that impacts do not exceed assigned limits.

• Wetland activities should comply with community plans for sewer, water, roads, dikes, levees, and other public works and not place a disproportionately heavy burden upon the community for these services. These regulations may take the form of zoning and subdivision regulations either prohibiting or carefully controlling uses in flood hazard, erosion, and similar areas where roads and sewers are disproportionately expensive to construct and maintain. Subdivision regulations may require that developers at their own expense install roads, sewers, and water supply systems that meet community standards.

Standard Six: Activities should be conducted to minimize their impact upon wetlands.

Where it is not desirable or possible to locate damaging activities at upland sites, all reasonable measures should be taken to minimize impact upon natural wetland functions.

Approaches for minimizing impact include many of those listed above and in Chapter 7. The approaches include:

• Development should be located on the upland portion of lots. The total area within each lot that may be filled, paved, or otherwise altered should be limited.

• Developers should be required to prepare environmental impact statements for larger projects.

• Proposed activities should be required to meet performance standards for construction and operation to minimize impact upon natural drainage, vegetation, wildlife, and other values.

• Land subdivisions should be required to incorporate open space. Structures should be clustered on upland sites to preserve wetland areas.

Standard Seven: "Compensation" in terms of wetland restoration or creation should be provided if wetland damage or destruction is permitted.

Conditions should be attached to zoning, subdivision control, building, sanitary, and other permits to require replanting of denuded areas, construction of settling ponds to protect wetlands from pollutants, and, in some instances, creation of new wetland areas or restoration of previously impaired wetlands where new development causes unavoidable wetland destruction or damage. (See Chapter 11.)

Endnotes

Association of State Wetland Managers, *State Wetland Regulation: Status of Programs and Emerging Trends* (1994).

R. Darnell, *Impacts of Construction Activities on Wetlands of the United States* (U.S. Environmental Protection Agency, Environmental Research Laboratory, 1976). EPA-600/3-76-045.

M. Strand, *Wetlands Deskbook* (Environmental Law Institute, 1996).

Reducing impacts to specific uses

The application of standards to the particular uses listed below may be incorporated into zoning ordinances or other regulations.

Agriculture

Agricultural practices are the principal threat to wetlands in many areas. Drainage destroys wetland vegetation and wildlife. Diking interferes with wetland water and nutrient supplies. Other impacts include nutrient enrichment from fertilizers and manure that results from agricultural runoff, sedimentation from the erosion and discharge of soil into waterways, introduction of toxic chemicals from agricultural pesticides and herbicides, disturbance of wetland water supplies by agricultural pumping, introduction of exotic species into wetland areas, and destruction of wetland vegetation and wildlife by plowing, harvesting, and other practices.

Wetland impacts may be minimized by:

❀ Utilizing minimum tillage farming techniques.

❀ Avoiding drainage and diking.

❀ Adopting soil conservation measures to control erosion and agricultural runoff.

❀ Maintaining wetland buffer areas.

❀ Fencing streamside wetlands and influent streams to reduce erosion and direct pollution by cattle.

❀ Reducing application of manure to frozen soils during the winter.

❀ Controlling pesticide and herbicide applications.

❀ Increasing wild crop harvesting and agriculture consistent with natural wetland characteristics.

Airports

Airports often are located in wetland areas along major lakes or the ocean where large tracts of undeveloped land are available at low price. Examples include the Washington, D.C.; San Francisco; and Boston airports. Wetland disturbance results from filling and grading for runway construction, interference with natural drainage patterns, and pollution from the runway surfaces and exhaust particles.

The impact of airport construction may be reduced by:

❀ Avoiding high-quality wetland sites.

❀ Providing a buffer strip of vegetation between runways and adjacent wetlands.

❊ Tightly regulating the dumping of aviation fuel and other wastes.

❊ Treating airport runoff before discharge into wetlands.

❊ Carefully designing drainage systems to maintain natural flow of waters.

Dams

Wetlands are directly destroyed by the construction of dams and reservoirs. Fluctuating water levels in reservoirs may prevent re-establishment of wetlands at the margins of the new water bodies. Dams also destroy and damage downstream wetlands by reducing flows and reducing or increasing nutrient and sediment supplies.

Adverse wetland impacts may be minimized by:

❊ Avoiding major wetlands as sites for dams or reservoirs.

❊ Designing reservoirs and maintaining reservoir water levels to encourage re-establishment of wetlands at reservoir boundaries.

❊ Designing dams so that water can be withdrawn from lower levels to ensure continued conveyance of nutrients to downstream wetlands.

❊ Timing water releases to benefit downstream aquatic and animal life.

Dikes, levees, and seawalls

Dikes, levees, and seawalls are constructed as flood or erosion control measures in wetlands along streams and at coastal locations. They interfere with natural flood and drainage patterns and nutrient supplies. Interference with water circulation is a particularly serious problem at coastal locations where salt marshes must be continually exposed to tidal action if they are to provide nutrients to estuarine areas and serve as spawning and feeding areas for coastal fish and shellfish. Inland dikes and levees deprive wetlands of rich alluvial soil, which is normally deposited by natural flooding. They may also deprive wetlands of water supply, ecologically separating them from nearby waters.

Wetland impacts may be reduced by:

❊ Avoiding high-quality wetlands.

❊ Equipping seawalls, levees, and dikes with floodgates to permit the normal circulation of waters except during times of flooding.

❊ Re-establishing vegetation on soil dikes and levees to reduce erosion.

Dredging

Dredging to deepen channel areas or create new channels is a major threat to wetland areas along rivers and streams used for

water transportation, at coastal sites used for ports, marinas, and water transport, and along lakes and at ocean sites where residential boat access is desired. Deepening, widening, and straightening of natural stream channels also is undertaken along streams and rivers to reduce flood heights and lower high groundwater levels. Wetlands that are dredged are permanently destroyed. Dredging damages downstream wetlands due to increased water turbidity and sediment. Dredging may also alter circulation patterns and salinity balance. Dredge spoil is highly erodible and difficult to stabilize.

Wetland impacts may be reduced by:

❊ Avoiding dredging in, adjacent to, or immediately upstream from high- and medium-value wetlands.

❊ Avoiding stream channelization for lowering of water levels.

❊ Avoiding dredging solely for the purpose of creating fill for residential or nonwater dependent development.

❊ Disposing of spoil at upland sites and quickly stabilizing it.

❊ Constructing channels at a minimum depth and width capable of achieving the intended purposes. Sides of channels should reflect an equilibrium shape to prevent slumping and erosion and allow revegetation.

❊ Conducting dredging at times of minimum biological activity to avoid disrupting fish migration and spawning.

Industries

Industries often are constructed in coastal and riverine wetland areas due to the low cost of the land and the availability of water for transport, cooling, manufacturing, and waste disposal. Industries destroy wetlands by filling and grading, and damage them by interfering with drainage, emitting pollutants, and extracting groundwater or surface water. Access roads and storage areas may also result in severe wetland impacts.

Impacts may be reduced by:

❊ Avoiding high-quality wetland sites.

❊ Vigorous enforcement of water and air pollution laws.

❊ Locating access roads, parking and storage areas, waste disposal, and ancillary uses at upland sites.

❊ Rehabilitating damaged wetland areas.

Marinas and piers

Marinas and piers often displace wetlands located along rivers and coastal sites. Other impacts include wetland destruction from dredging to maintain channels, increased water turbidity and disturbance of natural vegetation and wildlife by motor boats, and pollution of waters by motor fuels. Parking and boat storage areas may destroy wildlife habitats and contribute polluted runoff.

Impacts may be reduced by:

❋ Avoiding high-quality wetland sites.

❋ Locating marinas in naturally well flushed areas rather than in artificial channels where water circulation often is poor.

❋ Locating parking and boat storage areas at upland sites.

❋ Encouraging the use of "zonation mooring" at marinas (smaller draft boats use the shallower near-shore waters, and deeper draft boats are moored in deeper waters), thus reducing the amount of dredging necessary.

Mining

Sand and gravel operations threaten wetlands adjacent to some stream and marine habitats. Mining of shells and phosphates threatens coastal sites. Operations that remove the wetland substrate and vegetation cause direct damage and serious turbidity problems for downstream areas. Coal mining, oil and gas wells, and other extractive industries may cause water pollution, even if located far from wetland sites.

Impacts may be reduced by:

❋ Avoiding high-value wetland areas and immediate upstream areas.

❋ Rigorous enforcement of pollution controls.

❋ Avoiding coastal mining in the active surface zones.

❋ Using settling ponds and other water treatment facilities to reduce sediment runoff and other pollutants from sand and gravel and other mining activities.

❋ Using buffer strips between mining areas and adjacent wetlands to retard the runoff of sediment, chemicals, oils, and other pollutants.

❋ Reclaiming mine areas at upland sites to stabilize open surfaces and reduce sediment loadings.

❋ Rehabilitating damaged wetland areas.

Power plants

Power plants pose severe threats to both coastal and inland wetlands since they require large, low-cost sites and (in some instances) water access for transport of coal or oil and for cooling purposes. Wetland areas may be displaced or damaged by filling and grading, plant construction, access roads, cooling lakes, fuel storage areas, power transmission lines, waste disposal, and by dredging to install pipelines and to maintain access channels for fuel barges. Power plants may also destroy adjacent wetland areas by interfering with natural drainage patterns, polluting air and water, and increasing water temperature by dis-

charge of cooling waters. Fish and other organisms may be killed by impingement or entrainment in plant cooling systems.

Impacts may be reduced by:

❋ Avoiding high-quality wetland sites.

❋ Tightly controlling air and water pollution emissions.

❋ Designing plant cooling systems to prevent entrapment of fish and damaging increases in water temperature.

❋ Rehabilitating damaged wetland areas through planting and other techniques.

❋ Disposing of slag and other wastes at upland sites.

Residences

Residential development is an increasing threat to wetlands due to escalating land values that result in fill and drainage. Dredging and channelization to provide fill and boat access have been common for residential development on ocean shores and lakeshores. Other impacts of residential uses include damage to wetland wildlife from tree clearing and disturbance of wetland vegetation; sedimentation caused by grading, filling, and other construction activities; interference with wetland drainage and water supply by access roads, dikes, seawalls, and domestic wells; and increased groundwater and surface water nutrient loadings from septic tanks and lawn fertilizers.

Often wetland sites are poor residential sites even after reclamation. Low-lying sites continue to be flood-prone, and basement flooding and drainage problems are common. Uneven subsidence of wetland soils causes uneven stress to structures and may result in cracks or other damage. On-site waste disposal systems function poorly in high groundwater areas and in peaty soils where shallow fill is placed over natural wetland soils.

Impacts may be reduced by:

❋ Locating buildings and access roads on upland sites.

❋ Avoiding dredging and lagooning to provide fill and boat access for residential sites.

❋ Grading to maintain natural topographic contours and reduce erosion.

❋ Regulating tree-cutting and vegetation removal in wetlands and wetland buffers.

❋ Avoiding septic tanks in high groundwater areas and peaty soils.

❋ Carefully complying with flood elevation and floodway protection requirements.

❋ Constructing buildings on the upland portion of lots to lower the overall density of uses.

❋ Constructing access roads to maintain natural drainage.

❋ Treating storm drainage before discharge into wetlands.

Roads and bridges

Roads and bridges are constructed in wetlands in the normal course of roadbuilding and to provide access to shoreland areas for new residential, recreational, and other types of development. Damage results from roadbed fill, removal of wetland soils to provide a stable road or bridge base, interference with natural drainage, sedimentation from roadway construction, pollution by toxic chemicals from exhaust gases and road salting, oil runoff, and destruction of wetland wildlife by road traffic. In addition, roads and bridges often block flood flows, thereby increasing flood heights and velocities on other lands. Construction of roads through wetland areas encourages residential and other development.

Wetland impacts may be reduced by:

❋ Locating roads at upland sites and designing them to curve around wetland areas. This often will result in a more aesthetically pleasing roadway as well as reduced wetland impacts.

❋ Avoiding extension of minor roadways into wetland areas where they encourage private development.

❋ Designing roadways and bridges to maintain natural flow parallel to drainage, elevation of roadway surfaces on pile supports, design of bridge openings to convey storm flows, and installation of culverts.

❋ Erecting fences to protect deer, raccoons, and other wildlife from highway traffic.

❋ Minimizing the impact of construction through measures to reduce erosion, including the replanting of open surfaces and the construction of sediment retention facilities.

❋ Rehabilitating damaged wetland areas.

❋ Avoiding the use of road salt.

Septic tanks

In rural areas, domestic wastewaters are discharged into septic tanks and subsurface soil absorption systems. Soil absorption is severely limited in wetland areas by high groundwater and peaty soil conditions. Unable to flow into the soil, liquids back up into dwellings or flow out into the ground surface, causing odor nuisances, health problems, and nutrient enrichment of nearby waters.

Wetland impacts may be reduced by:

❋ Prohibiting new septic tank systems in high groundwater areas, including areas immediately adjacent to wetlands.

❋ Inspecting existing septic systems in flood hazard and high groundwater areas to ensure proper operation.

❋ Using holding tanks, gas incinerator toilets, public sewers, and other alternatives to septic tanks.

Solid waste disposal

Solid waste disposal sites often are located in inland and coastal wetlands due to their low cost and topographic contours. Solid waste disposal may destroy all wetland values. In addition, solid wastes may pollute downstream areas by contributing litter, nutrients, oils, and toxic chemicals to runoff. Groundwater pollution poses a severe problem, and air pollution may also result.

Wetland impacts may be reduced by:

❋ Avoiding use of high-value wetlands and adjacent floodplains where wastes may be dispersed by flooding. Waste disposal sites should also be located away from drainage courses.

❋ Avoiding discharge of toxic materials where they may pollute runoff waters or groundwaters.

❋ Recycling of materials to reduce the total quantity of solid waste. Other techniques for reducing quantity include compaction, incineration of materials, and reduction in use.

❋ Using settling basins and other measures to reduce water pollution.

❋ Maintaining buffer strips between solid waste disposal sites and wetlands.

Storm drains

Runoff from urban areas, residential subdivisions, marinas, and other developments may pollute wetland areas. Pollutants include but are not limited to trash, oils, pesticides and nutrients from lawn fertilizers and septic tanks, sediment, soap, and industrial chemicals. Natural vegetated drainage ways remove much of this material before it reaches wetland areas. However, storm drainage systems provide no filtering.

Wetland impacts may be reduced by:

❋ Maintaining natural, open, vegetated drainage ways, rather than concrete, enclosed storm sewers. If enclosed storm drain systems are necessary at a given location, place inlets in grass swales so that the storm water will be filtered before entering the closed system.

❋ Treating storm runoff before it enters wetlands through settling ponds, special treatment facilities, or combined storm drainage and sewer systems.

❋ Carefully controlling the use and discharge of pesticide applications, fertilizer use, oil spills, and other sources of damaging materials in the watershed.

❋ Limiting the rate of flow of storm water from the developed site to predevelopment rates through on-site detention ponds.

1885: The Mississippi River

A Raft and the Still Night Air

With his stories of Huck and Jim and their rafting adventures, Mark Twain spun a tale of robbers, kindly widows, and other vivid characters, but he also wrote a love song for the perilous, lazy river of his youth — the Mississippi — and the culture that lived alongside it. Take this passage from The Adventures of Huckleberry Finn:

". . . Not a sound anywheres — perfectly still — just like the whole world was asleep, only sometimes the bullfrogs a-cluttering, maybe. The first thing to see, looking away over the water, was a kind of dull line — that was the woods on t'other side; you couldn't make nothing else out; then a pale place in the sky; then more paleness spreading around; then the river softened up away off, and warn't black any more, but gray; you could see little dark spots drifting along ever so far away — trading-scows, and such things; and long black streaks — rafts; sometimes you could hear a sweep screaking; or jumbled-up voices, it was so still, and sounds come so far. . . ."

— from The Adventures of Huckleberry Finn *by Mark Twain (1885)*

Evaluating Permits

A variety of decisions must be made when development proposals are evaluated. Previous chapters have included information about issues surrounding that evaluation and standards for evaluating permits; Chapter 7 lays out those considerations in more detail. Use the chapter to help your community ensure that the effect of development on wetlands is minimized.

The federal Section 404 program, most state regulatory programs, and most local government regulatory programs do not prohibit all public and private wetland activities. Instead, regulatory agencies are authorized to evaluate activities on a case-by-case basis to determine their impact on wetland areas and whether they comply with regulatory standards. Usually regulatory agencies exercise broad discretion in evaluating the impact of a proposed development, determining whether the development is appropriate for the proposed site, and formulating conditions for the permit that will minimize adverse impacts to wetlands.

There are many important issues that arise in the permitting process, including the following:

• How will the impact to the wetland be determined?

• How will the necessary data be obtained?

• How are regulatory standards applied?

• What conditions are to be attached to the permit?

• How can the success of restoration and creation sites be assured?

• What monitoring and enforcement are needed?

How will the impact to the wetland be determined?

The impact of a proposed activity depends upon seven major factors: (1) the type and design of the proposed activity, including all ancillary uses; (2) the specific wetland characteristics, including all values and hazards at the site; (3) the location of the site in the wetland; (4) the relationship of wetland functions to broader hydrological and ecological systems; (5) existing uses and adjacent land uses that may be affected by the proposed activity; (6) available and planned public services such as sewers, water, and roads; and (7) broader community land and water use plans.

Often a quick review of a permit application will suggest factors that require special attention. For example, a proposed industrial use may result not only in filling of the wetland but also dredging to provide for barge access and the discharge of industrial wastes.

It is important that possible cumulative impacts as well as impacts on specific wetland functions be evaluated. This is not easy, but some procedures have been developed to facilitate cumulative impact analysis. For example, impact of the overall development scheme may be evaluated where a proposed permit application is part of a broader subdivision or other development plan.

Impacts of Construction Activities in Wetlands of the United States, a report prepared by Rezneat M. Darnell for the U.S. Environmental Protection Agency, analyzes in considerable depth the impact on wetlands of nine major steps in construction. The report suggests "factor train analysis" for evaluating impacts. Using this analysis, impacts of construction activities are analyzed in three general

"Protection of wetlands is based on the premise that preservation of a specific ecosystem type can be of sufficient common interest that its conversion or development should be prevented or restrained by law. . . ."

— National Research Council, *Wetlands: Characteristics and Boundaries* (1995)

time-related categories: (1) direct and immediate results that take place during the construction process; (2) effects that occur during the period of stabilization following completion of the construction; and (3) long-term effects of more or less permanent change brought about by the construction itself or by the subsequent human use and environmental management that results from the constructed facilities.

Most local and state wetland regulations require that developers prepare a formal impact statement or submit detailed information concerning the specifics of their proposed activity, wetland values and hazards at the proposed site, and the impact of the activity on those values and hazards. Some programs distinguish between activities with a high probability of impact on a wetland and those with low probability. More information is required from those with high probability.

The National Environmental Policy Act requires federal agencies to prepare environmental impact statements for federal or federally funded projects with significant impacts upon the environment. Executive Orders adopted by President Jimmy Carter establish criteria for projects in wetland and floodplain areas. In addition, at least 13 states have adopted statutes requiring that state agencies, local units of government, and, in some instances, private developers, prepare impact statements.

Melody Hopkins, Orange Beach, Alabama:

Stopping development in an island salt marsh

When a developer sought to build pile-supported houses in a barrier island salt marsh adjacent to Bayou St. John, Ono Island, Alabama, nearby-resident Melody Hopkins knew that she wanted the development stopped. She didn't know, however, that her efforts to do so would lead to changes in permitting conditions affecting the sensitive coastal region she calls home.

To stop the development, Hopkins first looked to the U.S. Army Corps of Engineers' Section 404 permit process. She convinced the Corps that an individual permit — rather than a general permit — was required because court decisions had limited the use of general permits for pile-supported structures. Through this process, Hopkins decided that the Alabama Department of Environmental Management had an important — and unrealized — potential to help regulate development in coastal wetlands, so she organized a campaign to encourage rulemaking and support final promulgation for changes to the department's regulations. Under the new regulations, the department joins the Corps in regulating the construction of pile-supported houses and other structures that affect water quality in coastal wetlands.

These broad environmental impact laws apply to many public projects, even those not regulated through state and local wetland protection efforts. By requiring a careful analysis of project impact, they encourage informed agency decision making.

How will the necessary data be obtained?

In permit analysis, much of the information needed to determine compliance with regulatory criteria is supplied by the permit applicant in the initial permit application or supplemental data gathering. This includes information needed to determine whether practical alternative sites are available, whether an activity needs a wetland location, the impacts of the proposed activity, and the adequacy of the mitigation and compensation measures.

For small projects, the permit applicant may be able to provide much of the needed information. For larger projects, the applicant often hires consultants to carry out studies and to collect the necessary information.

For larger projects, particularly if they are controversial, the data submitted by the developer often are field-checked by the regulatory agency. Existing topographic, soil, and flood maps, and other information sources are used to evaluate wetland values and hazards. Although these sources may not be sufficient in themselves to evaluate total impact, they are useful in determining groundwater and surface water flow systems; the general characteristics of wetland, watershed, and adjacent land use flood elevations; and the susceptibility of lands to erosion.

Where "red flags" or potential problems are identified, the regulatory agency often requires the permit applicant to conduct field surveys to determine wetland vegetation, soils, erosion, existing uses, and other parameters. Some of this information can be gathered quickly by a trained observer who can spot potential problem areas such as erosion or deep organic soils. However, the gathering of other information, such as subsurface geology, the relationship of the site to groundwater flow systems, and the presence of specific animal life is much more difficult.

Additional sources of information commonly are used:

• Data gathering and technical assistance may be sought from federal and state agencies with special expertise in particular topics. For example, local Natural Resources Conservation Service (formerly the Soil Conservation Service) personnel often are asked for soil evaluations. State Fish and Game personnel may be asked to conduct biological surveys. State heritage programs may supply information concerning endangered species and biodiversity.

• University personnel, conservation groups such as The Nature Conservancy and Audubon Society, and interested citizens may be able to supply useful information concerning the wetland, such as the plant and animal species that inhabit it.

• Public hearings may be used to gather raw data concerning the wetland characteristics, the possible impact of development, and to assess public attitudes. Usually anyone with an interest in the proposed activity is allowed to submit written evidence or testimony. While the quality of this evidence varies, it

Steps in evaluating permits

In evaluating permits, typically the regulatory agency follows these eight steps:

1. Discussion is held before a formal permit application is submitted. A landowner or developer often contacts the regulatory agency to discuss proposed fill, structure, or other related activities before he or she formulates specific project plans. He or she may even submit tentative "sketch" plans. Such informal contacts are desirable before the developer invests large sums in project plans and becomes less flexible.

The zoning administrator or other official may visit the proposed development site to determine whether it lies within a wetland, and, if so, to estimate the possible wetland impact. Often a permit applicant agrees to confine activity to the upland in order to avoid regulatory requirements and delays. Negotiations on project design may follow if all or a portion of the project lies within the wetland. All of this may take place before submission of a formal permit application.

2. A formal application is submitted. The permit applicant submits a formal permit application, usually on forms provided by the regulatory agency. Copies may be sent to adjacent landowners and other agencies. Usually the application must contain detailed information concerning the project design, location of the proposed activity, and the specific wetland characteristics at the site, including wet-land boundaries. An environmental impact statement may be required, particularly for larger projects if the proposed project is being funded or conducted by a federal agency or state law requires one.

Often the permit application is circulated by the regulatory agency to other agencies with review authority or special expertise. For example, a wetland regulatory agency may circulate a permit application to a floodplain management agency for assessment of flood hazards.

3. Agency staff make a field visit. If a regulatory agency field visit was not conducted at an earlier stage, regulatory agency personnel often conduct a field investigation to evaluate the impact of the proposed use, compliance with regulatory standards, possible problems, availability of alternative sites, and mitigation potential, including compensatory mitigation.

4. Additional studies are completed. If special problems or other "red flags" are identified in the field visit or through review of the application by the regulatory agency or other reviewers, additional studies may be required from the permit applicant. The regulatory agency may itself also carry out various studies on a controversial proposal. Considerable negotiation on the project design may follow between the project applicant and the regulatory agency.

5. A public hearing is held. Depending on the state statute or local ordinance, a public hearing may be held on the proposal. Public hearings are particularly common for large or controversial permit applications.

6. A decision on the permit is given. The regulatory agency approves, denies, or conditionally approves the proposed activity based on information supplied by the landowner or developer, the agency, reviewers, and participants in the public hearing. Often the proposed activity is permitted, subject to conditions relating to location, protection against flooding, erosion control measures, protection of natural vegetation, compensation for lost functions and values, and other matters.

7. The decision may be appealed. If dissatisfied with the decision of the regulatory agency, the applicant or other aggrieved party may appeal the decision to a court specified in the enabling statute or, less commonly, to a state appeals board.

8. The project is initiated. If the application has been approved and all necessary permits received, the landowner or developer then may initiate the proposed activity. In some instances, the developer is required to post a performance bond to ensure that the project is conducted in accordance with permit stipulations. The regulatory agency may inspect the development once it has been completed to determine compliance.

---

may assist the local agency in pinpointing problems and supplementing other sources of information.

How are regulatory standards applied?

Most regulations list both certain "bottom line" minimum regulatory criteria or standards and more general principles and factors that are to be applied by the regulatory agency in approving, denying, or conditionally approving a permit. Typically the agency first determines whether a permit application should be rejected because it fails to meet the minimum, preliminary criteria. If a permit application complies with these, the discretionary criteria then are applied. Conditions typically are attached to permits (particularly larger projects) to ensure compliance with the minimum and more discretionary criteria.

Minimum preliminary criteria often are those that relate to public health and safety and prevention of nuisances or to other critical "bottom line" determinations. For example, a permit application will be rejected if the proposed activity violates a:

• Prohibition of activities that block floodway areas.

• Prohibition of activities that threaten public safety or cause nuisances to adjacent lands.

• Prohibition of activities that violate state or local pollution control standards.

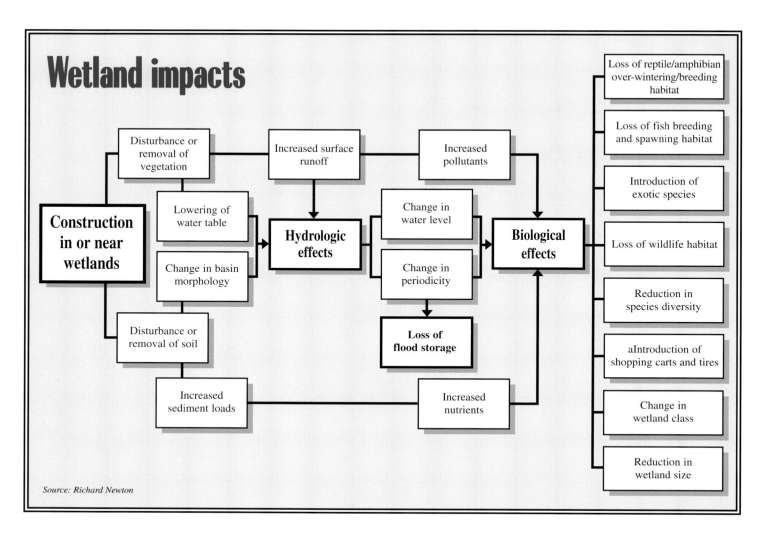

Wetland impacts

Source: Richard Newton

- Prohibition of septic-tank and soil absorption systems in high groundwater areas.
- Prohibition of activities that destroy storm beaches or dunes, which protect backlying areas from erosion.
- Prohibition of activities that threaten rare or endangered species.
- Prohibition of certain uses in an area as incompatible with zoning and nuisance-like in the surroundings (such as heavy industry in a residential area).
- Requirement that land subdivisions be free from flooding and suitable for intended uses.

If the permit application passes these tests, it then will be subjected to further determinations that require discretion in their application. Examples of these requirements include:

- It must be demonstrated that there is no "practical" upland alternative for the proposed activity.
- The proposed activity must be water-dependent or require a wetland location.
- New structures within floodplain areas must be elevated or "otherwise protected" to the elevation of the 100-year flood.

- All reasonable efforts must be made to reduce the impact of development upon a wetland.
- Wetland buffers must be created.
- There must be no net loss of wetland function (and acreage in some programs).

Programs sometimes establish a number of presumptions that may be rebutted in a given instance. Examples include requirements that:

- Compensatory storage be provided for any loss of flood storage due to fill, diking, or other alteration of a wetland area, unless it can be shown that storage is unimportant. Compensatory storage can be provided through creation of upland reservoirs or by excavation.
- On-site mitigation (compensation) be provided, unless it is impossible, impractical, or there are greater environmental benefits from an off-site location.
- Particular uses not be located in specific types of wetlands, unless compatibility of the uses with the wetland are demonstrated.

Finally, statutes, administrative regulations, and ordinances sometimes require that the regulatory agency weigh the environmental and economic costs and benefits of wetland development to determine the "public interest." Often the regulatory agency is required to consider regulatory goals and other factors set forth in the regulations, such as consistency with community public facility plans and broader land and water use plans. In determining the public interest, agencies often take into account public preferences expressed at public hearings as well as other sources of information.

What conditions are to be attached to a permit?

Regulatory agencies often attach conditions to permitted uses to ensure compliance with regulatory standards and criteria. Some conditions are attached to all permits, while others are applied only to particular permits. Conditions with widespread applicability include:

• Requirements that proposed uses comply with all applicable zoning, subdivision control, sediment control, and other regulations before work begins. Alternatively, all other permits may be required before a wetland permit is issued.

• Requirements that natural drainage be maintained through culverts, landscaping, or other measures.

• Requirements that grading, filling, and construction practices be used that reduce impact on systems.

• Limitations on removal of vegetation and requirements that denuded areas be quickly replanted.

• Requirements that on-site or off-site wetland creation or restoration be used to compensate for loss of wetlands functions and values and (in some instances) wetland acreage.

• Requirements that buildings be protected to the 100-year flood elevation.

• Requirements that siltation and erosion-control measures be applied to stabilize banks and other non-vegetated areas.

• Requirements that as little fill as possible be used; that it be confined to the margins of the wetland area; and that it be stabilized through plantings, riprap, and other techniques.

• Requirements that once a project has been completed, the applicant apply for a certificate of compliance.

• Requirements that there be monitoring and reporting on the success of wetland mitigation and compensation measures.

• Requirements that all facilities and equipment be operated and maintained to comply with the regulations.

Other more specific conditions may be attached, depending upon the specifics of the proposed use, wetland values and hazards, and other factors. Common specific conditions include:

• Time limitations for completion of the proposed activity.

• Tight restrictions upon filling or other activities within specified areas of the wetland.

• Deed restrictions that must be recorded to ensure that the applicant and successors protect particular areas and comply with conditions specified in the permit.

• Construction of vegetative screens and replanting of wetland buffer areas.

• Installation of sediment-settling ponds for storm runoff and tertiary treatment facilities for sewage disposal.

• Dedication of public access easements to wetlands.

How can the success of restoration and creation projects be assured?

Regulatory agencies usually require that wetland restoration or creation be undertaken by the project applicant to compensate for damage or destruction of a wetland, in order to achieve no net loss of function and value, acreage, or some combination of both. The regulatory agencies favor "on-site" and "in-kind" restoration so that no net loss will be achieved in the same area and for the same type of wetland. However, on-site and in-kind may not be practical or environmentally desirable in all instances.

Possible cumulative impacts as well as impacts on specific wetland functions must be evaluated.

Many restoration and creation projects constructed by regulatory permit applicants have failed over the last several decades to meet project goals in one or more respects. A 1990 study in Florida, for example, found that the rate of ecological success among 119 mitigation projects in that state was only 27 percent. Ecological success was defined as whether the site was functioning as, or clearly tending toward functioning as, a wetland of the type indicated. There are a number of factors that need to be considered to reduce project failure; see the table on page 124, in Chapter 11.

What monitoring and enforcement are needed?

Regulatory agencies may carry out site visits during project construction or at project completion to determine compliance with permit conditions. Site visits are likely for large-scale projects such as dams, dredging, or landfills. Violation of conditions may result in permit revocation or court action. Site visits for monitoring and to determine compliance are particularly important for projects involving compensatory wetland restoration or creation.

Several courses of action are available to an agency if a project does not comply with permit conditions. Typically, the applicant is given an opportunity to voluntarily comply if the violation or noncompliance is unintentional. For example, a restoration project may fail to produce desired vegetation.

A formal enforcement action involving fines, injunctions, and possible criminal penalties may be undertaken for flagrant and intentional violations. Often courts require restoration of a damaged wetland as a remedy in such enforcement actions.

Wetland impacts of steps in construction

Step	Specific activities	Impact	Suggestions for reducing impact
1. On-site activities before construction	1. Surveying carried out to define terrain features, minor clearing of vegetation, placement of stakes 2. Engineering borings 3. Percolation tests	1. Some destruction of natural vegetation, disturbance of wildlife due to transport of equipment to and from site, disposal of materials from drilling	1. Use of air photo survey techniques 2. Regulation of survey methods and equipment, including time of year in which borings occur
2. Construction of access roads	1. Tree cutting, vegetation removal 2. Excavating, filling	1. Destruction of natural vegetation, wildlife, interference with natural drainage, sedimentation	1. Location of roadways on upland sites, wherever possible 2. Confinement of tree cutting and filling to immediate roadway 3. Requirements that natural drainage and circulation be maintained through elevation of roadway on pilings, installation of culverts, requirements that measures be taken to reduce erosion and sedimentation
3. Establishment of construction camp (larger projects such as roads, bridges, dams, reservoirs)	1. Tree cutting, grading, filling 2. Installation of electricity, water supply, telephone	1. Destruction of wildlife, vegetation, interference with natural drainage, increased sedimentation	1. Location of construction camp at upland site wherever possible, maintenance if a wetland buffer strip
4. Materials storage	1. Grading, dumping, filling	1. Interference with drainage, pollution, and sedimentation from stored materials such as sand and gravel (depending upon materials)	1. Material storage on upland sites 2. Maintenance of wetland buffers 3. Installation of measures to reduce erosion from stored materials
5. Clearing of site	1. Vegetation removal	1. Destruction of wildlife habitat; destruction of storm and erosion barriers; destruction of scenic beauty; increased erosion; increased runoff	1. Vegetation removal only where absolutely necessary 2. Revegetation
6. Earth excavation and fill	1. Fill of wetland area, grading of natural wetland contours, removal of peaty soils		1. Confinement of fill to wetland margins and less sensitive wetland areas 2. Maintenance of natural drainage through fill and grading contours, currents 3. Rip-rap and revegetation to stabilize fill, reduce erosion
7. Foundation preparation and construction	1. Dumping of crusted stone and other foundation material; installation of piling, mixing, and pouring of concrete; installation of public facilities (sewer, water)	1. Water pollution (in some instances) from mixing and pouring concrete	1. Cofferdams, settling ponds to temporarily confine runoff from concrete mixing and pouring
8. Disposal of excess excavated materials		1. Erosion, water pollution, additional filling of wetland with consequential impacts	1. Disposal of excavated sites material at upland 2. Rip-rap and revegetation to quickly stabilize and fill denuded areas
9. Major construction activity	1. Erection of basic structure, accessory uses, roofing, siding, installation of major fixtures	1. Pollution by sediment, debris from construction site, oil and other residuals from installation of parking areas	1. Use construction design and practices to minimize wetland impact such as elevation of structure on pilings 2. Temporary settling ponds, other measures to reduce pollution
10. Site restoration and cleanup	1. Removal of litter, excess materials, back filling, landscaping, planting of trees and grasses, fertilization	1. Pollution from litter, backfilling, landscaping operations, use of fertilizers 2. Fill of wetland by landscaping	1. Confinement of fill to upland areas 2. Temporary settling ponds 3. Measures to reduce erosion on denuded surfaces

Endnotes

Association of State Wetland Managers, *State Wetland Regulation: Status of Programs and Emerging Trends* (1994).

R. Darnell, *Impacts of Construction Activities on Wetlands of the United States* (U.S. Environmental Protection Agency, Environmental Research Laboratory, 1976). EPA-600/3-76-045.

M. Strand, *Wetlands Deskbook* (Environmental Law Institute, 1996).

1800s: California

Laws of the Fish Dam

In 1916, Lucy Thompson, or Che-na-wah Weitch-ah-wah, wrote a book about her people, the Klamath/Yurok of California. In the book, Thompson described the strict sacred laws governing the ceremony of putting in fish dams before the ritual White Deerskin Dance, which was part of the annual World Renewal cycle of ceremonies during which people prayed that Earth's resources would continue:

"Families come in the morning and each one takes from the trap that which belongs to them, as many salmon as they need. . . . They must not let a single one go to waste, but must care for all they take, or suffer the penalty of the law, which was strictly enforced. . . . The Indians from up the river as far as they are able to come can get salmon, and down the river the same. In these traps there get to be a mass of salmon, so full that they make the whole structure of the fish dam quiver and tremble with their weight, by holding the water from passing through the lattice work freely.

"After all have taken what they want of the salmon, which must be done in the early part of the day, [those who put up the fish dam] open the upper gates of the traps and let the salmon pass on up the river, and at the same time, great numbers are passing through the open gap left on the south side of the river. This is done so that the Hoopas on up the Trinity River have a chance at salmon catching. But they keep a close watch to see that there are enough left to effect the spawning, by which the supply is kept up for the following year."

— from To the American Indian *by Lucy Thompson (self–published: 1916), as reprinted in* Native Heritage: Personal Accounts by American Indians 1790 to the Present, *edited by Arlene Hirschfelder (Macmillan: 1995)*

Using Federal Programs

Chapter 8 provides more detail on a variety of federal programs that address wetlands issues. Use the chapter to ascertain how federal programs can be used to advance your local wetland protection efforts.

Federal wetland protection and restoration efforts have become increasingly critical to wetland resources throughout the nation. The main regulatory vehicle, the Section 404 program of the Clean Water Act, has been strengthened in recent years, and the wetland conservation provisions of the 1996 Farm Bill provide significant protection on agricultural lands. Also, a broad range of nonregulatory assistance programs are available, such as the Wetlands Reserve Program. These federal initiatives offer many opportunities for citizens, land trusts, and local governments to advance wetland protection.

Federal moves toward wetland protection

As outlined in Chapter 1, a major shift in federal wetland policy began in the late 1960s and early 1970s. Before that time, the federal government pursued contradictory wetland policies. On the one hand, Congress authorized the U.S. Army Corps of Engineers, the Soil Conservation Service (now the Natural Resources Conservation Service), the Bureau of Reclamation, and other agencies to carry out water resources and flood control projects that destroyed or damaged millions of acres of wetlands through dredging, drainage, and construction of reservoirs, levees, seawalls, and groins. These agencies also offered grants-in-aid and other inducements to states, localities, and private landowners to drain valuable wetlands for agricultural purposes.

On the other hand, Congress authorized the U.S. Fish and Wildlife Service to protect

wetland areas through the Migratory Bird Conservation Act, the Wetland Acquisition Act, and the Land and Water Conservation Fund Act. Grants-in-aid and other inducements were offered to states, localities, and private landowners to protect wetlands under the Federal Aid to Wildlife Restoration Act, the Federal Aid to Fish Restoration Act, the Water Bank Program, and other programs.

Contradictions in the applications of these programs were particularly apparent in areas such as the prairie pothole region of the Midwest before 1975, where farmers on some parcels were draining wetlands with monies and technical assistance from the U.S. Department of Agriculture, while nearby farmers — or even the same farmers — were protecting their wetlands through easements from the U.S. Fish and Wildlife Service. In 1975, however, the Agriculture Department developed a policy of withholding technical or financial assistance for draining or altering certain types of wetlands in order to convert them to other uses.

Major advances in federal policy occurred when Congress adopted the National Environmental Policy Act of 1969, the Water Pollution Control Act Amendments of 1972 (today, these amendments commonly are referred to as the Clean Water Act), and the Coastal Zone Management Act of 1972. Further advances occurred when President Jimmy Carter adopted a Wetland Protection Executive Order in 1977, and Presidents Bush and Clinton endorsed a goal of no net loss of the nation's wetlands resources in 1988 and 1993, respectively. Congress endorsed the no net loss goal for water projects in 1990 and included wetland protection provisions in the 1985, 1990, and 1996 Farm Bills.

President Carter's Executive Order, No. 11990, Protection of Wetlands, established wet-

"We recommend that the nation establish a national wetlands protection policy to achieve no overall net loss of the nation's remaining wetlands base, as defined by acreage and function, and to restore and create wetlands, where feasible, to increase the quality and quantity of the nation's wetlands resource base."

— The Conservation Foundation, *Protecting America's Wetlands: An Action Agenda* (1988)

land protection as the official policy of all federal agencies. The Order, which continues to form the formal basis for federal policy (along with the Clean Water Act) stipulates that ". . . Each agency shall provide leadership and shall take action to minimize the destruction, loss or degradation of wetlands, and to preserve and enhance the natural and beneficial values of wetlands in carrying out the agency's responsibilities . . . ."

Important federal programs

Today, there are several federal programs that offer particularly important opportunities for citizens, land trusts, and local governments to protect and restore wetlands:

Regulation of fills and discharges

Section 404 of the Clean Water Act established the first nationwide regulations for discharges of fills into waters of the United States, which has been administratively and judicially defined to include wetlands. However, Congress had adopted an earlier regulatory act that has provided some protection to wetlands. Under Section 10 of the Rivers and Harbors Act of 1899, permits from the U.S. Army Corps of Engineers are required for any dredging, filling, or obstruction of navigable waters. Until the 1960s, the Rivers and Harbors Act was interpreted narrowly to protect waters for commercial navigation and was not applied to wetlands above the mean high water mark.

Protection for public lands

The federal government directly manages the one-third of the nation's lands that are in federal ownership. In addition, it acquires additional properties for national parks and recreation areas, water resource projects, federal buildings and works, and wildlife refuges. Principal federal land management agencies include the U.S. Fish and Wildlife Service, the National Park Service, the Bureau of Land Management, the U.S. Forest Service, and the U.S. Department of Defense. These agencies also carry out some activities on non-federal lands, such as construction of reservoirs and dredging of rivers and harbors.

Wetland protection is required or encouraged in the conduct of all federal activities on both federal and non-federal lands by a variety of measures:

Executive Orders on wetland protection and floodplain management establish a strong general wetland protection policy for all federal activities, including for land management, dredging, fills, and construction of federal buildings.

The Federal Land Policy and Management Act of 1976 requires the inventory and assessment of and planning for federal lands, including the assessment of aquatic habitats.

The Fish and Wildlife Coordination Act, as amended in 1958, requires that "equal consideration" be

given to wildlife conservation with other features of water resource development projects of the U.S. Army Corps of Engineers, Bureau of Reclamation, and other agencies. This Act requires that the Fish and Wildlife Service evaluate the impact on fish and wildlife of all new federal projects on existing federal lands and elsewhere (including the Corps of Engineers' dredging). The "equal consideration" requirement has given rise to a concept of mitigation of impacts by avoiding adverse consequences to wildlife or wetlands habitat and by replacing public wildlife conservation opportunities destroyed by federal projects through public acquisition of private lands offering similar opportunities.

The Endangered Species Act of 1972, as amended, places restrictions on federal agencies undertaking or funding a project that may adversely impact rare or endangered species.

In addition, federal activities are in some instances subject to state wetland and pollution controls. Section 404(t) of the Clean Water Act requires that federal projects comply with state regulations for the discharge of dredged and fill materials in the waters of the United States, including adjacent wetlands. However, a partial exemption is provided for federal projects individually authorized by Congress. Similarly, Section 301 of the Coastal Zone

Management Act requires that federal agencies comply with state coastal zone programs.

Guidelines developed by the Environmental Protection Agency pursuant to Section 404(b) of the Clean Water Act apply to most federal discharges of dredged or fill material into the waters of the United States or adjacent wetlands. Federal projects require permits from the Army Corps of Engineers consistent with these guidelines unless the project has been specifically and individually authorized by Congress, and the agency has prepared an environmental impact statement before authorization that complies with the guidelines.

The National Environmental Policy Act establishes a general federal policy to "fulfill the responsibilities of each generation as trustee of the environment for succeeding generations." Environmental impact statements must be prepared for federal activities with major impacts upon the environment, such as flood control projects, dredging, and land sales. The National Environmental Policy Act does not prohibit or otherwise control federal activities once the statement has been prepared. Nevertheless, impact statement requirements help ensure agency evaluation of the impacts of proposed projects and facilitate public review.

In response to increased national concern over environmental protection, the Corps in 1968 amended its permit regulations to broaden permit criteria so that it evaluated all relevant factors, including the effect of the proposed work on navigation, fish and wildlife, conservation, pollution, aesthetics, ecology, and the general public interest. These broadened criteria were sustained by the U.S. Court of Appeals for the Fifth Circuit in a landmark case, *Zabel v. Tabb*. In this case, the court upheld the right of the Department of the Army to refuse a permit to fill 11 acres of mangrove wetland in Boca Ciega Bay, Florida, based solely on grounds of environmental damage. The Corps now provides broad environmental review of wetland activities below the mean high water mark under Section 10 of the Rivers and Harbors Act.

As mentioned earlier, Section 404 of the Clean Water Act requires that permits be obtained from the Army Corps of Engineers or the states for discharge of dredged and fill materials into the "waters of the U.S." At first, Section 404 was interpreted narrowly by the Corps to apply only to traditionally navigable waters. However, this position was challenged in *Natural Resources Defense Council v. Callaway*, in which the U.S. District Court for the District of Columbia held that Section 404 applied to all waters, including wetlands. Based upon this ruling, the Corps adopted new regulations controlling activities in coastal and inland wetlands and provided a phased-in implementation of the Act.

The Section 404 administrative regulations provide that the District Engineer of the Corps is not to issue an individual or general permit for important wetlands (see the criteria listed below) unless he or she concludes that issuance is in "the public interest," considering all factors, including "conservation, economics, aesthetics, general environmental concerns, historic values, fish and wildlife values, flood damage prevention, land use navigation, recreation, water supply, water quality, energy needs, safety, food production, and, in general, the needs and welfare of the people." (See the figure on page 91 for the overall procedures for obtaining a Section 404 permit.)

In determining whether a proposed alteration is necessary, the District Engineer must "consider whether the proposed activity is primarily dependent on being located in, or in close proximity to, the aquatic environment and whether feasible alternative sites are available." The applicant "must provide sufficient information on the need to locate the proposed activity in the wetland and must provide data on the basis of which the availability of feasible alternative sites can be evaluated."

If the applicant shows that there are no "practicable alternatives" to locating the project in the wetland, the guidelines then state that the filling activities must be performed so that the adverse impacts are minimal. Finally, the applicant must provide

> ❋
>
> **The Section 404 program of the Clean Water Act has been strengthened in recent years, and the Farm Bill provides significant protection for wetlands on agricultural lands.**

compensation for any remaining unavoidable impacts through activities to restore or create wetlands.

An agreement between the Environmental Protection Agency and the Department of the Army, which oversees the Corps, lays out this "mitigation sequencing":

• *Avoidance.* An applicant must mitigate the impact of a project in the first instance by avoiding the filling of any wetlands in order to fulfill the project purpose.

• *Project modifications.* If impacts cannot be avoided, they must be reduced or minimized to the extent practicable through project modifications, such as design changes.

• *Compensation.* If all practicable project modifications have been accomplished and the project nonetheless will result in the loss of wetlands, the applicant must compensate for the loss. The compensation may take several forms, including on-site and off-site restoration or creation of wetlands.

Under the regulations, wetlands considered to perform functions important to the public interest include:

i. Wetlands which serve significant natural biological functions, including food chain production, general habitat and nesting, spawning, rearing and resting sites for aquatic or land species;

ii. Wetlands set aside for study of the aquatic environment or as sanctuaries or refuges;

iii. Wetlands the destruction or alteration of which would affect detrimentally natural drainage characteristics, sedimentation patterns, salinity distribution, flushing characteristics, current patterns, or other environmental characteristics;

iv. Wetlands which are significant in shielding other areas from wave action, erosion, or storm damage. Such wetlands are often associated with barrier beaches, islands, reefs and bars;

v. Wetlands which serve as valuable storage areas for storm and flood waters;

vi. Wetlands which are ground water discharge areas that maintain minimum baseflows important to aquatic resources and those which are prime natural recharge areas;

vii. Wetlands which serve significant water purification functions; and

viii. Wetlands which are unique in nature or scarce in quantity to the region or local areas.

. . . Although a particular alteration of wetlands may constitute a minor change, the cumulative effect of such numerous piecemeal changes often results in a major impairment of the wetland resources. Thus, the particular wetland site for which an application is made will be evaluated with the recognition that it is part of a complete and interrelated wetland area. . . .

Geographic areas regulated under Section 404

Activities affecting less than 10 acres of wetlands above headwaters may be authorized under Nationwide Permit 26

Headwaters
(Average annual flow less than 5 cubic feet per second)

Tributary to navigable waters (subject to Section 404)

Navigable River
(Used or susceptible of use in interstate commerce — subject to Section 404 and Section 10 Rivers and Harbors Act of 1899)

Adjacent freshwater wetland (subject to Section 404)

Extent of tidal influence

Isolated Wetlands
(Subject to Section 404 if destruction or degradation could affect interstate commerce)
Activities affecting less than 10 acres may be authorized under Nationwide Permit 26

High tide line

Estuarine
(Tidal waters subject to Section 404 and Section 10 Rivers and Harbors Act of 1899)
Adjacent wetlands above high tide line also subject to Section 404

Marine

Source: J. Goldman-Carter, A Citizens' Guide to Protecting Wetlands *(National Wildlife Federation, 1989)*

Over the years, the Corps has issued a number of types of supplementary guidance, including nationwide permits, programmatic permits, regulatory guidance letters, and memoranda of understanding. Although most U.S. wetlands now are regulated, quite a broad range of activities are exempted from the Section 404 program by statute and by various policies. For example, Section 404 permits are not required for:

• Established (ongoing) farming, ranching, and forestry activities, such as plowing, planting, and some minor drainage;

• Maintenance of structures, such as dikes, dams, ditches, levees, breakwaters, causeways, and bridge abutments;

• Construction of temporary sedimentation basins on construction sites; and

• "Prior converted cropland," which are wetlands that were drained, filled, and converted to agricultural production and no longer meet the current wetland definition.

To simplify the administration of the Clean Water Act and reduce the number of individual permits required for minor activities, the Corps has issued *nationwide permits* for those uses that have been determined to have relatively minor impact upon wetlands. Activities covered under nationwide permits can go forward without further Corps approval as long as the conditions set in the nationwide permit are met. Nationwide permits have been issued, for example, for:

• Discharges of dredged or fill material into non-tidal wetlands for the construction or expansion of a single-family home and features such as a garage (if the activity does not cause the loss of more than one-half acre of wetland) ("Nationwide 29");

• Minor discharges of less than 25 cubic yards of fill, which cause the loss of less than one-tenth of an acre of wetlands ("Nationwide 18"); and

• Discharges affecting no more than 10 acres of headwaters or isolated waters, including wetlands, with a "predischarge notification" required if the discharge will affect more than one acre ("Nationwide 26").

Corps districts can refuse to recognize and they can modify nationwide permits to fit local conditions. District Engineers also are authorized to issue *general permits* for particular activities of a similar kind that would not have severe individual impact upon the environment.

The Corps also has issued *state programmatic permits* to 13 states. State programmatic permits authorize the states to issue permits with respect to some activities or types of wetlands, and the Corps essentially "rubber stamps" the permits, where state regulations meet or exceed Corps permitting criteria.

In addition, the Clean Water Act authorizes states to adopt programs for the control of the placement of dredged or fill material into waters of the United States, including adjacent wetlands. Once a state has adopted a program meeting standards of the Environmental Protection Agency and EPA has approved the program, the state may assume permitting authority for all waters and wetlands except those susceptible to commercial navigation. Two state programs — for Michigan and New Jersey — have been approved.

Farm programs

Swampbuster, which was established in the 1985 Farm Bill and has been amended in the Farm Bill's 1990 and 1996 wetland conservation provisions, is designed to discourage conversion of wetlands to agricultural use. The Swampbuster program allows the continuation of farming practices. However, wetlands cannot be converted to cropland or wetland drainage increased. The program withholds federal farm program benefits from any person who converts a wetland by draining, dredging, filling, leveling, or any other means. In certain cases, landowners may perform certain activities if the effects are minimal on wetland functions. In addition, landowners may convert wetlands if their functions and values are mitigated.

The Wetlands Reserve Program (WRP), authorized by the 1990 Farm Bill, is a nonregulatory (voluntary) program offering landowners an opportunity to receive payments for restoring and protecting wetlands on their property. Under WRP, the Natural Resources Conservation Service obtains either permanent or 30-year conservation easements from participating landowners. Priority is given to permanent easements on lands that will be permanently protected by a third party. Beginning in 1996, a restoration-only, cost-share agreement option — which does not require a conservation easement — also was offered under WRP. Landowners are provided with 75 to 100 percent cost-sharing to pay for the required wetland restoration on permanent easements, 50-75 percent for 30-year easements, and 50-75 percent for the restoration cost-share agreements.

Lands that are eligible under the WRP program include restorable wetland areas that have been used intensively for cropping or forage production. Landowners are responsible for restoring, protecting, and maintaining the wetlands within the boundaries of the WRP easement, and they maintain control over access to the property. Acceptable uses of the land, which may include timber harvest, haying, grazing, or other activities, are spelled out in detail in the plan developed for the area. Activities that would degrade or diminish the wetland functions and values of the land under easement (such as cropping) are not allowed. As part of emergencies resulting from natural disasters, principally flooding, land can be entered into the WRP as authority and funds are provided by Congress.

Endangered Species Act

Under the Endangered Species Act, federal agencies are required to ensure "that any action authorized, funded or carried out by such agency . . . is not likely to jeopardize . . . any

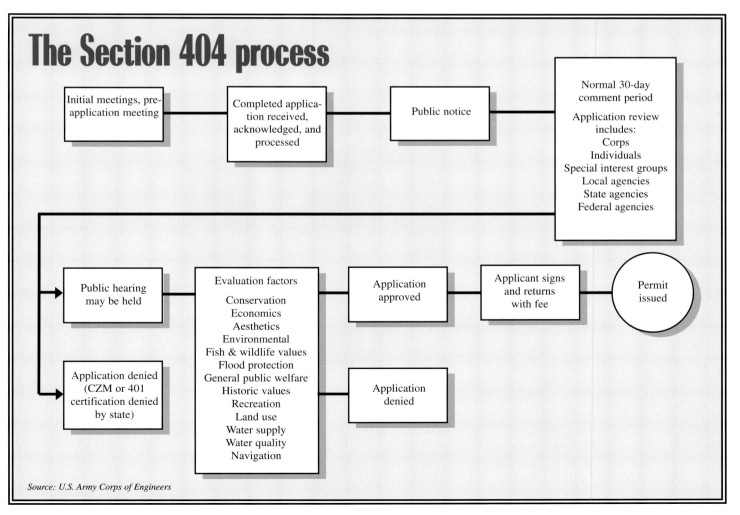

Source: U.S. Army Corps of Engineers

The Fagerlands, Langford, South Dakota:

Land stewardship in the prairie pothole region

For 20 years, Dennis and Jeanie Fagerland have farmed on top of the Prairie Coteau, a geological formation left by the last glacier 10,000 years ago. Originally, theirs was an area of profuse wetlands and tallgrass prairie; now part of that historical habitat is back due to the Fagerlands' land stewardship — and help from a variety of federal programs.

The Fagerlands have restored more than 30 drained wetlands, resulting in at least 120 surface acres of water. Wetlands are the centerpiece for the farm and provide habitat for shorebirds, waterfowl, and dozens of other species. More than 800 acres of cropland also have been planted to perennial grasses and legumes to protect the watersheds of the wetlands. The U.S. Fish and Wildlife Service, through Partners for Wildlife, has provided technical assistance to the Fagerlands, and the couple also has worked with the Natural Resources Conservation Service through the Great Plains Program and the Conservation Reserve Program. Ducks Unlimited also has provided expertise and funding for the Fagerlands' wetlands projects.

endangered or threatened species," or to adversely affect the species' critical habitat. The Army Corps of Engineers, then, in evaluating permit applications under the Section 404 program, must consider how any species listed as endangered or threatened would be impacted by the issuance of the permit. Major potential impacts on threatened and endangered species include covering or otherwise directly killing species and impairing or destroying their habitat. Regulations specifically direct that sites that have unique habitat or provide habitat for threatened and endangered species should be avoided when considering where to place dredged and fill material.

Generally, the Corps assesses the effects of permit activity on endangered species only in the permit area. However, the Corps will assess effects beyond the immediate permit area in three situations:

• When the activity authorized by the Corps has a physical effect on threatened or endangered species outside the permit area, the Corps will look outside this area to evaluate those effects.

• The Corps will consider activity effects beyond the permit area when the Corps is advised of a linear project, such as a pipeline, that will affect critical habitat outside the permit area and the Corps, through its control over the placement of a river

crossing, for example, can reasonably steer the route of the linear project around the critical habitat.

• The Corps also may enlarge the scope of the Endangered Species Act's review to include an entire project when "the linear project requires the Corps to issue such a significant number of permits, authorizing such a large portion of the project length, that by granting the permits, the Corps essentially would be authorizing the entire project or segments thereof."

The National Flood Insurance Program

The National Flood Insurance Program offers federally subsidized flood insurance as an incentive for state and local regulation of flood hazard areas. This program is important, because virtually all wetlands adjacent to rivers, streams, and the ocean are flood hazard areas. Other wetlands also may be flood areas. Tight floodplain regulations (particularly floodway regulations) may provide a considerable degree of protection for wetland areas. For example, the Federal Emergency Management Agency (FEMA), which administers this program, has adopted regulations requiring that communities with mangrove forests acting as coastal flood protection barriers adopt regulations protecting the mangroves in order to qualify for subsidized flood insurance.

Many communities now regulating wetland development do so through floodplain regulations designed not only to reduce flood problems but also to protect wetland functions. Combined wetland and floodplain ordinances not only can qualify communities for subsidized flood insurance but can meet broader water resources protection goals.

In 1993, FEMA established a voluntary community rating system, which provides an incentive — adjusted flood insurance premiums — for communities that do more than meet the minimum standards for the National Flood Insurance Program. The rating system encourages programs and projects that preserve or restore the natural state of floodplains by providing credit points for activities that address these functions. For example, credit is given for guaranteeing that a portion of a currently vacant floodplain will be kept free from development, for relocating flood-prone buildings so that they are out of the floodplain, and developing regulations that protect sand dunes.

Financial and technical assistance

President Carter's Wetland Protection Executive Order (11990) established a general wetland protection policy for all federal grants-in-aid and technical assistance to states and localities. These include not only aid for wetland protection but grants for land and water planning, construction of roads, airports and other facilities, construction of sewage treatment facilities, and open space acquisition. Grants-in-aid and technical assistance also are subject to the Flood Plain Management Executive Order (11988), which applies to most wetland areas adjacent to streams or the ocean.

Some agencies adopted wetland protection policies of providing grants-in-aid to states and localities before the Wetland Protection Executive Order was adopted. For example, the

Environmental Protection Agency adopted a wetland protection policy in 1973. Pursuant to this policy, EPA has attached conditions to grants for construction of sewage treatment plants to discourage secondary residential and commercial development in wetlands in Fairfield, California, and Block Island, Rhode Island. Several categories of grants-in-aid more specifically encourage and support state, local, and private wetland protection and restoration efforts:

Financial aid for wetland acquisition, restoration, and enhancement

Congress has authorized several programs that may be used to acquire, restore, and enhance wetlands. These have been important during the mid-1980s through mid-1990s; however, federal funding cuts may limit their future use.

The *Federal Aid to Wildlife Restoration Act* (Pittman-Robertson Act) is the principal mechanism for federal assistance to states for acquisition, restoration, and maintenance of wildlife areas, including wetlands. Grants for up to 75 percent of the cost of projects are available to states from this fund, which is made up of monies gathered from federal excise taxes on the sale of firearms and ammunition. Grants for fish restoration are available under the *Federal Aid in Fish Restoration Act* (Dingell-Johnson Act), and for the protection of habitat for rare and endangered species under the *Endangered Species Act*.

The *Land and Water Conservation Fund Act* (a special fund in the U.S. Treasury) has been a second major source of funds for state and local acquisition of outdoor recreation and open space areas. Acquisitions must be in compliance with the state's comprehensive outdoor recreation plan. While this program is not directed to wetland areas, some wetland acquisitions have been carried out under the broad objectives of the act, and states have been required to identify wetland acquisition priorities as part of their state outdoor recreation plans.

The *Coastal Zone Management Act* is a third source of funds for certain types of wetland acquisition. Section 315 of the Act authorized the National Estuarine Research Reserve System (NERRS), a protected area network of federal, state, and local partnerships that promotes informed management of the nation's estuarine and coastal habitats through linked programs of stewardship, public education, and scientific understanding. Individual reserves are managed by state and local governments, while the National Oceanic and Atmospheric Administration designates sites and administers the overall reserve system. Reserves range in size from 571 acres at Old Woman Creek NERR in Ohio, to more than 193,000 acres at Apalachicola NERR in Florida.

Authorized by the Coastal Wetlands Planning Protection and Restoration Act of 1990, the *National Coastal Wetlands*

Conservation Grants Program provides matching grants for the acquisition, restoration, management, or enhancement of coastal wetlands. States that border the Atlantic and Pacific oceans, the Gulf of Mexico, and the Great Lakes are eligible for the program, which is run by the U.S. Fish and Wildlife Service. (One exception is Louisiana, which has its own coastal wetlands program under the Act.) Usually, the federal government provides matching funding of at least 50 percent.

The *North American Wetlands Conservation Act* provides matching grants to private and public agencies in the United States, Canada, and Mexico to carry out wetlands acquisition, restoration, and enhancement projects. The Act was passed in 1989 partially in support of the North American Waterfowl Management Plan, an international blueprint for long-term protection of migratory bird habitat in North America.

Maps and technical assistance

Several other important sources of technical assistance are available to localities to help them develop and implement wetland protection programs or broader land and water management programs with wetland components:

Section 208 of the Clean Water Act directs the Fish and Wildlife Service to provide technical assistance to states in developing regulatory programs for the discharge of dredged and fill materials into waters of the United States, including adjacent wetlands. It also authorizes the Fish and Wildlife Service to conduct a National Wetlands Inventory of the United States, based upon a comprehensive wetland classification system. This inventory, which will be available in both map and computer form, is based primarily upon air photos, with the use of supplementary data when available.

The Army Corps of Engineers provides *floodplain management technical services* to states and localities under its floodplain management program. Because this program stresses non-structural approaches, such as floodplain regulations for controlling flood losses, much of its assistance is important in wetland protection and management efforts.

The Natural Resources Conservation Service is authorized, pursuant to a number of statutes, to provide technical assistance to states, local governments, and private landowners in many aspects of resource conservation, including wetland restoration and management. (NRCS works closely with conservation districts in providing this assistance.) Soil surveys prepared by the NRCS have been used in many states to identify wetlands and apply management and protection policies. For example, through the use of soil maps, the state of Connecticut has mapped inland wetlands, which Connecticut defines to include alluvial, poorly drained, and very poorly drained soils.

> The Section 404 administrative regulations provide that the Army Corps of Engineers is not to issue an individual or general permit for important wetlands unless it concludes that issuance is in "the public interest."

The *Wetlands Reserve Program* is another excellent source of technical and financial assistance for wetlands restoration on private lands (see the discussion on WRP, above). The WRP, administered by the Natural Resources Conservation Service, provides an excellent protection opportunity for those who don't own wetlands as well: Citizens groups and local governments may be able to acquire wetlands for a lesser price if the wetlands are included in the WRP program, as an attached conservation easement makes property less costly. In fact, the federal government encourages this type of arrangement by giving high priority to areas where this is planned.

The *Conservation Reserve Program* (CRP) is yet another source of assistance for private lands. CRP offers landowners annual rental payments in return for placing environmentally sensitive cropland into a 10-year easement and implementing a conservation plan for the land. If wetlands are part of the cropland that meets the CRP criteria, they can be included. Also, beginning in 1996, certain cropped wetlands were eligible for CRP in order to protect wildlife values. The program places a high priority on enrolling riparian (filter) strips around any wetland, lake, or waterway. Many other wetlands not included in CRP benefit from the program as it keeps erodible agricultural soils from being deposited in the nation's waterways and wetlands. The CRP program pays 75 percent of the cost of establishing permanent cover (trees and grass) and restoring wetlands.

Another source of technical assistance and funding for conservation on agricultural lands is the *Environmental Quality Incentives Program* (EQIP), a program authorized under the 1996 Farm Bill to deal with significant water, soil, and related natural resource problems. EQIP establishes five- to 10-year contracts to provide technical assistance to landowners and pays up to 75 percent of the costs of conservation practices, such as manure management systems and erosion control. EQIP can provide cost-sharing for wetland restoration or creation. Also authorized under the 1996 Farm Bill is the *Wildlife Habitat Incentives Program*, which has available $50 million for wildlife habitat improvement.

Under the U.S. Fish and Wildlife Service's *Partners for Wildlife Program*, landowners enter into voluntary partnerships and receive technical and financial assistance for engaging in proactive stewardship of habitat, including wetlands. The program sometimes pays all of the costs of the landowner's project, but usually a portion of the costs is paid.

In addition to these efforts, a variety of mapping and technical services, which can assist states and localities in wetland protection, are available from the U.S. Geological Survey, the Environmental Protection Agency, and the National Oceanic and Atmospheric Administration.

Aid for land and water use planning

Several federal grants-in-aid have been available to states and localities for planning and managing land and water resources. Some principal programs include:

The *Water Resources Planning Acts of 1972 and 1974* provide sources of matching grants to states for water and related

Opportunities for participation in federal programs

❋ **Section 10 and Section 404 program regulatory permit processing procedures**
Comment on proposed permits, participate in public hearings, report violations, and help prepare local wetlands and watershed management plans.

❋ **Section 401 state water quality certification for federal regulatory permits**
Be involved in the establishment of water quality standards for state waters, including wetlands, comment on proposed federal permits, participate in public hearings, and report violations of federal regulations.

❋ **Coastal Zone Management Act consistency requirements for federal actions**
Federal actions, including federal approval of permits, must be consistent with an approved state coastal zone management plan. Public input is required in developing this plan.

❋ **Federal public land planning procedures**
Federal land management agencies must prepare plans for use of lands. Solicitation of public input is required.

❋ **National Flood Insurance Program Community Rating System**
Help local governments plan and regulate wetlands and floodplains to qualify communities and individuals for reduced flood insurance rates.

❋ **Wetland conservation, or Swampbuster, program**
Educate landowners and assist in mitigation and restoration efforts.

❋ **Wetlands Reserve Program**
Help educate landowners concerning financial incentives available from the Natural Resources Conservation Service for the purchase of wetland easements on agricultural lands, help NRCS determine funding priorities for acquisition and restoration, and help design and carry out restoration projects.

❋ **Partners for Wildlife program**
Work with the U.S. Fish and Wildlife Service to prepare wetland protection and restoration plans, educate landowners, and design and carry out restoration projects.

❋ **Environmental Impact Statement requirements**
Help federal agencies prepare environmental impact statements for actions that will have substantial impact on the environment. Comment on draft statements.

❋ **Endangered Species Act**
Help federal and state agencies identify sites of rare and endangered species, prepare protection and restoration plans, monitor public and private activities that may impact rare and endangered species, educate landowners, and help raise funds for acquisition of sites.

land resources planning, including regional water and land assessments and special projects.

The *State Wetlands Protection Grant Program*, administered by the Environmental Protection Agency, provides funds for state and tribal efforts to protect wetlands by providing funds to enhance existing programs or develop new ones.

Section 208 of the Clean Water Act provides grants-in-aid to states and regional planning agencies to develop area-wide waste management plans and implementation processes. These plans and processes include the identification and regulation of non-point pollutants from agriculture, forestry, mining, construction activities, and other sources.

Section 319 of the Clean Water Act establishes a national policy and delineates programs for control of nonpoint sources of pollution. The federal government provides 60 percent cost-share for implementing approved nonpoint source programs. Aid goes to the states, which pass it through to local agencies, conservation districts, and other groups.

In addition, aid for planning protection strategies for coastal ecosystems is available through the National Estuarine Research Reserve System (see above).

Aid for regulation

Three principal sources of federal funds are available to help states and localities adopt and administer regulatory programs, which may include wetland regulations.

A portion of the funds allocated to states by the Environmental Protection Agency pursuant to *Section 208 of the Clean Water Act* may be used to develop and administer regulatory programs to control nonpoint pollutants, including the discharge of dredge and fill materials into the waters of the United States. *Section 205 of the Clean Water Act* authorizes EPA to make available to each state up to $400,000 a year for administering pollution controls, including dredge and fill programs that meet EPA standards.

The *Coastal Zone Management Program* as amended provides up to 80 percent federal matching grants for the development of coastal management programs. Most states give high priority to wetland protection. This program provides grants-in-aid of up to $6 million a year to aid states in acquiring, developing, and operating estuarine sanctuaries. For states approved before 1990, 80 percent of development costs are paid and 50 percent matching funds for maintenance of the program after approval. For states approved after 1990, 80 percent of development costs are paid, and maintenance costs are paid between 50-80 percent. About 30 states have received approval for such program administration grants.

Most states have emphasized local and regional rather than state implementation of coastal zone policies, although the state

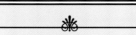

Several sources of technical assistance are available to localities to help them develop and implement wetland protection programs or broader land and water management programs with wetland components.

retains the power to directly regulate coastal areas in the event local units fail to adopt and administer regulations meeting state standards. States taking this approach include Maine, Minnesota, Oregon, Virginia, Washington, and Wisconsin.

Gaps in federal programs

Federal efforts have been extremely important to wetland protection, but they have several significant gaps. Also, several federal measures have questionable long-term political acceptability. Action by citizens, land trusts, and local governments is needed to fill in the missing pieces and assure that federal programs function effectively. Particularly critical needs include:

• Federal wetland planning, regulatory, restoration, grants-in-aid, and other efforts are complicated and only partially coordinated. They are difficult for landowners to understand. Citizens, land trusts, and local governments can help implement these efforts by carrying out public education programs and helping landowners understand and sort out the many programs.

• Many of the smaller, isolated wetlands have been exempted from federal regulatory efforts or are simply missed by regulatory agencies because of budgetary and staff constraints. In addition, quite a wide range of wetland impacts are not regulated. Local governments can adopt wetland regulations (such as special regulations, zoning, and subdivision control) that fill these gaps and "back up" federal and state efforts for larger wetlands.

• Federal wetland regulatory efforts operate on a case-by-case basis and do not consider the broader hydrologic regime or ecosystems. In addition, there is no federal control for buffer areas or water or land uses throughout watersheds. Citizens, land trusts, and local governments can provide comments on proposed Section 404 and Section 10 permits and provide testimony at hearings with regard to broader context. They can influence state Section 401 water quality certifications of Section 404 permits and state Coastal Zone Management consistency requirements for Section 404 permits and other activities. Local governments also can undertake wetlands and watershed management planning to provide a broader policy context for federal decision making.

• Federal budget and staff limitations mean inadequate technical assistance and other landowner assistance are available. Citizens, land trusts, and local governments can provide technical assistance to landowners to address these gaps.

• Finally, the federal Section 404 wetland regulatory program has not adopted maps and wetland delineation criteria are complicated, resulting in landowner uncertainties. Local governments can prepare or make available wetland maps and assist landowners in using them.

Endnotes

Environmental Law Institute, *Wetland Mitigation Banking* (1993).

J. Goldman-Carter, *A Citizens' Guide to Protecting Wetlands* (National Wildlife Federation, 1989).

National Research Council, *Restoration of Aquatic Ecosystems* (National Academy Press, 1992).

M. Strand, *Wetlands Deskbook* (Environmental Law Institute, 1996).

U.S. Environmental Protection Agency, *Wetland Fact Sheets* (Office of Wetlands, Oceans, and Watersheds, 1995). EPA 843-F-95-001.

White House Office of Environmental Policy, *Protecting America's Wetlands: A Fair, Flexible and Effective Approach* (1993 and updates).

1820s: Louisiana

A Haven from Slavery

In the first half of the 1800s, tales of "maroons," as long-escaped slaves were then known, finding refuge in swamps were legendary in the United States. Many Americans knew John James Audubon's famous encounter that took place in the late 1820s. The famous ornithologist was struggling in the Louisiana bayou muck to transport his heavy gun and six dead wood ibises when his dog began to yelp. Audubon then heard from a thicket the command to drop his gun. Out stepped "a tall, firmly-built Negro" holding a rusty musket. Audubon did not drop his gun, which both men recognized as more likely to fire than the maroon's old musket, so the man pleaded with him: "I am a runaway. I might shoot you down; but God forbids it ...[so] I ask mercy at your hands." Audubon's curiosity got the better of him and, persuaded that he was too far from his base, anyway, to reach it before nightfall, he agreed to accompany the maroon back to his camp. There Audubon was introduced to the runaway's wife and to his three children. They ate venison and potatoes, and Audubon heard their tale of separation through sale some 18 months before. The man had escaped, gathered his family from four separate plantations, and re-created family life deep within a canebrake.

— *from* Poquosin: A Study of Rural Landscape and Society
by Jack Temple Kirby
(University of North Carolina Press: 1995)

Using State Programs

Chapter 9 provides an overview of various state wetland protection programs. Use it to ascertain how state programs can be used to advance your local wetland protection efforts.

All but a few coastal states now provide some protection for coastal wetlands through wetland regulation statutes or broader coastal zone or shoreland acts with wetland components. At least 19 states regulate inland wetland areas. In addition, many others regulate floodplain areas that contain major wetlands.

Citizens and communities can help protect and restore wetlands by participating in these state efforts. They can help administer and enforce state regulations by informing landowners of requirements, educating landowners on wetland protection options, monitoring wetland activities and reporting violations, and participating in hearings on individual wetland permits. Communities also can supplement state regulations with their own and develop joint permit procedures.

In some states, citizens and communities also can participate in state wetland acquisition programs. State grants-in-aid and technical assistance may be available to assist communities. Over the last decade, state wetland programs across the nation have developed hundreds of helpful model ordinances, brochures, guidebooks, maps, films, and videos to help citizens and local governments protect and restore wetland areas.

State wetland programs have been prompted by several considerations. First, wetlands often cross local government jurisdictions, creating problems in managing wetlands on the local level. Second, wetland water supply is affected by watershed use. Watersheds often encompass several jurisdictions or even several states. Conversely, what happens to a wetland in one jurisdiction often affects flooding, water quality, and water supply in other areas. Third, local governments often lack the expertise and funds to identify and evaluate wildlife, floods, erosion, and other wetland values and hazards and to determine the impact of development. Fourth, control and protection of wetlands is linked closely with traditional state protection of wildlife and public rights in navigable waters.

State wetland protection programs, which are more extensively discussed in the Association of State Wetland Managers' report *State Wetland Regulation: Status of Programs and Emerging Trends*, include both regulatory and nonregulatory components.

Regulatory programs

Following the lead of Massachusetts in 1963, at least 20 states now require a permit for fill and structures in coastal wetland areas. Permits for regulated activities are evaluated on a case-by-case basis in light of statutory and administrative standards. In addition, six states authorize a state regulatory agency to adopt wetland protective orders resembling zoning regulations, require permits, and list permitted and prohibited wetland uses.

Coastal wetland protection efforts in most of the remaining coastal states are components of broader regulatory efforts. In some states, standards for local regulations are established in shoreland zoning programs. For example, Michigan regulates wetland areas along Lake Michigan through a shoreland zoning act. Washington requires that local governments in the coastal zone adopt regulations for natural areas and environmental areas. California provides some protection for wetland areas as part of a broader coastal zone regulatory program administered by special regional regulatory boards. Oregon has developed a coastal zone

"Protection efforts should be coherent and coordinated to make the most efficient use of scarce resources and minimize inconsistency among federal, state, and local programs."

— National Governor's Association (1992)

program with wetland components as part of a broader mandatory state land use program. Similarly, Florida has developed standards for the Florida Keys as part of a critical area program.

Inland wetlands have been afforded less protection. Explicit state inland wetland protection acts have been adopted in Connecticut, Florida, Illinois, Maine, Maryland, Massachusetts, Michigan, Minnesota, New Hampshire, New Jersey, New York, North Dakota, and Rhode Island. Massachusetts regulates inland wetlands through two statutes. The first requires review of proposed development by a local conservation commission. The second authorizes the state Commissioner of Environmental Protection to adopt inland wetland protection orders and issue permits. New Hampshire and Rhode Island regulate both coastal and inland wetlands through state permit requirements. Connecticut, Michigan, and New York establish standards for local wetland protection and directly regulate areas only in the event of local inaction.

In several states, inland wetland regulation is a component or an indirect result of broader state regulatory efforts applied to state waters, shorelands, floodplains, wild and scenic rivers, or other areas. For example, Michigan, Oregon, and Wisconsin protect some wetlands by controlling dredging and filling in state waters. State shoreland zoning programs that apply to lake and stream shore areas have been adopted in Maine, Minnesota, Vermont, Washington, and Wisconsin. These programs require or encourage local units to adopt special standards for wetland areas.

Direct state floodplain or floodway regulations or state standards for local regulations have been adopted in at least 30 states. Protection of ecological values is rarely an explicit objective, although a large measure of wetland protection may in fact be achieved by the very restrictive controls typically applied to floodway areas.

Scenic and wild river programs adopted in one-half of the states provide some protection for wetland areas. The Florida critical area program has adopted standards for local regulation of lands in Big Cypress Swamp. Dam permit laws in at least 30 states provide a measure of protection to wetland areas, although their primary emphasis is on navigation and other public rights to navigable waters and control of water pollution.

In addition to these acts aimed at controlling water-related uses, many states regulate on-site waste disposal systems in areas of high groundwater through plumbing and sanitary codes. These codes provide some protection for inland and coastal areas without sewers. Some protection also is provided in Florida and Vermont through regulation of large-scale development. Additional protection is achieved through state power plant siting controls and strip mining regulations.

> ❋
>
> **Citizens and communities can help administer and enforce state regulations by educating landowners on wetland protection options and participating in hearings on individual wetland permits.**

Non-regulatory efforts

Non-regulatory wetland protection efforts provide a valuable supplement to coastal and inland regulatory programs. Non-regulatory efforts can take many forms:

• *Waterfowl and wildlife protection programs.* All states have adopted wildlife protection and conservation programs. Programs include hunting regulations, acquisition of wildlife protection areas, propagation and stocking of fish and waterfowl, protection of rare and endangered species, and conservation education efforts. Many programs involve the acquisition and management of wetland areas. Communities often can help establish priorities for acquisition.

• *Environmental impact review acts.* Many states promote informed decision making by requiring the assessment of impacts before a project is carried out.

• *Public land management programs.* Wetland management often is a component of state public land management programs. These include state forestry, park, trust land (beaches, lake bottoms), scientific area, and scenic and wild river programs. Communities and citizens can review and comment upon management policies for lands within their jurisdiction.

• *Flood control efforts.* Wetland acquisition is a component of a few state flood control programs. For example, Massachusetts has recommended acquisition of wetlands along the Neponsit River to protect flood storage. Communities and citizens often can influence state plans or comment upon permits.

• *Public education.* Universities in several states, including the University of Wisconsin and the University of Minnesota, have acquired wetlands for educational and scientific purposes.

• *Tax incentive programs.* Some states, including California, Connecticut, Michigan, New Hampshire, Pennsylvania, Rhode Island, and Washington, authorize tax relief for wetland and open space areas (See Chapter 11.)

Implementation of wetland statutes

Budgets and staff

Most state programs are handicapped by small budgets and limited staff. Community assistance in data gathering, monitoring, permit evaluation, and other activities is welcomed. State staff typically divide their time among such tasks as mapping, adopting orders and rules, and conducting workshops and maintaining liaison with local governments and other agencies. They also hold discussions with landowners, process permits, and conduct public hearings, field investigations (to determine precise wetland boundaries and evaluate permit applications), enforcement activities, and, in some instances, wetland acquisitions. Wetland mapping, whether carried out by the staff or consultants, often is a principal budget item during early phases of program implementation. The evaluation of wetland permits, another major staff function, varies in its demand on staff time. Because of the many responsibilities and inadequate staff, monitoring wetland activities often is a low priority.

Data gathering

State wetland data gathering often includes preparing new wetland maps (if necessary), and conducting field surveys to evaluate the impact of proposed development. Some state regulatory programs have prepared formal wetland maps at scales from 1:200 (one inch equals 200 feet) to 1:2,000. Maps typically are based upon interpretation of black and white, color, or color-infrared air photos, although other data sources, such as soil surveys and tidal records, are used in some efforts.

The scale of wetland mapping often is an issue. Not all programs agree with the need for large-scale and accurate maps. Field surveys are needed to resolve boundary disputes and to evaluate individual development proposals, even where very detailed maps are available. Large-scale mapping is very expensive and may create a false impression that wetlands can be located with mathematical certainty.

A mapping approach advocated by some states (such as Maryland and Wisconsin) is to adopt wetland maps with less initial accuracy and use field surveys to apply vegetative or other criteria to resolve boundary disputes. Some states rely solely on vegetative criteria, not mapping, in applying regulations. (The Georgia Marshland program and the New York interim regulations for freshwater areas are examples.) Only a small number of wetland regulatory programs have completed mapping on a statewide basis, although efforts now are underway in Michigan, New York, Wisconsin, and other states in cooperation with the National Wetland Inventory.

State wetland regulatory programs rarely have mapped specific subzones within wetland areas. However, New York administratively divides tidal wetlands into more specific subzones. They include coastal fresh marsh, intertidal marsh, coastal shoals, bars and flats, littoral zones, high marsh or salt meadow, formerly connected tidal wetlands, and unclassified tidal wetlands. Virginia has adopted guidelines for coastal wetlands that suggest variations in use potential for various vegetation zones. North Carolina administrative regulations place special emphasis on protecting coastal low marshes.

Data gathering to calculate the impact of individual development proposals is conducted on a case-by-case basis to assess natural values and hazards and the probable impact of the particular development. Site-specific data usually are derived from two sources: (1) information is supplied by the developer in his or her application form, environmental impact statement (if one is required), or special studies, and (2) information is generated by the regulatory agency through air photos, topographic maps, field surveys, and other available sources of information. Usually, a field investigation is conducted for each permit. A

staff engineer or biologist determines the precise wetland boundary and evaluates the probable impact of the project on wetland soils, hydrology, water quality, vegetation, and other parameters. The specific data gathered depend on the proposed project design and the characteristics of the site. Community assistance in permit evaluation can be particularly important.

Administrative rules and orders

Most states have adopted administrative rules and regulations to supplement standards and criteria contained in enabling statutes. Typically these regulations repeat much of the language of enabling statutes pertaining to program objectives, wetland definitions, criteria, and penalties, but they add new, more detailed definitions for basic terms, specify permit application procedures in detail, and establish specific standards and criteria for processing permits. The latter may include lists of permitted, prohibited, and special permit uses.

Wetland orders are authorized by the statutes of at least six states. This approach, designed to provide "once and for all" regulatory policies for particular wetlands, has worked with varied success. Orders consist of a map and written text. The written text typically contains language from a model order designed by the agency but for specific circumstances. Most

Leo Kenney, Reading, Massachusetts:
Student association leads to statewide wetland protection

A few years ago, Leo Kenney, a teacher at Reading Memorial High School, developed a wetlands curriculum for his students that has resulted in not only an excellent field biology course but a significant contribution to wetlands protection in the state as well. Kenney's curriculum focused on vernal pools, which are shallow, intermittently flooded wet meadows, and his students became so interested in the topic that they formed a Vernal Pool Association. The Association has been active with a number of activities, including presenting workshops on vernal pool natural history, and designing and distributing T–shirts depicting the frogs, salamanders, and other wildlife that utilize vernal pools.

The Association's most important contribution has been to the Massachusetts Natural Heritage Program. Vernal pools are afforded protection under the Massachusetts Wetlands Protection Act only if they first have been certified, which involves documenting evidence of breeding of vernal pool obligate species by gathering biological data and submitting the evidence to the state's program. Since 1992, Kenney and his students have "certified" more than 200 vernal pools, close to one-third of all the pools certified for the Massachusetts program.

orders adopted to date have applied to coastal wetlands. However, Massachusetts has adopted protective orders for between 5,000 and 6,000 acres of inland wetlands. Adoption of orders has been hindered by the detailed map requirements of most acts (map scales of 1:2,400 in Connecticut and Rhode Island) and the requirement that landowners be notified in writing before the order's adoption. Written notification of regulations is not required by traditional zoning approaches. This spe-

cial requirement has increased greatly the time and expense of order procedures. There is some evidence, however, that written notice procedures facilitate enforcement. Written notice also may strengthen regulations against legal challenge, particularly where the right to contest the constitutionality of an order is forever barred after a specified period, as provided by some statutes. Regulatory agencies typically negotiate with landowners in preparing final boundaries for the regulatory order. Lines

What's in a statute?

Coastal and inland wetland regulatory statutes often contain the following types of provisions:

1. Legislative findings of fact concerning wetland losses and the need for protection. Most statutes stress the importance of wetlands to fisheries, waterfowl, and other forms of wildlife. Others stress pollution control, flood storage, recreation, educational and scientific values, and water supply. These findings help establish the policy basis for the statutes, educate landowners and the general public to the need for regulation, and aid the regulatory agency in interpreting the act and administering permits.

2. Statement of statutory purposes and policies. Statutes generally establish strong protection policies, although some balance preservation and economic or development goals.

3. Wetland definitions. Most statutes define wetlands with considerable specificity. Coastal definitions usually combine tidal action criteria with vegetation type. Inland definitions usually combine periodic surface water inundation or high groundwater levels with vegetation type.

4. Authorization for a designated agency to map wetlands. Wetland regulatory statutes usually contain several types of provisions that indirectly or directly require gathering particular types and scales of data. Many acts contain explicit data gathering requirements pertaining to data scale and format, such as the Connecticut Coastal Wetland Act, which required mapping at a scale of 1:200 (one inch equals 200 feet). Other acts indirectly require gathering particular types of data by requiring the regulatory agency to adopt wetland maps and orders complying with statutory wetland definition criteria.

5. Delegation of power to a designated agency either to directly regulate wetlands or establish standards for regulation by local governments. Most statutes authorizing direct state regulation of wetlands apply to coastal wetlands, although the Rhode Island and New Hampshire acts apply to both inland and coastal wetlands. The responsible agency usually is a natural resources or water resources agency. In contrast, most inland wetland statutes rely primarily upon

local governments for the administration and enforcement of state minimum standards. Virtually all statutes authorize the regulatory agency to adopt administrative rules and regulations to supplement statutory standards. Some statutes authorize the agency to adopt formal orders for particular wetlands as well as general written rules for all wetlands. Many statutes authorize the regulatory agency to undertake a number of additional wetland protection and management functions, including acquiring wetlands in fee or easement and providing assistance to local governments.

6. A requirement that landowners seek permits for specified kinds of uses in wetland areas (piers, fills, dredging, structures) from the state agency or local government. The statute usually contains partial or complete exemptions for activities of state and federal agencies, public utilities, local political subdivisions, agriculture, and mosquito control projects. The statute may also list permitted and prohibited uses. Statutes contain criteria for evaluating permits and procedures for applying for and issuing permits.

7. Penalties for violating regulatory standards. Statutes generally provide that any person violating any provision of the statute shall be liable for a fine ranging from $100 to $10,000, with each violation usually considered a separate offense. In case of continuing violations, each day of continuance generally is viewed as a separate offense. Some statutes authorize imprisonment of up to one year as well as fines. Under many statutes, the regulatory agency or the court can order restoration of the wetland or assess the cost of restoration against the offending landowner.

8. Appeal procedures. Most statutes provide that any party with an interest in the proceedings who is dissatisfied with the action of the regulatory agency on the proposed permit may appeal to a specified court. Administrative appeals to an appeals board or regulatory agency also are provided in Massachusetts, North Carolina, Maryland, Virginia, New York, Washington, and Delaware. Appeal procedures also may establish standards for determining whether a "taking" of property has occurred and provide remedies.

may be shifted somewhat to accommodate private needs where the essential integrity of the wetland still can be maintained.

Processing permits

Most statutes require case-by-case evaluation of proposals for excavations, fills, or structures in wetland areas. The vast majority of permits are conditionally approved. However, many developers are discouraged in early discussion from submitting formal permit applications. They are likely to do so only if they believe that the permits will be approved or if they wish to initiate a formal court challenge. In addition, extensive negotiation sometimes occurs on the developers' plans before final disapproval or approval of the permit application. Performance bonds have been required in some instances to ensure that projects are carried out as specified.

Regulatory administrators cite several major problems in processing permits. First, the cumulative impact of development from piecemeal issuance of permits may gradually destroy a wetland. It is difficult to evaluate the probable cumulative impact of development or deny a permit because of future anticipated development. Second, difficulties are encountered in the application of general performance standards that do not provide minimums based on quantity (such as protection of structures to the 100-year flood elevation). Agencies may be reluctant to refuse permits when there is no violation of a minimum quantified standard. Communities can adopt supplementary regulations to help address these problems.

Enforcement

Monitoring and enforcement of state regulations often are hindered by the lack of staff. This is particularly true for inland wetlands. Enforcement is less a problem in coastal wetland programs, due in part to their more limited geographical scope and more easily identified physical characteristics.

Monitoring techniques vary from state to state and range from principal reliance upon reporting of violations to systematic surveys. Experiments also have been made with monitoring through satellite imagery in Georgia and New Jersey, although the scale of the imagery is too small for most monitoring purposes.

Despite some misgivings, most state wetland programs have moved toward increased local involvement. For example, the Massachusetts program, which originally stressed permitting at the state level, has shifted much of the task of permit evaluation to local conservation commissions. Basic enabling statutes in Connecticut (inland wetlands), New York (inland wetlands), and Virginia place primary responsibility for wetland regulation at the local level. Only New Jersey regulates wetlands exclusively at the state level. Whatever the mix of state and local responsibility in your state, there are many opportunities for using the state program to strengthen your local protection efforts.

Endnotes

Association of State Wetland Managers, *State Wetland Regulation: Status of Programs and Emerging Trends* (1994).

S. Crane, J. Goldman-Carter, H. Sherk, and M. Senatore, *Wetlands Conservation: Tools for State and Local Action* (World Wildlife Fund, 1995).

U.S. Environmental Protection Agency, *Wetlands Regulation Guidebook for New York State* (1993). EPA-902-R- 93-004.

T. Henderson, W. Smith, and D. Burke, *Non-Tidal Wetlands Protection: A Handbook for Maryland Local Governments* (Maryland Department of Natural Resources, 1983).

Michigan Department of Natural Resources, *Michigan's Wetlands* (1982).

Pennsylvania Department of Environmental Resources, *Wetlands Protection: A Handbook for Local Officials* (1990).

World Wildlife Fund, *Statewide Wetland Strategies: A Guide to Protecting and Managing the Resource* (Island Press, 1992).

1947: Florida

The Grassy Waters

"There are no other Everglades in the world," Marjory Stoneman Douglas wrote in her book The Everglades: River of Grass. *"The miracle of the light pours over the green and brown expanse of saw grass and of water, shining and slow-moving below, the grass and water that is the meaning and the central fact of the Everglades of Florida."*

Stoneman Douglas's book was five years in the making, but its influence has been almost fifty. Through it, South Floridians and others were told tales about the Native Americans who were the original inhabitants of the Everglades, Spanish conquerors, and the drainage that had been going on even a century before Stoneman Douglas arrived in Miami in 1915. The final description in Stoneman Douglas's book is prescient: She discusses the region's booming cities and the great challenge of reconciling development and wetland protection. With population expected to more than double in portions of South Florida over the next 30 years, that challenge is even greater today.

— from sources including
The Everglades: River of Grass
(Hurricane House Publishers: 1947)

Making the Most of Local Regulation

Chapter 10 provides more detail on wetland zoning and other local regulations, including types of ordinances, issues that come up in their implementation, and examples of specific zoning and special bylaw provisions. When you promulgate or revise your local wetland protection regulations, use this chapter to guide your efforts.

There are many reasons for a community to consider implementing its own wetland regulations. Regulations can help your community achieve a variety of land and water use planning objectives, such as reasonable minimization of natural hazards, provision for open space and recreation areas, and prevention of drainage and flood problems. Regulation also can help with other objectives, such as prohibiting septic tanks in unsuitable areas, allocating lands throughout the community to the most appropriate uses, and protecting water supplies. Rarely are sufficient funds available at the local level to purchase more than a small portion of community wetlands to serve these objectives, and it often is politically unacceptable to remove large acreages of land totally from the tax rolls. Land use regulations restrict activities in wetlands while permitting some continued private use of lands.

Local regulation of wetland activities is required by state wetland protection acts in Connecticut, Massachusetts, New York, and Virginia. The Washington and Wisconsin shoreland zoning programs and the Florida critical area program, which applies to Big Cypress and Green Swamps, also require local controls. More than 3,000 local communities have adopted wetland protection regulations in these states. A larger number of other communities have adopted land use regulations for broader land use zoning or subdivision programs.

Local adoption of wetland regulations has been encouraged not only by state wetland acts but also by the National Flood Insurance Program, which requires local regulation of the 100-year floodplain in order to qualify for federally subsidized flood insurance. More than 17,000 communities have adopted or indicated an intent to adopt floodplain regulations to qualify for this program. Other federal incentives for wetland protection by localities include the Coastal Zone Management Act of 1972 and the Clean Water Act Section 404 permit requirements. The U.S. Army Corps of Engineers, which administers the Section 404 program, ordinarily will not issue a permit when a locality already has denied a permit, thereby strengthening local controls.

Ordinance types

There are two main regulatory approaches applied to wetland areas — a broad exclusion of virtually all uses that might damage wetlands (through public acquisition or tight regulations), and application of less restrictive performance standards. (See Chapter 6.) Applying performance standards is most common to reduce flood losses, reduce impact upon wildlife, and serve a wide range of other objectives, although many communities also have adopted very restrictive controls.

Wetland protection provisions typically are incorporated in several types of ordinances:

Zoning regulations. The most common type of local wetland regulation is a wetland or conservation zone, which is adopted as part of a comprehensive zoning ordinance, or, alternatively, as a separate wetland ordinance. Zoning regulations consist of a map showing wetland boundaries and text listing prohibited and permitted uses and establishing general standards for special permit uses. Usually a zoning board of

"An owner of land has no absolute and unlimited right to change the essential natural character of his land so as to use it for a purpose . . . which injures the rights of others."

— *Just v. Marinette County* (1972)

adjustment, planning board, or special board (a conservation commission) is authorized to evaluate applications for special permits within wetland areas. Lot-size restrictions typically are combined with siting controls and regulation of tree-cutting, grading, filling, dredging, construction of roads, and other activities. A considerable degree of wetland protection may be achieved if each proposed use is carefully evaluated and efforts are made to shift development to upland areas. In addition, large-lot zoning reduces the density of wetland development.

Special wetland protection bylaws and ordinances. Special bylaws also are quite common. They may be adopted pursuant to home rule powers given under special state wetland protection statutes. For example, a Massachusetts statute authorizes local units of government to regulate directly or comment upon wetland uses. These bylaws and ordinances also may be adopted pursuant to statutes authorizing local control of grading and filling, tree-cutting, and other activities. Special bylaws or ordinances typically contain text setting forth prohibited, permitted, and special permit uses. Wetlands may be defined by description or with reference to a map.

Floodplain zoning. Floodplain zoning ordinances with wetland protection provisions are a third common approach. Floodplain zoning regulations are, like wetland regulations, adopted either as part of broader zoning efforts or as separate ordinances. Usually, floodplain regulations apply only to mapped flood zones along major streams and the ocean. Independent wetland areas not associated with rivers or streams generally are not affected. Flood maps for urban areas often are based upon engineering studies defining the 100-year floodplain, and for some riverine areas, the 100-year floodway. Flood maps also may be based upon historic flood records, soil maps, or air photos.

Where wetland protection is not an explicit regulatory objective, minor amendments can strengthen wetland protection by adding tight control of structures, fills, and dredging in wetland areas. Separate but overlapping floodplain and wetland regulations may also be applied to provide an independent factual base for evaluating development permits. Wetland regulations also should be applied to wetland areas not lying within mapped floodplain zones.

Subdivision regulations. Subdivision regulations typically require that subdividers prepare detailed maps or "plats," which must be approved by the local planning board before the division of lots for sale or the construction of buildings. For approval, plats must comply with zoning and special subdivision regulations pertaining to lot size and width, access roads, the suitability of land for subdivision purposes, drainage and flooding, and the adequacy of public facilities. Subdividers usually must provide roads, sewers, drainage systems, and parks needed for subdivision residents. Although most subdivision ordinances do not specifically mention wetlands, many contain specific pro-

Regulation can help your community achieve land and water use planning objectives, such as reasonable minimization of natural hazards.

visions prohibiting the subdivision of flood-prone areas and require that lots be suitable for building and on-site waste disposal if public sewers are not provided. This, combined with requirements that subdividers provide recreation and open spaces, provides communities with bargaining power for the protection of wetlands. Additional bargaining power may be provided by "cluster" subdivision provisions, which encourage subdividers to group buildings together in upland areas (maintaining the overall density of the subdivision) so that other low lying areas can be maintained as open space.

Building codes. Many communities have adopted building codes to control the design and materials used in structures. These rarely contain references to wetlands, although several provisions, such as requirements that buildings be elevated above flood protection elevations and that buildings be located on suitable foundation material, may provide some protection for wetland areas.

Sanitary codes. Many communities have adopted sanitary codes regulating or prohibiting the use of septic tank and soil absorption systems in high groundwater areas and within specified distances of lakes and streams. If adequately enforced, these regulations can control building development in rural wetlands.

Special codes. Communities often adopt special codes for tree-cutting, grading, mosquito control, application of pesticides, solid waste disposal, storm sewers, air and water pollution emissions, and surface and groundwater extraction. These regulations, if adequately enforced, provide some protection for wetland areas, including the quality and quantity of waters entering wetlands from watershed lands.

Implementing local regulations

A variety of issues must be addressed in implementing local regulations, including the following:

• *The adequacy of wetland maps* is a widespread issue for several reasons. Detailed wetland maps rarely are available except for some coastal wetland areas (such as in Maryland and New Jersey) where detailed state mapping has occurred. Often soil, topographic, and generalized wetland maps are used for regulatory purposes in the absence of more detailed data. These maps may be outdated or of too small a scale for regulation, and they may not cover the community as a whole.

The accuracy of maps and map scale has been more of a problem for inland than coastal wetlands since coastal wetlands are more readily identifiable, even without maps, due to tidal actions and a relatively small number of characteristic plant species. Some communities have adopted both maps and written definition criteria for wetland areas and have required that field surveys be conducted to apply the written definition criteria in case of boundary disputes.

Local zoning administrators and government officials often are uncomfortable with wetland zone boundaries that lack certainty and do not coincide with property lines. There is a general belief that the zoning ordinance should contain quite precise boundary locations so that by inspecting the map, any boundary question could be settled. However, wetland boundaries are not precise, since saturated soils and wetland vegetation types grade into upland soils and vegetation. Fluctuating water levels over a period of years complicate the problem. Any attempt to define boundaries with mathematical precision, therefore, is bound to fail. Some landowners are able to exploit feelings of uneasiness on the part of zoning administrators and local legislative bodies by claiming that they will challenge the sufficiency of maps in court.

In some instances, problems with boundary location are minimized by mapping wetland boundaries directly on large-scale air photos and incorporating the photos in official zoning maps. If a landowner wishes to develop a particular site, the precise location of the site and its relationship to wetland boundaries usually can be located with reference to trees, roads, buildings, and other features visible on the photo.

Only a small number of communities have conducted data gathering efforts sufficient to rank wetlands for regulatory purposes, although informal ranking based upon size, threats, land ownership, and special values and hazards is quite common for acquisition. A ranking procedure based upon wetland values alone may be of relatively limited value for regulations based primarily upon flood or other hazards. In addition, a ranking procedure may encourage development of wetlands with a low ranking.

Many communities in New York and Wisconsin have applied regulations only to larger and readily mappable wetlands. This approach has proven politically expedient and minimizes administrative problems while preserving the more important wetlands.

All communities have found that wetland maps provide only a portion of the data required for evaluating proposed development. Field investigations usually are required to evaluate the seriousness of flood hazards at a site, suitability for on-site waste disposal, hydrologic characteristics, and other factors. Flood hazard maps, soil maps, and detailed air photos widely are used to make these additional determinations.

• **Budget restrictions** plague most local programs. Local programs are faced with limited funds and personnel for wetland mapping, site investigations, and enforcement actions. However, there are a variety of approaches that may be taken to reduce program costs. First, to help communities evaluate proposed development, developers often are required to file environmental impact statements or undertake other data gathering. Second, a fee may be charged to help defray the costs of field inspections and the processing of permits. Third, interest groups often are encouraged to testify at public hearings on proposed permits in order to generate free information on the permits. Fourth, local regulatory programs make do with existing wetland maps rather than produce their own. Finally, volunteer groups, such as The Nature Conservancy and Audubon

Mike Houck, Portland, Oregon:
Local planning requirements advance protection

Creekside Marsh is a significant Portland, Oregon, wildlife viewing area — and an excellent model for how wetlands, streams, and upland forests can be integrated with an office park development. A variety of partners helped make the site a model, including Mike Houck, Urban Naturalist for the Portland Audubon Society.

The Creekside Marsh project began in the mid-1980s, when a developer applied for permits to build on the site. Earlier Houck had completed an inventory for the city of Beaverton, a requirement under Oregon's statewide land use program, and he had identified Creekside Marsh as a "highly significant" natural area. Houck's inventory helped convince Beaverton officials and other regulators that the site was worth protecting. The result of the Section 404 and state permit processes? One building was put on pilings at the far end of the marsh, leaving the wetland largely protected. The owner then donated the marsh to the local park district. Since then, Houck has developed a brochure on and interpretive signs for Fanno Creek (where the marsh is located), helped form the group Fans of Fanno Creek, and held a stewardship workshop for those who manage office parks, featuring the Creekside Marsh site.

Society, may be used to monitor development and report violations of regulations.

• **Education and community support** will determine the success of local wetland programs. Some communities, such as Concord, Massachusetts, and Sanibel, Florida, have met with all individual wetland landowners to discuss their laws and the need for wetland protection. Other communities and interest groups have conducted public education efforts through lectures, slide shows, workshops, and lobbying. For example, the Massachusetts Audubon Society completed a three-year project, funded by the Rockefeller Foundation, to assist local conservation commissions in wetland protection. Universities have played major educational roles in assisting communities in Massachusetts, Washington, Wisconsin, and other states.

• **Legal issues** often are a challenge for communities. Landowners' concern that regulations will "take" private property without just compensation often is an impediment to adopting and tightly enforcing wetland regulations. A variety of approaches have been taken to achieve wetland protection while avoiding the takings issue; some of these are outlined in Chapter 5. Performance standards rather than outright prohibition of all structural uses can be applied. Also, negotiation can occur between the governmental body and the landowner in the processing of individual development permits. For example, the local regulatory body may agree upon wetland boundaries that preserve most but not all of a wetland. In return the landowner may agree to minimize impact upon the wetland by locating most if not all of a regulated activity in upland areas. Issues subject to negotiation commonly include the size, design, and precise location of the proposed project. Communities also can carefully coordinate tax policies with regulations to alleviate the burden of restrictive land use controls.

• *The advisability of regulating land solely to protect wetlands* sometimes is questioned. Broader regulations to reduce flood hazards, prevent septic tank systems in high groundwater areas, control filling and grading, and control tree-cutting may be more effective alternatives. Often a considerable degree of wetland protection can be achieved through the vigorous enforcement of regulations applying to these broader objectives without clearly confronting the political issue of wetland regulations.

The applicability of a particular approach depends upon the physical circumstances and the political climate. Considerable wetland protection is achieved in some areas through vigorous enforcement of sanitary codes prohibiting septic tanks in high groundwater areas and subdivision regulations prohibiting the division of floodprone areas. Wetlands in urbanizing and urban areas may be effectively protected through vigorous enforcement of floodway and coastal high-hazard restrictions that prohibit all fills and structures in these areas.

Only a small number of communities have conducted data gathering efforts sufficient to rank wetlands for regulatory purposes.

Careful evaluation, strong enforcement

Careful evaluation of permits is essential to a strong local program, and yet evaluation may be handicapped by limited budgets, an inadequate database, and a lack of expertise in the local regulatory agency. As a result, local governments rely upon environmental impact statements provided by developers and seek help from nearby universities, state agencies with hydrological and biological expertise, and federal employees such as Natural Resources Conservation Service soil scientists. The success of local programs often depends upon this outside assistance.

Permit applications submitted to local units of government typically are approved but usually with conditions — sometimes stringent ones — attached to minimize development impact. Before that even happens, developers with unacceptable projects may be discouraged from applying for permits.

Evaluation of the cumulative impact of development frequently is a serious problem in processing permits. Two approaches may be taken. First, all new uses may be prohibited based upon arguments of cumulative impact. Or, the density of new uses may be limited through lot-size restrictions or restrictions on the percentage of wetland areas that may be altered

within a parcel. In this way, the total impact of uses may be held within acceptable limits.

Once a permit is issued, enforcement is, of course, the key. Strong public education programs and watchdog interest groups who report violations and appear at public hearings can facilitate local enforcement. Periodic surveys of wetland areas and consistent prosecutional violations of not only wetland regulations but of floodplain zoning and septic tank permit requirements can help ensure that the permit is being followed.

Zoning and special bylaw provisions: Some examples

The rest of this chapter is devoted to the elements that often are contained in wetland zoning and special bylaw regulations.

These elements, which either are set out as a separate wetlands ordinance or integrated into a broader zoning or other code, include: (1) purposes; (2) wetland definition criteria and maps; (3) prohibited, permitted, and special permit uses; and (4) penalties.

Purposes

Local wetland ordinances typically list objectives for control of wetland development related to both natural hazards and values. A strong statement of public purpose establishes public intent and may be helpful in later court suits. The City Council of Boulder, Colorado, for example, has adopted a policy to "protect all wetlands in the Boulder Valley. This goal aims to ensure 'no net loss' of wetland acreage or function." No net loss goals also have been adopted by Thurston County, Washington, and West Eugene, Oregon.

Another example of a strong statement of public purpose is a Lexington, Massachusetts, ordinance, which provides:

Purpose of District. The purposes of the Wetland Protection District are to preserve and maintain the groundwater table; to protect the public health and safety by protecting persons and property against the hazards of flood water inundation; and to protect the community against the costs which may be incurred when unsuitable development occurs in swamps, marshes, along water courses or in areas subject to floods.

More detailed standards are included in an Orono, Minnesota, ordinance, which provides in part:

In addition to (other) general purposes, the specific intent of this ordinance is to:

(a) reduce danger to health by protecting surface and groundwater supplies from the impairment which results from incompatible land uses by providing safe and sanitary drainage.

(b) reduce the financial burdens imposed both on this community and on communities within the Minnehaha Creek Watershed District and the individuals therein by frequent floods and overflow of water on lands.

(c) Permit and encourage planned development land uses which will not impede the flow of flood water or cause danger to life or property.

(d) Permit and encourage land uses compatible with the preservation of the natural vegetation and marshes which are a principal factor in the maintenance of constant rates of water flow through the year and which sustain many species of wildlife and plant growth.

(e) Avoid fast runoff of surface waters from development areas to prevent pollutional materials such as animal feces, motor oils, paper, sand, salt and other debris, garbage, and foreign materials from being carried directly into the nearest natural stream, lake, or other public waters.

(f) Encourage a suitable system of ponding areas to permit the temporary withholding of rapid water runoff which presently contributes to downstream flooding and general water pollution giving preference to areas which contribute to groundwater infiltration and recharge, thereby reducing the need for public projects to contain, store, and control such runoff.

(g) Provide sufficient land areas to carry abnormal flows of storm water in periods of heavy precipitation, and to prevent needless expenditures of public funds for storm sewers and flood protection devices which proper planning could have avoided.

(h) Prevent the development of structures in areas unfit for human usage by reason of danger from flooding, unsanitary conditions, or other hazards.

(i) Prevent the placement of artificial obstructions which restrict the right of public passage and use of the bed, bank and water of any creeks, marshes, or watercourses within the Village.

Wetland definition criteria

Most local wetland ordinances include general written wetland definitions and rely on wetland maps to specifically delineate the wetlands that are subject to the ordinance. Wetland maps, discussed earlier, include air photos with wetland boundary delineations, soil maps, U.S. Geological Survey topographic maps, and special maps. Wetland maps and regulations often "overlay" and supplement other zoning and mapping efforts. For example, a Lincoln, Massachusetts, ordinance provides:

Overlay Districts. The C–Open Space Conservation District, the W–Wetlands and Watershed Protection District, the FP–Flood Plain District . . . are hereby established as overlay districts and shall be superimposed on other districts established by this Bylaw. Any land lying within such overlay districts shall also be subject to the development and use regulations for the applicable overlay district or districts and shall, in addition, conform to the additional requirements of the one or more overlay districts in which the land lies.

Where a state statute has defined wetland areas for regulatory purposes, local permits generally incorporate this definition. For example, a Glastonbury, Connecticut, ordinance incorporates a state wetland definition based upon soils:

"Wetlands" means land, including submerged land as defined in Section . . . which consists of any of the soil types designated as poorly drained, very poorly drained, alluvial, and flood plain by the National Cooperative Soils Survey, as may be amended from time to time by the Soil Conservation Service of the U.S. Department of Agriculture (USDA). Such areas may include filled, graded, or excavated sites or made land which possess a saturated, acrid soil moisture regime as defined by the USDA Cooperative Soil Survey.

A model shoreland zoning ordinance promulgated by the Wisconsin Department of Natural Resources and adopted by many counties for wetland areas suggests two alternative approaches for mapping wetland conservancy districts:

Destination. This district includes all shorelands designated as swamps or marshes on the United States Geological Survey Quadrangle map sheets which have been designated the Shoreland Zoning Map of _____ County, Wisconsin or on the detailed Insert Shoreland Zoning Maps.

In a Brockton, Massachusetts, ordinance, wetlands were separated into three subdistricts for regulatory purposes:

Scope

The Flood Plain, Watershed, and Wetlands Protection Zone overlies the basic zoning in an area and its provisions apply in addition to those of the basic zone, and of any other City regulations and ordinances, and any State laws.

The District is divided into three subdistricts reflecting the sensitivities and limitations of the wetlands involved. These are the: (1) Major Importance, (2) Moderate Importance and (3) Minor Importance subdistricts.

In Major Importance subdistricts the complete Flood Plain, Watershed, and Wetlands land use regulations and special permit procedures apply to all actions. In addition, all proposed actions must be submitted to the City Engineer and the Highway Division of the Department of Public Works for engineering plan review, and to the Conservation Commission as required under Chapter 131, Section 40 of the General Laws.

In Moderate Importance subdistricts, the complete land use regulations and special permit procedures apply to all actions in which combined building coverage and paving and filling of land exceeds five thousand square feet (5000 sq. ft.) or thirty-five percent (35%) of the site area. In addition, all actions must be submitted to the City Engineer and the Highway

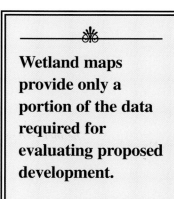

Wetland maps provide only a portion of the data required for evaluating proposed development.

Division of the Department of Public Works for engineering plan review, and to the Conservation Commission as required under Chapter 131, Section 40 of the General Laws.

In areas of Minor Importance, all actions must be submitted to the Conservation Commission as required by Chapter 131, Section 40 of the General Laws.

Interpretation of boundaries of zones

The Flood Plain, Watershed, and Wetland Protection Zone.

This zone (which is divided into three subdistricts) covers all property so identified on the map entitled "The city of Brockton, Massachusetts Zoning District Map." To simplify interpretation, small partially affected parcels have been included in their entirety.

Distinctions between areas of Major, Moderate, and Minor wetlands importance reflect their relative hydrological and ecological significance and the extent and duration of their high water tables.

Steps in local wetland regulation

1. Data gathering

Often the most expensive and time-consuming step in the adoption of legally sound and politically acceptable regulations. A variety of data may be needed to identify wetland boundaries.

All data need not be gathered at once. The ultimate data uses for regulation will determine the rationality of the regulation. Two approaches often are combined: 1) initial data gathering to identify wetland limits gathered in advance of adoption of regulations; and 2) case-by-case gathering of more specific data when building permit applications are submitted.

Zoning may require wetland maps. With subdivisions, mapping of wetland boundaries is desirable before adoption of regulations, but such boundaries may be determined on a case-by-case basis.

2. Planning

Planning can help ensure that wetland policies reflect not only environmental values but transportation, housing, and other needs. Planning usually is the responsibility of consultants or in-house land use planners acting under the direction of a local planning commission.

While zoning enabling acts often require adoption of a "comprehensive plan" before zoning maps are prepared, this has not been strictly enforced by the courts. With subdivisions, some enabling acts require adoption of a "master plan" before subdivision regulations are adopted, though often this is

not strictly enforced. Master plans showing proposed community public works are important if the subdivider is required to install sewer, water, roads, and drainage facilities consistent with overall community needs.

3. Drafting of regulation

Drafting often is the responsibility of a consultant, a resident land-use planner, or a member of the local conservation commission cooperating with the city attorney, planning commission, city council, or conservation commission.

For zoning, both a text and map generally are required. Subdivisions usually are drafted by the planning commission cooperating with the city or county officials.

4. Notice of public hearings

At least one hearing must be held before regulations are adopted. Often several hearings are held. Regulations and maps often are modified based upon the hearings.

For zoning, public hearings are required before regulations are adopted. A zoning map that determines where particular regulations will apply often is the most controversial subject at the hearing. For subdivisions, hearings are required before regulations are adopted.

5. Adoption of regulations

Adoption usually requires a majority of the local legislative body (city, county, town, village, borough council). Regulations must be published in the local newspaper. Regulations must be

available at a public place (such as a zoning office) for inspection by interested individuals.

For zoning, generally adoption is the responsibility of the local governing body. For subdivisions, generally adoption is the responsibility of the local municipal governing body or the planning commission.

6. Administration

Administration of ordinances requires engineering and biological expertise to ensure that proposed development meets ordinance standards. Widespread issuance of exceptions and variances undermines ordinance policies.

For zoning, building permits generally are issued by the zoning administration or the conservation commission. Enabling acts typically authorize the issuance of variances and special exceptions by the zoning board of appeals. For subdivisions, enabling acts typically designate planning commissions as "plat review" agencies. Preliminary and final plat procedures and specifications may be defined in some detail.

7. Enforcement

Ordinances establish fines and other penalties, including jail sentences, for violations. Courts enforce fines and wetland restoration requirements (in some instances) but rarely require jail sentences.

For both zoning and subdivisions, penalties vary.

The Major Importance subdistrict includes surface water bodies and their banks to the contour or distance noted below, areas subject to flooding, as described below, and areas where the water table is at or near the surface most of the year.

The Moderate Importance subdistrict includes areas with the water table at or near the surface seven months of the year.

The Minor Importance subdistrict includes areas where the water table is within 18 inches of the surface in winter and early spring.

Prohibited, permitted, and special permit uses

Local ordinances typically specify "prohibited," "permitted," and "special permit" uses. Some ordinances list the prohibited uses. For example, a Lexington, Massachusetts, ordinance mandates:

No landfill or dumping or excavation of any kind.

No drainage work other than by an authorized public agency.

No damming or relocation of any watercourse except as part of an overall drainage basin plan.

No building or structure.

No permanent storage of materials or equipment.

Sometimes qualifications are placed on the prohibited uses. For example, a Wayland, Massachusetts, zoning bylaw provides:

a) No building, wall, dam, or other structure shall be erected, constructed, altered, enlarged or otherwise created or moved for any living or other purpose, provided that noncommercial signs not exceeding four feet square in size, tents, fences, wildlife management shelters, foot paths, bicycle paths, horse paths, and foot bridges are permitted if:

(i) they are accessory to lawful primary uses in a single residence district and

(ii) they do not affect the natural flow pattern of any watercourse.

b) Dumping, filling, excavating or transferring of any material which will reduce the natural floodwater storage capacity or interfere with the natural flow patterns of any watercourse within the District are prohibited.

Most ordinances also contain a list of "permitted uses" (whereby no permit is required or one is issued automatically). This list is similar for most coastal and inland wetland protection ordinances. A list from Lincoln, Massachusetts, is typical:

Uses Permitted.

(a) conservation of water, plants, and wildlife;

(b) recreation, including nature study, boating, fishing and hunting where otherwise legally permitted;

(c) grazing and farming, including truck gardening and harvesting and storage of crops;

(d) forestry;

(e) boat houses, duck-walks, landings, and small structures for non-commercial recreational uses;

(f) dams and ponds consistent within the purposes of the C–Open Space Conservation District . . . .

Ordinances also establish a list of "special permit" uses which the ordinances neither prohibit nor permit outright. These uses must be evaluated on a case-by-case basis. Special permit uses (also termed special exceptions or conditional uses) generally are those that may or may not have serious wetland impact, depending upon circumstances. A board of adjustment, planning commission, conservation commission, or other local board is authorized to issue special permits. Usually ordinances establish standards and procedures for the evaluation of special permits. A Wayland, Massachusetts, zoning bylaw contains a typical list of special permit uses:

Upon the issuance of a special permit for an exception by the Board of Appeals, and subject to the conditions hereinafter specified and such other special conditions and safeguards as the Board of Appeals deems necessary to fulfill the purposes set forth in paragraph 1, the following uses, structures and actions, as permitted in single residence districts are permitted.

(1) Duck-walks and boat landings;

(2) Appropriate municipal use, such as waterworks pumping stations and parks;

(3) Temporary storage of materials or equipment;

(4) Dams, excavations, or grading, consistent with the purposes of this section to create ponds, pools, or other changes in watercourses, for swimming, fishing, or other recreational uses, agricultural uses, scenic features or drainage improvements;

(5) Driveways and roads;

(6) Any other filling, excavating, or transferring of any material, or erection, construction, alteration, enlargement, or removal or demolition of any structure, upon the condition that with respect to each such action and structure the Board of Appeals determines that granting a special permit therefore would not result in any substantial risk of pollution or contamination of any waterway or pond, substantial reduction of seasonal high water storage areas, substantial reduction of groundwater absorption areas, which serve the public water supply or other derogation from the intent and purpose of this Section X–C.

A Lexington, Massachusetts, ordinance illustrates general standards for such permits:

Special Permits for Uses in Harmony With General Purposes of the District. The Board of Appeals may issue a special permit for any use of land which would otherwise be permitted if such land were not, by operation of this section, in the Wetland Protection District if the Board finds (1) that such land within the District is . . . not subject to flooding or is not unsuitable because of drainage conditions for such use, and (2) that the use of such land for any such use will not interfere with the general purposes for which Wetland Protection Districts have been established, and (3) that such use will not be detrimental to the public health, safety, or welfare.

Ordinances usually do not establish detailed standards for special permits and instead apply general performance guidelines. However, some ordinances list factors to be considered by the regulatory board. An inland wetland protection regulation from Ledyard, Connecticut, directs the regulatory agency to consider the following factors in evaluating the importance of the wetland at the site of a proposed activity:

The existing or potential use of the area as a surface or groundwater supply.

The extent to which the area serves as a recharge area or purifier of surface or ground waters.

The function of the area as part of the natural drainage system for the watershed.

The extent to which the area serves as a natural wildlife feeding or breeding area.

The existence of rare or unusual concentrations of botanical species.

The existing and potential use of the area for recreation purposes.

The availability of other open space in the surrounding area.

The size of the wetland and its relationship to other wetlands or watercourses which may be affected by the proposed activity.

The importance of the area in preventing leaching or siltation or otherwise affecting water quality.

The regulation also directs the regulatory agency to consider the following environmental impacts of the proposed activity:

The ability of the regulated area to continue to absorb, store, or purify water or prevent flooding.

Increased erosion problems resulting from changes in grades, ground cover, or drainage features.

The extent of additional siltation or leaching and its effect on water quality and aquatic life.

The influence of toxic materials on water supplies, aquatic organisms, or wildlife.

Changes in the volume, velocity, temperature, or course of a waterway and their resulting effects on plant, animal, or aquatic life.

Some wetland ordinances establish minimum lot size requirements of one to 15 acres for structural uses. In other instances, zoning ordinances place restrictions upon the use of wetland areas to meet traditional lot area restrictions (such as 20,000 square feet in residential areas). This, in effect, requires

larger lot sizes in wetland areas. For example, a Brockton, Massachusetts, wetland overlay ordinance permitted a landowner to use wetland areas to meet *"up to 60 ft of the lot area requirements for uses allowed in the underlying zone. The actual development must be confined to the portion of the site (a minimum of 40 feet of the total required area) which is outside the Flood Plain, Watershed, and Wetlands Protection District."*

Often the applicant is required to submit detailed information to help the regulatory board apply special permit criteria. For example, a model local wetland protection ordinance promulgated by the State of New York provides:

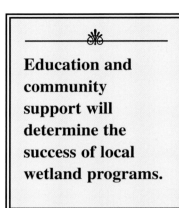

Education and community support will determine the success of local wetland programs.

An application for a permit shall be filed by the applicant on a form prescribed by the Agency. Such application shall set forth the purpose, character and extent of the proposed regulated activity. The application shall include a detailed description of the regulated activity, a map showing the area of freshwater wetland or adjacent area directly affected, with the location of the proposed regulated activity thereon, a deed or other legal description describing the subject property and such additional information as the Agency deems sufficient to enable it to make the findings and determinations required under this law.

The application shall be accompanied by a list of the names of the owners of record of lands adjacent to the freshwater wetland or adjacent area upon which the project is to be undertaken and the names of known claimants of water rights, of whom the applicant has notice, which related to any land within, or within one hundred feet of the boundary of, the property on which the proposed regulated activity will be located.

An application shall not be deemed to be completed or received until the Agency determines that all such information, including any additional information requested, has been supplied in a complete and satisfactory form.

Generally the regulatory agency is authorized to attach conditions to permits to minimize development impact such as restrictions on the amount and location of fill.

Some ordinances authorize the regulatory agency to require a permit processing fee and to require a performance bond from an applicant to ensure that conditions are carried out. For example, an Easton, Connecticut, ordinance provides:

Upon approval of the application and prior to issuance of a permit, the applicant may, at the discretion of the Agency, be required to file a bond with such surety in such amount and in a form approved by the Board of Selectmen.

The bond and surety shall be conditioned on compliance with all provisions of these regulations and the terms, conditions and limitations established in the permit.

The Agency may require the applicant to certify that it has public liability insurance against liability which might result from the proposed operation or use of the wetlands or watercourses covering any and all damage which might occur within two (2) years of completion of such operations, in an amount to be determined by the Agency commensurate with the regulated activity.

Penalties

Most ordinances provide a combination of fines and possible jail sentences for violation of ordinance provisions. Many require that the affected wetland area be restored. A statute from Connecticut provides:

Any person who commits, takes part in, or assists in any violation of any provision of sections . . ., including regulations adopted by the commissioner and ordinances and regulations promulgated by municipalities or districts pursuant to the grant of authority herein contained, shall be assessed a civil penalty of not more than one thousand dollars for each offense. Each violation of said sections shall be a separate and distinct offense, and in the case of a continuing violation, each day's continuance thereof shall be deemed to be a separate and distinct offense. The Superior Court, in any action brought by the commissioner, municipality, district or any person, shall have jurisdiction to restrain a continuing violation of said sections, to issue orders directing that the violation be corrected or removed and to assess civil penalties pursuant to this section. All costs, fees and expenses in connection with such action shall be assessed as damages against the violator together with reasonable attorney's fees which may be allowed, all of which shall be awarded to the commissioner, municipality, district or person which brought such action. The moneys collected pursuant to this section shall be used by the commissioner of environmental protection, to restore the affected wetlands or watercourse to their condition prior to the violation, wherever possible.

Endnotes

Association of State Wetland Managers, *Wetlands and Watershed Management: A Guidebook for Local Governments* (1997).

D. Burke, *Protecting Non-tidal Wetlands* (American Planning Association, 1989).

C. Thurow, W. Toner, and D. Erley, *Performance Controls for Sensitive Lands* (American Society of Planning Officials, 1975).

S. Crane, J. Goldman-Carter, H. Sherk, and M. Senatore, *Wetlands Conservation: Tools for State and Local Action* (World Wildlife Fund, 1995).

1890s: San Francisco Bay

The Fish Patrol

Author of The Call of the Wild *and* The Sea Wolf, *Jack London (1876–1916) packed his tales full of suspense that often had resulted from his real-life adventures. It was an anything-but-quiet childhood on the San Francisco Bay that provided fodder for many of London's tales. In his youth, London's family settled on the Oakland water-front, and he spent his hours sailing a skiff through the Bay. By the age of 16, London had travailed with an opium-smuggling yacht, robbed oyster beds, and generally drank a lot before becoming — briefly — a member of the fish patrol. As London recounted in* Tales of the Fish Patrol:

"San Francisco Bay is so large that often its storms are more disastrous to ocean-going craft than is the ocean itself in its violent moments. The waters of the bay contain all manner of fish, wherefore its surface is ploughed by the keels of all manner of fishing boats manned by all manner of fishermen. To protect the fish from this motley float-ing population many wise laws have been passed, and there is a fish patrol to see that these laws are enforced. Exciting times are the lot of the fish patrol: in its history more than one dead patrolman has marked defeat, and more often dead fishermen across their illegal nets have marked success."

— from Tales of the Fish Patrol
by Jack London and other sources

More on Nonregulatory Approaches

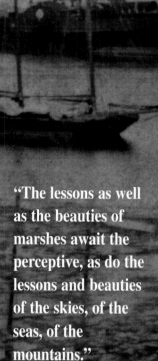

Chapter 11 expands on a variety of nonregulatory approaches that can be applied on the local level to protect and restore wetlands. Use the chapter to choose the wetland protection techniques that will protect the functions and values and lessen the hazards discussed in Chapter 1, implement watershed planning, as suggested in Chapter 4, and follow the standards set forth in Chapter 6.

Regulations have been the backbone of wetland protection programs and, therefore have been discussed extensively in this book. They also have an important role in guiding future private and public activities. However, as we have mentioned, regulations are subject to political, legal, and administrative drawbacks. Landowners will not comply with regulations if they are not aware of them and what they require. Local zoning controls generally exempt a broad range of activities and do not apply to agricultural, governmental, or existing uses that damage wetland areas. Because of their negative approach to land uses (landowners are told what they cannot do but not what they should do), regulations alone cannot restore wetlands and repair lost damage. Regulations cannot, by themselves, achieve public access to private wetland areas for birdwatching, hunting, and nature study. Further, since regulations can be altered at the whim of the local legislative body, they may offer only temporary protection and lull conservationists into a false sense of security. Finally, regulations raise "property rights" and "takings" issues with landowners.

Nonregulatory techniques have limitations as well, such as the high cost of acquisition. However, they are critically needed to supplement regulations and, in some contexts, to achieve wetland protection and restoration without regulation at all. Acquisition of fee and easement interests in property on a voluntary basis can address landowners' "takings" complaints while providing permanent wetland protection and active public use for nature watching or other uses. Public education can reduce landowner complaints and encourage voluntary stewardship. Real estate tax incentives also can reduce the economic burdens of regulations and can encourage private stewardship in the absence of regulation. Wetland restoration can address past mistakes. Finally, creation of wetland interpretation sites provides public education and recreational opportunities.

Chapter 11 discusses these five nonregulatory wetland protection techniques: public education, acquisition, real estate tax incentives, wetland restoration, and creation of wetland interpretation sites. These techniques can be used independently, in combination with each other, or in combination with regulatory programs.

Public education

Landowners, developers, public works planners, and other land and water use decision makers comply with policies and regulations to protect and restore wetlands only if they: (1) are aware of the regulations and policies and understand them; (2) know what wetlands are and their boundaries; and (3) have "how to" information available to them on compliance with restoration policies and guidelines. They also must be motivated to protect and restore wetlands.

Unfortunately, federal, state, and local wetland regulatory efforts rarely have been accompanied with parallel educational efforts. Landowners may know that the wetlands on their lands are subject to regulations, but they lack specific information with regard to wetland boundaries, exempted and regulated activities, and management and restoration techniques.

"The lessons as well as the beauties of marshes await the perceptive, as do the lessons and beauties of the skies, of the seas, of the mountains."

— Paul Errington,
Of Men and Marshes (1957)

Tips for providing wetland education

❋ Understand wetlands yourself. Without personal knowledge, you will not be a good teacher.

❋ Understand your audiences and address the subject from their perspectives.

❋ Do not lose your audience by being too technical; on the other hand, do not underestimate your audience. Often people understand a lot more than you think.

❋ Talk to your audience. Do not lecture them.

❋ Get your audience into the field. There is no substitute for real places and real issues.

❋ Be specific. Provide "how to" information.

❋ Utilize available educational materials such as videos, guidebooks, books, and pamphlets. There is a lot out there to use.

A variety of approaches can be undertaken by citizens, land trusts, and local governments to help meet these educational needs:

• *Talk with your neighbors.* Because people learn best from friends and trusted acquaintances, the best way to educate fellow citizens is simply to talk with them. For example, a group of interested and informed citizens in Lincoln, Massachusetts, visited all of the wetland landowners in putting together a wetland plan and strategy for that town.

• *Set an example.* You can set examples for others in a community by undertaking wetland restoration projects, creating wetland trails, enhancing wetlands with duck nesting boxes, and undertaking other protection measures.

• *Distribute booklets, videos, and pamphlets.* In the last decade, many educational materials have been developed by nonprofit organizations, federal and state agencies, and local governments that explain why wetlands should be protected or restored and how. (See Appendix E for examples.)

• *Disseminate wetland maps.* Wetland maps such as National Wetland Inventory maps can help the public become aware of wetland resources and help identify wetland boundaries. The maps must be readily available, such as in local zoning offices. Local distribution of wetland regulatory maps is particularly important where local governments wish to help implement the federal Section 404 program. The Section 404 program has not mapped wetlands; the distribution of local, state, or federal wetland maps to landowners can reduce landowner uncertainties and establish presumptions that areas may be regulatory wetlands, even if the maps do not coincide perfectly with Section 404 boundaries.

• *Conduct educational workshops.* Many local governments, such as West Eugene, Oregon, and Madison, Wisconsin, have conducted educational workshops for the public and public

officials concerning wetland functions and values, wetland maps, restoration, and the specifics of various planning and regulatory programs.

• *Create wetland interpretive trails, boardwalks, and centers.* The creation of wetland interpretive sites is one of the best ways for educating the public and local legislators. Examples include the Hackensack Meadowlands Development Commission in New Jersey and Huntley Meadows in Alexandria, Virginia. See the discussion on Interpretation, below.

• *Conduct wetland and river festivals, art fairs, and celebrations.* Everyone loves a party! Many communities, such as Boulder, Colorado, now celebrate their riverfronts with a festival. A huge waterfowl festival, including a wildlife art fair, is held on the eastern shore of Maryland, and a festival is held by the Wetland Conservancy in New Jersey each year.

• *Work with teachers and children.* Many land trusts and local governments work with elementary, high school, and college teachers to provide wetland educational programs for children. Numerous wetland teaching guidebooks, videos, and other educational materials are available from the U.S. Fish and Wildlife Service, organizations such as Environmental Concern, and universities, such as the University of Montana. (See Appendix E.)

Coordinating tax and special assessment policies with protection and restoration

A second technique for relieving regulatory burdens and providing landowners with incentives for protection and restoration of wetlands is coordination of real estate tax and special assessment policies with wetland protection policies and regulations. Landowners often complain (and with considerable cause) when their wetlands are tightly regulated but taxed as if fully developable, or if the wetlands are charged special assessments for sewer, water, flood control, or other purposes as if the lands were developable. Reductions in real estate tax rates and special assessments can encourage private protection and restoration of wetlands, even where regulations have not been adopted.

Local tax assessors generally value land for its "highest and best use" (see the box on page 121), and development potential is reflected in that assessment where development is possible. However, the combination of wetland regulations at multi-levels of government (federal, state, regional, and local) and other regulations such as floodway restrictions and buffer setbacks effectively preclude development of wetlands in many instances. Real estate tax assessments should reflect these restrictions if they are correctly carried out. The issue becomes even more clear-cut where a landowner has executed a deed restriction or granted an easement, precluding any future development. At least 45 states now specifically allow certain properties in real estate tax abatement programs.

It also makes sense to reduce sewer, water, flood control, and other existing assessments for property that will not be developed in the future. Future assessments can be reduced when community public works and public facilities planning are

Taxes and wetlands

Tax codes and ordinances can provide many incentives for wetland protection — and can also encourage wetland destruction, depending on whether available conservation provisions in them are used and used wisely. Four types of federal, state, and local taxes that affect the use of wetlands are presented here: real property, estate, gift, and income taxes. (Tax laws are complicated and have different impacts on individuals; a tax expert or lawyer should be consulted by anyone contemplating use of various tax provisions.)

Real property taxes

Real property taxes, the largest source of revenue for local governments, are based on the values of lands and structures as determined by local assessors in accordance with state-established guidelines. Some states tax the full-market value of the land. Land value usually includes potential development value, a factor that encourages the development of wetlands.

Preferential real estate tax assessment policies are available in many states for conservation lands. Several states provide for preferential assessment of wetlands through wetland regulations and other environmental statutes. Others have special real estate tax incentive laws and regulatory statutes with tax incentive provisions.

Statutes that afford preferential tax treatment are premised on the theory that there are individuals who may want to preserve their land in an undisturbed state but who are forced, through rising property taxes (caused by development pressures and the need for more services), to sell their land for development. Three approaches are applied in state differential tax assessment programs. The first is pure preferential assessment, whereby taxes are assessed based on how the land is used (open space or recreational use, for example), rather than its market or development value. With the second approach, a deferred taxation system, land is taxed at its use value, but owners of eligible land who convert their land to noneligible uses must pay some or all of the taxes that would have accrued (absent the tax abatement) during the years of preferential assessment. The third system is like the second, with the additional requirement that qualifying owners sign contracts restricting development for a term of years.

The key to wetland protection through preferential assessment is providing landowner incentives for maintaining lands in an undeveloped state while, at the same time, preventing the abuse of the preferential treatment as a privilege. Otherwise, landowners avail themselves of reduced taxes until development pressures and market values increase sufficiently to warrant subdivision. For this reason, deferred taxation and particularly restrictive agreement approaches are desirable.

Despite their advantages, deferred taxation and restrictive agreements often are insufficient in themselves to prevent conversion of agricultural and open space lands in urbanizing areas. In addition, landowners often are unwilling to agree to permanent restrictions in areas of intense development, because they do not want to forego future profit options. Consequently, experts advocate that use value assessment schemes supplement, but not replace, regulatory programs to protect open spaces and ecologically critical areas. One study contends that preferential assessment will be beneficial primarily in semi-rural areas where it can help "buy time" before the adoption of regulatory programs.

Income taxes

Income tax advantages are available to those who donate full title of wetlands or conservation restrictions and easements to governmental bodies, publicly supported charities, or private charitable foundations. Upon making such donations (which are widely sought by private organizations), landowners may take charitable deductions for the value of the gift from their federal income tax and, in many states, from their state income taxes. Where land or an interest in land has appreciated greatly in value since the original acquisition, the tax savings may be substantial.

Section 170(b) of the Internal Revenue Code allows landowners to deduct the fair market value of long-term capital gain on property donated to a government or qualifying charitable organization, provided that the total amount of the contribution does not exceed 30 percent of the landowner's gross income in the year of the donation. If the amount exceeds 30 percent of the taxpayer's adjusted gross income, he or she can carry over the excess during five succeeding tax years. Or a taxpayer can deduct the gift up to 50 percent of adjusted gross income if he or she reduces the value of the gift to its cost or basis. Gifts of ordinary income property are deductible in an amount equal to the cost or basis of the property.

There are some restrictions on the use of the charitable deduction for gifts of partial interests in property, and the deduction is limited to those donations that are "exclusively for conservation purposes" and granted in perpetuity, pursuant to the rules established under Section 170(h) of the Code.

Tax savings also are available when appreciated property is sold at less than fair market value to a charitable organization as a "bargain sale" under Section 1011(b) of the Code. This provision allows the difference between the fair market value and the selling price to be used as a charitable contribution to improve the net financial return to the landowner.

Estate taxes

Upon an individual's death, estate taxes become payable to the federal government. These are calculated on a progressive scale in direct proportion to the value of assets in the decedent's estate. The greater the value of the estate, the higher the taxes. At the state level, inheritance taxes are levied on the transfer of property from one generation to another.

Estate taxes have a particularly harsh impact when the decedent's estate is composed largely of land. Unless cash can be obtained from other assets, the property may have to be sold to pay estate taxes. Thus, wetlands and open spaces that the decedent and his or her heirs had hoped to protect may become the victims of development.

There are several ways to reduce estate taxes while simultaneously protecting wetland areas. Section 2055(a) of the Internal Revenue Code permits deduction from the gross estate of the value of all bequests of property to qualified charitable organizations or government bodies. The effect of this provision is that the value of the donated land or interest will be excluded from the value of the assets of the estate, thereby enabling the estate to enjoy a reduction in estate tax liability.

Gift taxes

Gift taxes resemble estate taxes in that they are progressive and are imposed upon the transfer of an interest in property. Unlike estate taxes, however, gift taxes are imposed during the life of the donor, not at his or her death. For a number of years, the Internal Revenue Code has provided that gifts (that qualify for charitable contribution treatment under Section 170) to governmental units and to qualifying charitable organizations are not subject to lifetime gift taxes.

consistent with wetland protection and restoration goals, such as the avoidance of public works projects for wetland areas.

Acquisition of wetlands

Land acquisition of a fee or lesser interest in a private property is a third major approach to relieve regulatory burdens and achieve a variety of wetland protection and restoration objectives that cannot be accomplished through regulations alone, such as public access to land. Land acquisition, including conservation easements, can be accomplished through the variety of techniques discussed in Chapter 4, including donation as gifts or devises in wills, conditioning subdivision approval upon donation for open space purposes, "bargain sales" with landowners, and outright purchase. Often local land acquisition is best a cooperative effort between a governmental unit and a local land trust or environmental organization.

A variety of questions arise when you consider acquiring wetlands: (1) Is acquisition needed for a particular type of wetland, or will regulation combined with landowner education, tax incentives, and other techniques suffice? (2) Which wetlands should be acquired? and (3) How can acquisition funds be obtained?

Virginia Michels Dent and Aurora Gareiss, Queens, New York:

Education crucial for Queens wetlands

Often stacks of papers submitted, speeches made, and phone calls placed are needed to protect wetlands, as Virginia Michels Dent and Aurora Gareiss will tell you. Dent and Gareiss have done all three to educate their neighbors about the need to protect the expansive salt marsh and freshwater wetland complexes surrounding Littleneck Bay in Queens, New York City.

The women's fight started back in 1971–72, when the nearby village of Great Neck Estates decided to fill in marshland for a golf course and parking lot. Dent and Gareiss launched a campaign to convince the village residents that they had a valuable resource that should be preserved. Gareiss purchased multiple copies of an *Audubon* magazine on the birdlife in wetlands and distributed them to the landowners who lived closest to the marsh. Both women helped organized a day to "walk the marsh," which received a lot of publicity when the mayor of New York City attended. (Reaching politicians is key, Dent says.) As a result of these actions and others, the people of Great Neck Estates later voted against the development and then bought out some of the private property owners, acquiring the first of many parcels of what today is called the Udalls Cove Park Preserve.

Is acquisition needed?

Acquisition of a fee interest and securing an easement interest both have important advantages. Acquiring a fee interest ensures public access and 100 percent public control over land. Depending on its terms, an easement may also permit public access. Because voluntary acquisition of either full or partial interests avoids the "takings" issue, acquisition often is a politically attractive alternative to regulation for landowners and local governments. Under certain circumstances, acquisition may ensure permanent protection of the wetland, whereas regulations are much more susceptible to changing political climates.

Despite advantages, outright public purchase of wetlands can be expensive, especially for coastal wetlands. Inland wetlands usually are less costly, except in urban areas. Public purchase of a fee interest removes the land from the tax roles (however, an agency or nonprofit organization may continue to pay the taxes in order to dampen criticism of acquisition efforts). Acquisition can be time-consuming and politically unpopular, especially if done by condemnation. Even if the acquisition is by gift, the community often must provide management and protection for the wetlands. Moreover, full control does not always guarantee absolute protection. If, for example, only a portion of a wetland is purchased, development on the remainder may destroy the ecological balance in the "protected" area.

To maximize the benefits of acquisition and minimize limitations, local governments generally avoid condemnation and undertake acquisition only on a willing seller basis. Often acquisition is carried out in cooperation with a local land trust or environmental organization, which negotiates with landowners and assumes long-term responsibility for management of the wetlands. Acquisition by donation, devise, and bargain sales are common to reduce costs.

Which wetlands should be acquired?

Wetland acquisition programs often are focused upon "priority wetlands" such as: (1) wetlands with unique natural functions and values or special hazards; (2) wetlands where all private actions must be prohibited because of the unique features of the land, such as habitat for rare and endangered species; (3) wetlands that are subject to severe development threats; (4) wetlands needed for active public use (such as birdwatching, recreation, or scientific study); and (5) wetlands with particularly strong restoration potential.

Despite these priorities, communities often acquire wetlands based more upon the willingness of landowners to donate or sell them than on rigorous acquisition criteria. Here the preferences of the donor, not the community, prevail.

Many communities and land trusts have elected to acquire only a partial interest in lands rather than full fee. Such landowners often wish to retain some ownership and use of wetlands. Acquisition of easements or development rights offers many of the protective advantages of acquiring the full title but does not provide public access. Moreover, because the original owner retains title to the property, local governments can continue to collect some property taxes (although the assessment must

Local opportunities for wetland restoration and creation

✽ **Restoration or creation carried out by private landowners and developers pursuant to federal, state, and local regulations to compensate for damage or loss.** These are the most common restoration projects, but they often partially fail to meet project objectives.

✽ **Restoration, enhancement, or creation of wetlands on public lands to compensate for public wetland impacts of roads, bridges, dikes, and dams, including forestry lands, margins of water supply reservoirs, stormwater management ponds, and margins of lakes and rivers.** Public projects are increasingly common to compensate for adverse public impacts on wetlands. These projects are designed to enhance fish and wildlife, or to protect and enhance water quality.

✽ **Bioengineering and wetland restoration for stream banks to control erosion and reduce flood losses.** Bioengineering projects also are increasingly common and may be carried out as part of erosion control, pollution control, stream restoration, floodplain management, fisheries enhancement, or stormwater management efforts.

✽ **Restoration of gravel pits and mined lands by landowners, governmental units.** Federal, state, and local mining regulations generally require "reclamation" of mined sites. Creation of wetlands often is possible at modest costs.

✽ **Restoration and enhancement as part of public park, recreation, and wildlife projects.** Public wildlife management and recreation agencies increasingly are carrying out wetland restoration and enhancement projects to enhance wildlife and fisheries, enhance recreation opportunities, and provide outdoor education.

✽ **Restoration projects in conjunction with construction of roads, sewers, water supply systems, and other public works.** Often major wetland restoration (and sometimes creation opportunities arise when public works projects are undertaken. Such projects may be initiated independent of adverse public works impacts on wetlands (see above).

✽ **Restoration in conjunction with post-flood disaster recovery.** Many wetland restoration projects have been carried out along the Mississippi and Missouri rivers as part of post-flood response following the Great Flood of 1993.

✽ **Private landowner, land trust, and environmental organization voluntary restoration projects.** Thousands of private projects are being carried out to protect endangered species or unique ecosystems (heritage programs), protect or enhance water quality, enhance wildlife or fisheries, or achieve other objectives.

✽ **Private and public "mitigation banks" and cooperative ventures.** Many states and some local governments are experimenting with the use of mitigation banks and cooperative ventures to provide "credits" for damage to wetlands by public and private activities.

be reduced to reflect the decreased value of the land resulting from the sale of development rights). Federal and state tax incentives also are available to individuals who donate less than total interest in their property to the government or private conservation organizations.

What sources of funds are available?

As noted above, most local wetland acquisition is through donation, devise, or bargain sale, although outright purchase of fee or easement interests does take place. Funds for wetland acquisition may come from several sources. Private sources include donated funds from individuals or corporations. General revenues from property taxes or revenues generated by specially enacted sales taxes also have been used.

Matching federal grants for state and local wetland acquisition often are the most important source of funds. Although money allocated to states and communities by the Land and Water Conservation Fund for acquisition of open space lands is not directly earmarked for wetlands acquisition, wetlands may be included in the land actually purchased. The Natural Resources Conservation Service provides funds directly to landowners pursuant to the Wetlands Reserve Program. The U.S. Fish and Wildlife Service provides grants under the Pittman-Robertson Act for state acquisition of wildlife areas, and the Coastal Zone Management Act also funds acquisition of estuarine sanctuaries. (See Chapter 8 for information on a variety of these programs.)

Steps in acquiring wetlands

The methods and types of wetland acquisition vary. Formal purchase by a local government must be consistent with statutory procedures for purchase of land, and these may be quite specific and cumbersome. Fewer procedures are provided for acquisition through donation or negotiated fee. A local land trust is free to follow any procedures it wishes (and these often are fairly informal).

There are several steps that local governments, land trusts, and environmental organizations undertake in formal land acquisition, although these are not rigorously followed:

1. Mapping and evaluation of wetlands. Conceptually, the first step in acquisition of wetlands is to identify the wetlands in a community or region and determine their relative priority for acquisition in terms of goals such as biodiversity, rare and endangered species, birdwatching, recreation, education, waterfowl production, and flood storage. If undertaken, an inventory should not only indicate the relative importance of the wetlands, but also the degree to which the threat of development exists.

2. Identifying wetlands-related legislation. Along with the inventory, the agency interested in acquisition should identify all legislation and implementing regulations that affect the use of wetlands, including regulatory statutes. Statutes, regulations, and land ownership information can be checked against the inventoried wetlands to determine which wetlands are already protected by public purchase, easement, or deed restriction; which wetlands may be at least partially protected by regulation; and which are unprotected and possible priorities for acquisition.

Ensuring success in wetland restoration and creation

❋ **Consider restoration versus creation.** In general, wetland restoration projects have been much more successful than creation because it is much easier to restore preexisting wetland hydrology and soils than to start from scratch.

❋ **Understand the hydrologic and sediment regimes.** An understanding of hydrologic and sediment regimes has been critical to successful restoration or creation. Restoration projects do not succeed if there is inadequate water supply, too much sediment, and too much high velocity water.

❋ **Provide design expertise consistent with wetland type.** It has been much easier to restore certain types of wetlands than others, depending, in large measure, on how easily hydrology can be assessed and restored or created. In general, it is easiest to restore or create estuarine wetlands. Coastal wetlands rank second. Groundwater-controlled shrub and forested wetlands are most difficult.

❋ **Increase size.** In general, larger wetland restoration projects have been more successful than small.

❋ **Find nearby reference wetlands.** The availability of nearby "reference wetlands" has been helpful to guide restoration or creation efforts. Nearby wetlands may also provide seed stocks for wetland plants.

❋ **Find a project sponsor with a long-term interest in maintaining the wetland.** In general, wetland restoration, enhancement, and creation projects undertaken by government natural resources or wildlife agencies, or by land trusts or conservation groups are more successful than those undertaken by private landowners seeking regulatory permits, due to the higher level of commitment to project success.

❋ **Use multidisciplinary expertise in design and construction.** As one would expect, more expertly designed projects have a higher success rate. Construction practices also are critical since a matter of inches in grading may make the difference between project success and failure.

❋ **Design to anticipate hydrology and extreme events.** Project designs need to anticipate extreme events, such as high velocity water, which can otherwise destroy a wetland. They also need to anticipate changes in watershed hydrology due to urbanization or other factors. A wetland will not be a wetland if it is too dry or too wet.

❋ **Maintain buffers.** Buffers can protect projects from pollution and provide an ecotone (or boundary between adjacent ecosystem types) for many wetland species.

❋ **Mid-course correction capability.** Projects are most successful where monitoring occurs and there is the ability to change water levels or carry out corrected measures if original design was inadequate or conditions change.

❋ **Long-term management.** Projects are most successful where long-term management is provided for restored or created wetlands, such as control of exotics, fire management (controlled burns), periodic deepening of areas, and construction of duck boxes.

3. Establishing priorities. Because of economic constraints, local governments should first acquire lands that are both subject to special values (for example, if they harbor endangered species) and are threatened by development. The timing and criteria for acquisition will depend on the amount of money available.

4. Preliminary negotiations and approvals. After specific wetlands have been selected, the agency or land trust contemplating acquisition often begins discussion with landowners, the local legislative body, and private organizations that may assist in the acquisition effort; and federal and state agencies that may help fund such acquisition. Priorities often are modified in this negotiation process as landowner interests are determined.

5. Appraising the land. Land appraisal is the next step for formal local government purchases. If localities rely on federal funding, they must comply with the requirements of the Uniform Relocation Assistance and Real Property Acquisition Policies Program. This law requires that real property must be appraised before the initiation of negotiation and that the owner or his or her representative must be given an opportunity to accompany the appraiser during inspection of the property. The owner may not be offered less than the value set by the appraiser. Several factors influence the appraised value of the land. The soil structure, the productivity of the land, the amount of water on the land, the potential for development, and the value of similar land in the neighborhood all are considered.

6. Preparation of impact statements. In states with environmental impact requirements for land acquisition and where federal funds are used, a determination must be made on whether an environmental impact statement is required. This is rare, but if one is necessary, it must be prepared before the acquisition occurs.

7. Final negotiations with the landowner. If all has gone smoothly up to this point, the agency then can begin final negotiations with the landowner with regard to terms, the content of easements (if easements are to be used), and other specifics.

8. Closing. Assuming that an agreement for purchase of the land, an easement, or another type of restriction is reached, the following general steps may be followed. These usually require legal assistance.

• All terms and conditions of the sales contract must be developed and fulfilled.

• The deed must be drawn and executed.

• The mortgage deed and note, if any, must be drawn and executed.

• Any exceptions listed on the title policy must meet with the approval of the acquiring agency.

• The survey must be certified, and the description in the deed must conform with the survey.

• Real property taxes must be prorated to the date of closing.

Wetland restoration, enhancement, and creation

A fourth important nonregulatory technique is the restoration, enhancement, or creation of wetland areas. A wide variety of opportunities exist for citizens, land trusts, and local governments to restore and create wetlands in order to remedy past problems. The table on page 123 outlines some of the principal opportunities.

Tens of thousands of wetland restoration and creation projects have been carried out over the last three decades by agencies at federal, state, and local levels and by the private sector. These projects range in size from a 60,000-acre wetland restoration now underway for an area north of the Everglades, to private projects of a few tenths of an acre on an urban residential lot by a birding enthusiast. Restoration and creation projects involve almost all types of wetlands, although restoration and creation are more difficult for some than for others. Costs vary from a few hundreds of dollars an acre for restoration of partially drained agricultural land by blocking a drainage ditch or crushing drainage tiles, to hundreds of thousands of dollars an acre in an urban wetland for detailed hydrologic studies, fill removal, and replanting of wetland vegetation. Wetland restoration, enhancement, and creation projects have had a mixed record of success, depending on a number of factors.

Wetland restoration, enhancement, and creation projects are of three principal types:

• *Federal, state, and local government restoration projects on public lands.* Many restoration projects have been conducted on Fish and Wildlife Service Refuge lands, such as Horicon Marsh in Wisconsin. These wetlands often have water control structures and are actively managed for specific waterfowl and other wildlife objectives. These projects have been quite successful in achieving project goals because of expertise in design, their large size, a long-term commitment to maintenance and protection, and a long-term capability to manipulate water levels.

• *Voluntary landowner and land trust restoration projects.* Many projects have been undertaken on private lands, often financed in whole or in part through Partners for Wildlife, the Wetlands Reserve Program, and other programs. Overall, these projects also have been successful, particularly where restoration rather than creation is used. Landowner commitment to design and implementation, and long-term maintenance and protection of the projects have been key elements in success.

• *Private and public landowner "compensatory mitigation" projects.* These have been conducted in response to the federal Section 404 program, state wetland regulation, local wetland regulation, or other regulations that require restoration and creation as a condition to the granting of permits. Compensatory mitigation projects have been much less successful in achieving vegetative cover and fish and wildlife objectives. Some are never constructed or are incorrectly constructed. Many are very small, have not been expertly designed, do not include protective buffers, and are not actively managed over time. Water pollution and sedimentation are severe problems. Getting the hydrology "right" is particularly problematic in urban contexts where runoff and hydrology are changing quickly. Wetlands may end up as lakes (too wet) or as uplands (too dry).

Suggestions for reducing costs of interpretive sites

❋ Develop interpretive facilities on sites already in public or private nonprofit ownership.

❋ Use volunteers for most aspects of planning, construction, and operation. Professionals may be hired on a limited basis as supervisors.

❋ Design and locate trails, boardwalks, signs, and interpretive centers so that they are as low-maintenance and as vandalism-resistant as possible.

❋ Design boardwalks, viewing platforms, and towers with an adequate margin of structural safety but do not overdesign (a common practice that can add greatly to the cost).

❋ Design and locate trails, boardwalks, signs, and interpretive centers with consideration of flooding and fluctuations in water levels (the most common source of damage other than vandalism).

❋ Use simple, inexpensive signs (made of wood or metal) and place them out of reach, wherever possible, to reduce vandalism.

❋ Use inexpensive wood chip-covered trails where the trails are not too steep or subject to frequent flooding.

❋ Design trail maps and interpretive information so that they can be easily recycled.

This does not mean that private compensatory mitigation projects fail in all respects. Many of these projects at least partially restore flood storage and conveyance, erosion control, pollution control, and some habitat values. But low success rates for compensatory mitigation projects have produced increased interest in concepts such as mitigation banking, where larger off-site wetland areas are used to mitigate for habitat losses from a number of independent wetland development conversions.

There is great potential for a variety of creative restoration schemes between individual private landowners or groups of landowners, environmental organizations, and government agencies. The Grand Kankakee Marsh Restoration Project is an example. At the turn of the century, the Grand Marsh of the Kankakee River was an ecologically complex and biologically rich wetland of between 400,000 and one million acres (depending on water levels) in northern Indiana. In the years following, the marsh was drained, and channels and ditches were dug in the wetlands for agriculture and development. In 1993, a diverse group from governmental agencies and the private sector came together to form the project, which has a goal of restoring 26,500 acres of wetland and associated uplands in the next decade. Among the partners in the project are the North America Wetlands Conservation Council (coordinated by the U.S. Fish and Wildlife Service), which has funded a large portion of the restoration work through the North American Wetlands Conservation Act; the primary power utility serving northern Indiana, which donated 840 acres to the project; and local realtors and other businessmen and women who are able to use their long-standing contacts to generate support for the project.

Several other lessons about wetland restoration, enhancement, and creation have been learned over the past decade, including:

• Restoration of an area that once was a wetland is almost always simpler, less costly, and often more successful than creation of a new wetland area. In general, wetland creation should be avoided because it is difficult to simulate natural water levels.

• Both short-term and long-term hydrology are the key to successful restoration, creation, and enhancement. Average water depths and seasonal and long-term fluctuations are critical components.

• Protection of wetland water quality, including sediment control, is an important consideration, particularly in urban areas.

• Creation of saltwater and freshwater marshes is easier than creation of shrub and forested wetlands, because saltwater and freshwater marshes have wider hydrologic tolerances.

• To the extent possible, a wetland system should be designed to be self-sustaining. However, water control structures may be needed, particularly where natural hydrologic regimes have been substantially modified.

• Replanting of a restored area often is unnecessary, particularly where existing soil is intact. However, replanting may be needed in high-velocity areas or where it is desirable to give vegetation a competitive edge.

• All wetland restoration, creation, and enhancement projects must, to some extent, be viewed as an experiment. The capability to make mid-course corrections and long-term management are needed.

Creation of wetland interpretive sites

Creation of local wetland interpretive sites is a fifth nonregulatory wetland protection and restoration approach with large educational and other benefits. Wetland interpretation sites involving — at a minimum — a trail, interpretative markers, and a brochure can serve a broad range of educational, research, and tourism functions. (Many sites also involve boardwalks, observation towers, and interpretive centers as well.) Interpretation sites can be used to explain wetland functions and values and management needs to legislators and the public. They can provide outdoor recreational opportunities for birdwatchers, hikers, photo enthusiasts, and eco-tourists. They can be used to demonstrate protection and restoration measures, and they can help educate students and serve as research sites for universities.

Creating a wetland interpretation site involves a combination of acquisition, public education, and wetland management. Steps include:

Techniques for limiting impacts of visitors upon wetlands and conflicts between visitors

1. Limit types of uses. Typically all types of motorized vehicles, including outboard motors, motorbikes, and all-terrain vehicles are prohibited at wetland interpretive sites.

2. Limit seasons, months, or hours of use. The hours in which users may gain access to the interpretive site are limited at some sites. Special restrictions on use also may be imposed during nesting seasons.

3. Limit intensity of uses. Intensity of use is indirectly limited at many sites by controlling parking, limiting the size of the parking lots, and, in some instances, limiting the number of visitors permitted at a site through individual use permits.

4. Control location of uses to avoid sensitive areas through careful siting of roads, trails, boardwalks, towers, signs, septic tanks, and parking lots.

5. Establish conditions of use. A wide variety of conditions are imposed upon uses at many sites. Visitors may be instructed that there is no hunting, picking, or collecting; and they may be limited to marked trails, asked to be quiet, and asked not to litter.

---

1. A group or organization interested in protecting, restoring, and interpreting wetlands decides that wetland interpretation should be provided at a wetland already in public or nonprofit ownership or that a wetland needs to be acquired. Quite often this has been a group or organization that already owns a wetland (such as staff of a unit of a National Park or Refuge system). In other instances, it is a new group, such as local birdwatchers.

2. The group meets and sets some goals.

3. A specific site is located and secured for interpretive purposes through a land management plan, agreements with landowners, acquisition, or other approaches. Most sites have been on lands already in public or nonprofit ownership.

4. The site is assessed through maps, air photographs, and field inspections to identify potential trail sites, boardwalks, special features needing protection, including areas that may be sensitive to development, and potential problem areas (such as flooding and poison ivy).

5. Decisions are made to determine the type and design of trails, boardwalks, trail markers, displays, and interpretive centers. Often such decisions are not made all at once. For example, a trail may first be created, then trail markers may be added, then a boardwalk, then displays.

6. Necessary permits are sought. Permits are not needed for trails and interpretive markers; however, local, state, or federal permits may be needed for the construction of an interpre-

tive center, large boardwalks, substantial fills, grading, or other alterations of wetland areas.

7. Funding is obtained. (This is needed at an early point if the land for the interpretive site is not already in public or non-profit ownership.)

8. Construction begins on roads, parking lots, signs, interpretive trails, trail markers, and interpretive centers. Often this simply involves cutting of vegetation for trails, establishment of trail markers, and construction of a boardwalk.

9. Damaged wetland areas may be restored and enhanced. Restoration is a fairly common element at sites but is not needed and does not take place at many sites.

10. The site is operated and maintained. Operation and maintenance vary from simple maintenance of trails and signs with volunteer staff, to full-time operation of interpretive centers, parking lots, and roads by professional staff.

11. Active interpretation programs are carried out (at some but not all sites). These interpretive programs may range from interpretation by volunteers (such as birdwatchers and science teachers) to sophisticated courses. A 1989 Symposium on urban wetlands held in Oakland, California, concluded with a general recommendation that a wetland interpretation site be created in every large and mid-sized city. Hundreds of such sites have been created across the nation in the last several decades by federal agencies (such as the National Park Service and the Fish and Wildlife Service), state fish and wildlife agencies, local governments, and land trusts and conservation organizations.

South Platte Park in Littleton, Colorado, is an example. The Park, which is the former site of a 425-acre gravel operation, is a floodplain to the Platte River, with wetlands at various points along its length. Owned by the city and managed by the South Suburban Park and Recreation District, the park includes a nature center, a paved trail that winds along the river corridor, forested trails, and an extensive volunteer network to assist with interpretation and restoration activities.

Another example is the Tifft Nature Preserve in Buffalo, New York. This preserve includes a 75-acre marsh, some shrub and forested wetland — and rolling hills made up of mounds of garbage covered with soil and planted to grasses and clumps of trees. In 1972, when the city acquired the site, it planned to use it to dump municipal refuse. Concerned citizens convinced city officials to construct a landfill on a concentrated 40-acre upland site and designate the entire 264 acres as a nature preserve and environmental education center. Available today at Tifft Nature Preserve, which is administered by the Buffalo Museum of Science, is a visitor center, a self-guided nature trail, and various guides to aid interpretation.

Endnotes

Association of State Wetland Managers, *Guidebook for Creating Wetland Interpretation Sites Including Wetlands and Ecotourism* (1994).

Environmental Concern, *WOW — The Wonders of Wetlands* (1995).

D. Hammer, *Constructed Wetlands for Wastewater Treatment — Municipal, Industrial, and Agricultural* (Lewis Publishers, 1990).

J. Kusler and M. Kentula, *Wetland Creation and Restoration: The Status of the Science* (Island Press, 1990).

Land Trust Alliance, *Doing Deals: A Guide to Buying Land for Conservation* (1995).

Lane Council of Governments, *Interpretive Center Report: Wetlands Interpretation in West Eugene, Oregon* (1992).

B. Lynn, *Discover Wetlands: A Curriculum Guide* (Washington State Department of Ecology, 1988).

Washington State Department of Ecology, *A Guide to Washington's Wetland Walks* (1990).

G. Whitaker, *Wetlands Assistance Guide template* (National Wetlands Conservation Alliance, updated regularly).

APPENDIX A

Federal Programs and Initiatives and Contacts

Multi-agency programs

Clean Water Act: Section 404
Section 404 of the Clean Water Act requires permits for the discharge of dredged or fill material into waters of the United States. The program is jointly administered by the U.S. Army Corps of Engineers and the U.S. Environmental Protection Agency; other agencies have supporting roles. *(Authority: Federal Water Pollution Control Act Amendments of 1972, 33 U.S.C. Section 1344)* **Contact:** Regulatory Branch, U.S. Army Corps of Engineers, 202/761-0199. Wetlands Division, U.S. Environmental Protection Agency, 202/260-1991.

National Environmental Policy Act (NEPA)
NEPA establishes national environmental policy and goals for the protection, maintenance, and enhancement of the environment. NEPA requires all federal agencies to prepare detailed environmental impact statements to assess the impacts of and alternatives to "major federal actions significantly affecting the environment." *(Authority: National Environmental Policy Act of 1970, as amended, 42 U.S.C. Sections 4321-4370a)* **Contact:** Council on Environmental Quality, 202/395-5750.

Land and Water Conservation Fund
The Fund supports purchases of natural areas, including wetlands. Under the amended Land and Water Conservation Fund Act, states are required to include acquisition of wetlands as part of their statewide wetlands plans. *(Authority: Land and Water Conservation Fund Act of 1965, as amended, 16 U.S.C. Section 4601)* **Contact:** Director, Land Resources Division, National Park Service, 202/343-4828.

Fish and Wildlife Coordination Act
This Act requires the U.S. Army Corps of Engineers to consult with and give strong consideration to the views of the U.S. Fish and Wildlife Service, the National Marine Fisheries Service, and state wildlife agencies regarding the impacts of projects that propose to impound, divert, channel, or otherwise alter a body of water on fish and wildlife. *(Authority: Fish and Wildlife Coordination Act, 16 U.S.C. Sections 661-666c)* **Contact:** Branch of Federal Activities, Division of Habitat Conservation, U.S. Fish and Wildlife Service, 703/358-2183.

The Wild and Scenic Rivers Act
The National Wild and Scenic Rivers System provides federal protection for river segments that possess scenic, recreational, geologic, fish and wildlife, historic, cultural, or other similar values. Wetlands within the corridors of designated rivers receive special protection under the Act. *(Authority: The Wild and Scenic Rivers Act, as amended, 16 U.S.C. Sections 1271 et seq)* **Contact:** Planning Division, National Park Service, 202/208-4290. Recreation Staff, U.S. Forest Service, 202/205-0925.

Coastal Wetlands Planning, Protection, and Restoration Act (CWPPRA)
CWPPRA authorizes appropriations to develop priority restoration projects for Louisiana and, to a lesser extent, other states. *(Authority: Coastal Wetlands Planning, Protection, and Restoration Act of 1990, 16 U.S.C. Sections 3951-3956)* **Contact:** Wetlands Division, U.S. Environmental Protection Agency, 202/260-1991. Central Planning Branch, U.S. Army Corps of Engineers, 202/761-8529.

Coastal America
Coastal America joins the efforts of federal agencies with those of state, local, and private alliances to collaboratively address coastal environmental problems. *(Authority: Established through a Memorandum of Understanding between participating partners)* **Contact:** Director, Coastal America, 301/713-3160.

U.S. Environmental Protection Agency (EPA)

U.S. EPA Wetland Information Hotline
This toll-free hotline provides information on wetlands laws, regulations, internal agency documents affecting the administration of wetlands protection, and educational materials. The Hotline provides contacts and references for further information and educational literature and agency publications free of charge. **Contact:** 800/832-7828.

Wetlands Research
EPA conducts wetlands-related research in order to improve the scientific basis for wetland decision making and policy formulation. **Contact:** Office of Research and Development, U.S. Environmental Protection Agency, 202/260-7676. Corvallis Lab Wetlands Program, 503/754-4478. Duluth Lab Water Quality Research, 218/720-5723.

National Estuary Program (NEP)
The mission of the NEP is to protect and restore the health of the nation's estuaries while supporting economic and recreational activities. EPA helps create local NEPs by developing partnerships between government agencies and people working at the local level. *(Authority: Clean Water Act, as amended (Section 320), 33 U.S.C. Section 1330)* **Contact:** Office of Wetlands, Oceans, and Watersheds, U.S. Environmental Protection Agency, 202/260-7166.

State Wetlands Conservation Plans
EPA provides State Wetland Development Grants to states for development of State Wetlands Conservation Plans. The Plans are meant to outline a comprehensive strategy to coordinate and improve the effectiveness of the programs affecting wetlands in the state. *(Authority: Clean Water Act, as amended (Section 104(b)(3), 33 U.S.C. Section 1254)* **Contact:** Wetlands Division, U.S. Environmental Protection Agency, 202/260-1991.

Nonpoint Source Program
EPA provides funding for nonpoint source grants and technical assistance to states to help them develop programs for reducing nonpoint sources of pollution, including preserving and restoring wetlands. *(Authority: Water Quality Act of 1987 (Section 316(a)); Clean Water Act, as amended, 33 U.S.C. Section 1329)* **Contact:** Nonpoint Source Control Branch, U.S. Environmental Protection Agency, 202/260-7101.

U.S. Department of Defense, U.S. Army Corps of Engineers (Corps)

Rivers and Harbors Act: Section 10
Section 10 of the Act requires authorization from the Corps for the construction of any structure in or over any navigable water of the United States, the excavation, dredging, or deposition of material in these waters, or any obstruction or alteration in a navigable water. *(Authority: Rivers and Harbors Act of 1890, as amended, 33 U.S.C. Sections 403 et seq)* **Contact:** Regulatory Branch, U.S. Army Corps of Engineers, 202/761-0199.

Wetlands Research
The Corps conducts wetlands research to improve existing wetlands, reduce wetlands loss and impacts, and provide better environmental accountability in water resource projects. **Contact:** Waterways Experiment Station, U.S. Army Corps of Engineers, 601/634-2664.

APPENDIX A

U.S. Department of Commerce

The Coastal Zone Management Act (CZMA)
The CZMA was designed to protect and restore the natural resources of the coastal zone, including wetlands, while balancing the need for "reasonable" growth. The CZMA provides grants and technical assistance for coastal states to develop a coastal management program. *(Authority: Coastal Zone Management Act of 1972, as amended, 16 U.S.C. Sections 1451, et seq; Subtitle C of Title VI of The Omnibus Budget Reconciliation Act of 1990, Pub. L. No. 101-508, 104 Stat. 1388, as amended by the reauthorized CZMA of 1996, Pub. L. No. 104-150)* **Contact:** Office of Ocean and Coastal Resources Management, Department of Commerce, 301/713-3086 x100. Coastal Guidance Hotline, 800/226-1234.

U.S. Department of Agriculture (USDA)

For additional information on the listed USDA programs, contact your local conservation district, your Natural Resources Conservation Service (NRCS) State Conservationist, or the NRCS, Division of Watersheds and Wetlands, at 202/690-0848. For the name and number of your NRCS State Conservationist, contact the U.S. Environmental Protection Agency Wetlands Information Hotline at 800/832-7828.

Swampbuster
Swampbuster was created to discourage drainage of wetlands for agriculture by withholding most federal farm program benefits to farmers who drain wetlands or otherwise convert a wetland to make it suitable, or more suitable, for agricultural production. *(Authority: Food Security Act of 1985, as amended by the Federal Agriculture, Conservation, and Trade Act of 1990, and the Federal Agriculture Improvement and Reform Act of 1996; 16 U.S.C. Section 3821).*

Wetland Reserve Program (WRP)
WRP provides landowners federal cost sharing for reestablishment of wetlands vegetation and hydrology if they enroll in permanent or 30-year easements or if they sign a voluntary restoration agreement. *(Authority: Food Security Act of 1985, as amended by the Federal Agriculture, Conservation, and Trade Act of 1990 and the Federal Agriculture Improvement and Reform Act of 1996; 16 U.S.C. Section 3837).*

National Natural Resources Conservation Foundation
The National Natural Resources Conservation Foundation was established to fund research and educational activities related to conservation on private lands and to promote innovative solutions to conservation problems through public-private partnerships. *(Authority: Federal Agriculture Improvement and Reform Act of 1996; Pub. L. No. 104-127, 110 Stat. 888, 1010).*

Environmental Quality Incentives Program (EQIP)
EQIP allows landowners to enter into five- to 10-year contracts to provide technical and financial assistance for conservation practices such as manure management systems, pest management, wetland restoration, and erosion control. *(Authority: Federal Agriculture Improvement and Reform Act of 1996; Pub. L. No. 104-127, 110 Stat. 888, 996).*

Farmland Protection Program (FPP)
FPP helps state and local governments purchase conservation easements for land that farmers want to preserve in agriculture. *(Authority: Federal Agriculture Improvement and Reform Act of 1996; Pub. L. No. 104-127, 110 Stat. 888, 1020).*

Wildlife Habitat Incentives Program (WHIP)
WHIP helps landowners improve wildlife habitat on their lands. The program provides cost-sharing for developing habitat for upland wildlife, wetlands wildlife, endangered species, and fisheries. *(Authority: Federal Agriculture Improvement and Reform Act of 1996; Pub. L. No. 104-127, 110 Stat. 888, 1020).*

Conservation Reserve Program (CRP)
CRP offers landowners annual payments in return for placing environmentally sensitive cropland into an easement and implementing a conservation plan for the land. *(Authority: Food Security Act of 1985, as amended by the Federal Agriculture, Conservation, and Trade Act of 1990, and the Federal Agriculture Improvement and Reform Act of 1996; 16 U.S.C. Section 3831).*

Farm Credit Program
Formerly under the Farmers Home Administration, this program accepts conservation easements as partial payment for USDA loans. Conservation easements are established on portions of the land that contain wetlands and on other sensitive lands. *(Authority: Agriculture Credit Act of 1987; 7 U.S.C. Section 1977).*

Flood Risk Reduction Program
This program pays a lump sum payment to landowners who farm land with high flood potential in lieu of their expected seven-year marked transition payments. The landowner must comply with requirements for wetlands and highly erodible land and give up commodity loans, crop insurance, conservation program payments, and disaster payments. *(Authority: Federal Agriculture Improvement and Reform Act of 1996; Pub. L. No. 104-127, 110 Stat. 888, 1016).*

U.S. Forest Service

Forest Stewardship Program (FSP)
FSP encourages long-term stewardship of non-industrial private forest land by assisting owners in managing their forest for multiple resource benefits. *(Authority: 16 U.S.C. Section 2103a)* **Contact:** Division of Cooperative Forestry, U.S. Forest Service, 202/205-1389.

Stewardship Incentive Program (SIP)
SIP is designed to provide landowners with money to implement stewardship plans, including wetland protection and improvement efforts, developed under the Forestry Stewardship Program. *(Authority: 16 U.S.C. Section 2103b)* **Contact:** Division of Cooperative Forestry, U.S. Forest Service, 202/205-1389.

U.S. Department of Interior

U.S. Fish and Wildlife Service

Partners for Wildlife (FWS)
Partners for Wildlife is a voluntary partnership program that provides financial and technical assistance to private landowners who engage in proactive stewardship of habitat. *(Authority: 16 U.S.C.A. Section 3741)* **Contact:** Division of Habitat Conservation, U.S. Fish and Wildlife Service, 703/358-2161.

Endangered Species Act (ESA)
The ESA requires federal agencies to protect endangered and threatened species and their habitat. The Fish and Wildlife Service and the National Marine Fisheries Service administer the program in cooperation with other federal agencies. *(Authority: The Endangered Species Act of 1973, as amended, 16 U.S.C. Sections 1531 et seq)* **Contact:** Division of Endangered Species, U.S. Fish and Wildlife Service, 703/358-2171.

National Wetlands Inventory (NWI)
The Fish and Wildlife Service's National Wetlands Inventory maps and reports on the nation's wetlands. *(Authority: Fish and Wildlife Act, 16 U.S.C. Sections 742a et seq; Fish and Wildlife Coordination Act, 16 U.S.C. Sections 661-666c)* **Contact:** Division of Habitat Conservation, U.S. Fish and Wildlife Service, 703/358-2161.

North American Waterfowl Management Plan (NAWMP)
NAWMP is an international agreement between the United States, Canada, and Mexico that creates a framework for increasing the quantity and quality of waterfowl habitat. NAWMP is designed to coordinate action of federal, state, provincial, and local governments, businesses, conservation organizations, and individual citizens. *(Authority: North American Wetlands Conservation Act of 1989, 16 U.S.C.A. Sections 4401 et seq)* **Contact:** Executive Director, North American Waterfowl and Wetlands Office, U.S. Fish and Wildlife Service, 703/358-1784.

APPENDIX A

Coastal Barrier Resources Act
The Coastal Barrier Resources Act prohibits most new federal expenditures and financial assistance for development on property in the Coastal Barrier Resource System (CBRS). *(Authority: Coastal Barrier Resources Act of 1982, 16 U.S.C. Sections 3501-3510)* **Contact:** Branch of Habitat Resources, U.S. Fish and Wildlife Service, 703/358-2201.

Migratory Bird Hunting Stamp Act
The Act provides funds for the acquisition of habitat for migratory waterfowl by requiring waterfowl hunters to purchase "duck stamps." The proceeds from the program are maintained in the Migratory Bird Conservation Fund. *(Authority: Migratory Bird Hunting Stamp Act of 1934, 16 U.S.C. Sections 718 et seq)* **Contact:** Division of Realty, U.S. Fish and Wildlife Service, 703/358-2403.

National Biological Service (NBS)
NBS works with other federal agencies to provide the scientific understanding and technologies needed to support the sound management and conservation of our nation's biological resources. *(Authority: Established by Secretary's Order Number 3173, December 29, 1993)* **Contact:** Public Affairs Office, National Biological Service, 202/482-3048.

Bureau of Land Management (BLM)
BLM administers approximately 270 million acres of land owned by the federal government, including nearly 23.7 million acres of wetlands. The Bureau has developed the Riparian Wetland Initiative, under which BLM will review the status and management of riparian wetlands on its lands and expand wetland areas through land exchanges. *(Authority: Federal Land Policy and Management Act, 43 U.S.C. Sections 1701 et seq)* **Contact:** Bureau of Land Management, 202/653-9210.

National Park Service (NPS)
The Park Service carries out resource inventories and research programs, such as the Wild and Scenic Rivers Program, Land and Water Conservation Fund Grants, and watershed protection and research programs. *(Authority: National Park Service Organic Act of 1916, 16 U.S.C. Sections 1-3, Sections 460 et seq)* **Contact:** Wetlands Coordinator, National Park Service, 303/969-2955.

Office of Surface Mining (OSM)
OSM, which operates a regulatory program to assure permitting and reclamation of surface and underground coal mines and a reclamation program for abandoned mine sites, has experimental practice sites around the country where it conducts reclamation research, including several sites that involve wetlands restoration and creation. *(Authority: Surface Mining Control and Reclamation Act, 43 U.S.C. Sections 411 et seq)* **Contact:** Office of Surface Mining, 202/208-2553.

Bureau of Reclamation
The Bureau of Reclamation is responsible for the construction of large, western irrigation projects, managing existing facilities, and improving water conservation and water quality — including wetlands management and conservation. *(Authority: Reclamation Act, 43 U.S.C. Sections 4411 et seq.)* **Contact:** Public Affairs Office, Bureau of Reclamation, 202/208-4662.

Federal Emergency Management Agency (FEMA)

National Flood Insurance Program
The program makes the availability of government-guaranteed flood insurance contingent upon implementation of approved local plans that limit development in floodplains. *(Authority: National Flood Insurance Act of 1968, as amended, 42 U.S.C. Sections 4001-4128)* **Contact:** National Flood Insurance Program, 800/638-6620.

Department of Transportation (DOT)

Under the "National Highway System" and "Surface Transportation Program" provisions of the Intermodal Surface Transportation Efficiency Act (ISTEA), wetland mitigation banking projects are eligible for federal funding support. The Department is involved in several nationwide banking projects. *(Authority: 23 U.S.C. Sections 109(h), 133, 138; 42 U.S.C. Sections 4321 et seq)* **Contact:** Office of Environment and Planning, Federal Highway Administration, U.S. Department of Transportation, 202/366-5004.

APPENDIX B

Selected Organizations That Work for Wetland Protection

American Farmland Trust
1920 North St., NW
Washington, DC 20036
202/659-5170

American Rivers
1025 Vermont Ave., NW, Suite 720
Washington, DC 20005
202/547-6900

Association of State Wetland Managers
P.O. Box 269
Berne, NY 12023
518/872-1804

Chesapeake Bay Foundation
162 Prince George St.
Annapolis, MD 21401
410/268-8816

Coalition to Restore Urban Waters
1250 Addison St., Suite 107
Berkeley, CA 94702
510/848-2211

The Conservation Fund
1800 N. Kent St., Suite 1120
Arlington, VA 22209
703/525-6300

Ducks Unlimited
One Waterfowl Way
Memphis, TN 38120
901/758-3825

Environmental Defense Fund
In Washington, DC: 1875 Connecticut Ave., NW
Washington, DC 20009
202/387-0070
In New York: 257 Park Ave., S
New York, NY 10010
212/505-2100

Environmental Law Institute
1616 P St., NW, Suite 200
Washington, DC 20036
202/939-3800

Friends of the Earth
In Washington, DC: 1025 Vermont Ave., NW,
Third Floor
Washington, DC 20005
202/783-7400
In Washington State: 4512 University Way, NE
Seattle, WA 98105
206/633-1661

Izaak Walton League
707 Conservation Lane
Gaithersburg, MD 20878
301/548-0150

Land Trust Alliance
900 17th St., NW, Suite 410
Washington, DC 20006
202/785-1410

National Association of Conservation Districts
509 Capitol Court, NE
Washington, DC 20002
202/547-6223

National Audubon Society
700 Broadway
New York, NY 10003
212/979-3000

National Fish and Wildlife Foundation
1120 Connecticut Ave., NW, Suite 900
Washington, DC 20036
202/857-0166

National Wetlands Conservation Alliance
509 Capitol Court, NE
Washington, DC 20002
202/547-6223

National Wildlife Federation
1400 16th St., NW
Washington, DC 20036
202/797-6800

Natural Resources Defense Council
In New York: 40 West 20th St.
New York, NY 10011
212/727-2700
In Washington, DC: 1200 New York Ave., NW,
Suite 400
Washington, DC 20005
202/289-6868

The Nature Conservancy
1815 North Lynn St.
Arlington, VA 22209
703/841-5300

Sierra Club Legal Defense Fund
180 Montgomery St., Suite 1400
San Francisco, CA 94104
415/627-6700

Southern Environmental Law Center
137 East Franklin St., Suite 404
Chapel Hill, NC 27514
919/967-1450

Trout Unlimited
1500 Wilson Blvd., Suite 310
Arlington, VA 22209
703/522-0200

The Trust for Public Land
116 New Montgomery St.
San Francisco, CA 94105
415/495-4014

Wildlife Management Institute
1101 14th St., NW, Suite 725
Washington, DC 20005
202/371-1808

World Wildlife Fund
1250 24th St., NW
Washington, DC 20037
202/293-4800

This is only a partial list of primarily national and large regional organizations. Many other organizations, including numerous local and statewide groups, exist that are very important to wetland protection.

Sample Conservation Easement and Other Conveyance Documents

In this Appendix, we include three legal documents often used to protect wetlands: A conveyance of fee simple title with a condition subsequent and power of termination; a restrictive covenant; and a conservation easement. These documents are presented here as samples only; consult a lawyer to tailor these and other legal conveyance tools to the particular circumstances you encounter in your wetland protection efforts.

Restriction to Nature Preserve — Non-automatic Reverter

In this example, The Nature Conservancy conveys fee simple title on a condition subsequent and retains power of termination:

This conveyance is made subject to the express conditions that (1) the property herein conveyed shall be used and maintained forever as a nature preserve for the preservation of the natural characteristics and features of the property for scientific, educational, and aesthetic purposes and (2) the property shall be managed and maintained to the fullest extent possible in its natural state, except for the undertaking of scientific and educational research, ecological management, and maintenance of fences and foot trails as may be appropriate to effectuate the foregoing purposes without impairing the essential natural character of the property.

The Grantor hereby reserves for itself and its successors and assigns a power of termination in the nature of a right of re-entry, which right may be used by the Grantor to terminate the estate hereby granted to the Grantee if the property is no longer used in accordance with the conditions set forth herein or upon a breach of any of the conditions set forth herein. This right, if exercised by the Grantor upon violation of the above conditions, shall be exercised by mailing a notice of violation by certified mail to the Grantee or its successors or assigns at the last known address of the Grantee or its successors or assigns; provided, however, that this right may not be executed unless the Grantee has first been given written notification of the violation (by certified mail to such last known address) and an opportunity to cure the violation within 60 days thereafter. The notice exercising the power of termination shall declare that the power of termination has been exercised, shall state the violation which caused the action, and shall note that the violation has not been cured in a timely manner. A copy of the notice exercising the power of termination shall simultaneously be recorded on the appropriate land records and the property conveyed herein shall then revert to the Grantor and its successors and assigns forever.

Restrictive Covenant

In this example, The Nature Conservancy conveys subject to a restrictive covenant. The remedy for breach is an injunction or damages:

This conveyance is made subject to the express covenants of the Grantee that (1) the property herein conveyed shall be used and maintained forever as a nature preserve for the preservation of the natural characteristics and features of the property for scientific, educational, and aesthetic purposes and (2) the property shall be managed and maintained to the fullest extent possible in its natural state, except for the undertaking of scientific and educational research, ecological management, and maintenance of fences and foot trails as may be appropriate to effectuate the foregoing purposes without impairing the essential natural character of the property.

These restrictive covenants shall be construed to carry out the intent of the parties to the fullest extent possible. These restrictive covenants are for the benefit of that adjacent property owned by the Grantor [legally described in attached Exhibit _____/ and known as the _____ Preserve]. These restrictions shall run with the land and be binding upon the Grantee and its successors and assigns and all future owners of the property in perpetuity. The Grantor or its successors or assigns shall have the right to enforce these restrictions by proceedings at law or in equity. By acceptance of this deed of conveyance, the Grantee for itself and its successors and assigns hereby acknowledges that injunctive or other appropriate equitable relief is among the available remedies in the event of a breach of these restrictive covenants.

Draft Conservation Easement

STATE OF SOUTH CAROLINA

COUNTY OF _____

CONSERVATION EASEMENT

THIS INDENTURE, made this _____ day of _____, 19_____, by and between _____ ("Grantor"), of Georgetown (city), Georgetown (county), South Carolina (state}, and Wetlands America Trust, Inc. ("Grantee"), a nonprofit corporation organized under the laws of the District of Columbia and an eligible donee as described under Treasury Reg. 1.170A-14(c)(1).

WHEREAS, the Grantor is the owner in fee simple of certain real property (hereinafter referred to as the "Protected Property") which has aesthetic, scientific, educational, and ecological value in its present state as a natural area which has not been subject to development or exploitation, which property is referred to as Salt Marsh Plantation and is more particularly described in Exhibit A attached hereto and by this reference incorporated herein.

WHEREAS, the Protected Property consists of natural areas of historic and scenic value and has substantial value as a natural, ecological, and scientific resource; and

WHEREAS the Grantee is a nonprofit corporation whose purpose is to preserve and conserve natural areas for aesthetic, scientific, charitable, and educational purposes; and

WHEREAS, Sections 27-8-10 et seq. of the South Carolina Code of Laws of 1976, as amended, permit the creation of conservation easements for the purposes of inter alia retaining land or water areas predominantly in their natural, scenic, open, or wooded condition or as suitable habitat for fish, plants, or wildlife; and

WHEREAS, Grantor and Grantee recognize the natural, scenic, aesthetic, and special character of the Protected Property, and have the common purpose of the conservation and protection in perpetuity of the Protected Property as "a relatively natural habitat of fish, wildlife, or plants or similar ecosystem" as that phrase is used in Public Law 96-541, 26 USC 170(h)(4)(A)(ii), and Section 170(h)(4)(A)(ii) of the Internal Revenue Code of 1986, as amended and in regulations promulgated thereunder by placing voluntary restrictions upon the use of the Protected Property and by providing for the transfer from the Grantor to Grantee of affirmative rights for the protection of the Protected Property; and so as to qualify as a contribution of a "qualified conservation contribution" as that term is defined under Section 170(h)(2)(C) of the Code;

WHEREAS, "natural, scientific, educational, aesthetic, scenic, and recreational resource," as used herein shall, without limiting the generality of the terms, mean the condition of the Protected Property at the time of this grant, evidenced by the Conservation Easement Documentation Report for _____ dated _____, a copy of which is on file with both Grantor and Grantee, which documentation establishes the condition of the property at the time of the gift as provided by Treasury Reg. 1.170A-14(g)(5), and may include:

A) The appropriate survey maps from the United States Geological Survey, showing the property line of the Protected Property and other contiguous or nearby protected areas;

B) A map of the area drawn to scale showing all existing man-made improvements or incursions (such as roads, buildings, fences, or gravel pits), vegetation and identification of flora and fauna (including, for example, rare species locations, animal breeding and roosting areas, and migration routes);

land use history (including present uses and recent past disturbances), and distinct natural features (such as large trees and aquatic areas);

C) An aerial photograph of the Protected Property at an appropriate scale taken as close as possible to the date the donation is made; and

D) On-site photographs taken at appropriate locations on the Protected Property; and other documentation possessed (at present or in the future) by the Grantor which the Grantor shall make available to the Grantee, its successors and assigns, which documentation establishes the conditions of the property at the time of the gift as provided by Treasury Reg. 1.170A-14(g)(5).

NOW, THEREFORE, the Grantor for good and valuable consideration paid by the Grantee, for receipt of which is hereby acknowledged by the Grantor, and of the covenants, mutual agreements, conditions and promises herein contained, the Grantor does hereby freely give, grant, bargain, sell, and convey unto the Grantee, its successors and assigns, forever, a conservation easement over the Protected Property consisting of the following:

SECTION 1
AFFIRMATIVE RIGHTS

1.1 Visual Access. The right of the Grantee to have visual access to and view of the Protected Property in its natural, scenic, open, and undisturbed condition, provided, however, that said right shall not be construed to permit general public accession over or upon the Protected Property.

1.2 Right of Entry. The right of the Grantee to enter the Protected Property for the purposes of inspecting same to determine compliance herewith, to enforce by proceedings at law or in equity the covenants hereinafter set forth including, but not limited to, the right to require the restoration of the Protected Property to its condition at the time of this grant. The Grantee, their successors or assigns, do not waive or forfeit the right to take action as may be necessary to insure compliance with the Covenants, hereinafter set forth, (the "Covenants"), and purposes of this grant by any prior failure to act. Nothing herein shall be construed to entitle the Grantee to institute any proceedings against Grantor for any changes to the Protected Property due to causes beyond the Grantor's control such as changes caused by fire, floods, earthquake, storm, or unauthorized wrongful acts of third persons.

1.3 Management Plan. The right of the Grantee to develop one or more management plans to be implemented with Grantor's permission, which permission shall not be unreasonably withheld or delayed, for the protection of Conservation Values. Costs for such a plan shall be borne by Grantee.

SECTION 2
RESTRICTIONS AND COVENANTS

AND IN FURTHERANCE of the foregoing rights, the Grantor, on behalf of the Grantor, his heirs, successors, and assigns, and with the intent that the same shall run with and bind the Protected Property in perpetuity, does hereby make, with respect to the Protected Property, and subject to the rights reserved in Section 3 the following covenants:

2.1 Uses. There shall be no agricultural, commercial, or industrial activity undertaken or allowed, nor shall any right of passage across or upon the Protected Property be allowed or granted if that right of passage is used in conjunction with uses which are expressly prohibited by the terms of this Easement on or about the Protected Property.

2.2 Structures. There shall be no construction or placing of advertising signs, billboards, or any advertising materials on any of the Protected Property. There shall be no construction or placing of temporary or permanent buildings, docks, bridges, piers, or other structures excepting maintenance and replacement of existing structures. There shall be no mobile homes or trailers placed on property.

2.3 Roads. There shall be no building of any new roads, nor widening of existing roads. Maintenance of roads shall be limited to normal practices for non-paved roads, such as the removal of dead vegetation, necessary pruning or removal of hazardous trees and plants, application of permeable materials necessary (e.g., sand, gravel, crushed stone) to correct erosion, placement of culverts,

water control structures, and bridges, and maintenance of roadside ditches.

2.4 Timber. There shall be no timber harvesting.

2.5 Topography and Minerals. There shall be no filling, excavating, dredging, mining, or drilling; no removal of topsoil, sand, gravel, rock, peat, minerals, or other materials, nor any dumping of ashes, trash, garbage, or any other unsightly or offensive materials and no change in the topography of the land in any manner.

2.6 Exotics. There shall be no introduction of exotic plant or animal species except those traditionally and prevalently used as of or prior to the date hereof for wildlife food planting or for agricultural planting traditional to the area.

2.7 Agriculture. There shall be no commercial agricultural-related (e.g., a nursery, cattle, livestock) enterprises of farming, horticulture, or husbandry. Agricultural planting for wildlife is permissible.

2.8 Wetlands. There shall be no dredging, construction of ponds, groins, or dikes, nor any manipulation of natural water courses within any salt or brackish marsh.

2.9 Subdivision. There shall be no subdivision of the Protected Property, and title of the Protected Property shall be held by the same owner at all times.

2.10 Use Inconsistent with Purpose. The parties recognize that this Conservation Easement cannot address every circumstance that may arise in the future and the parties agree that the purpose of this Conservation Easement is to preserve the Protected Property predominantly in its present condition and to protect the Property's environmental systems (the "Purpose"). Any use or activity not reserved in Section 3 which is inconsistent with the Purpose of this Easement or which materially threatens the Purpose of this Easement is prohibited. In the event that there is a dispute between the Grantor and the Grantee as to whether or not an activity or use is prohibited under this Section, the parties shall arbitrate the matter in accordance with the provisions of Section 4.11.

SECTION 3
RESERVED RIGHTS

3.1 Grantor's Reserved Rights. Notwithstanding any provision to the contrary contained in this Conservation Easement, the Grantor reserves for himself, his heirs, successors, and assigns the "Reserved Rights" set forth in this Section 3. The exercise of all reserved rights shall be in full accordance with all applicable local, state, and federal laws and regulations.

3.2 Structures and Roads. The right to maintain and replace the existing structures and roads at the same location with roads and structures of like size and function and new temporary roads permitted in this paragraph. The right to construct one additional single family structure and other auxiliary buildings as are normal to a private plantation in the Lowcountry of South Carolina. The single family structure shall not exceed 40' in height and contain no more than 3,000 square feet of heated space. The right to construct firebreaks as necessary, to build temporary roads for access to timber, and to widen existing roads for utility rights-of-way and timber removal. The Right to use roads for all agricultural, or timber harvest uses permitted under this easement.

3.3 Hunting and Fishing. The right to hunt and fish on the Property, including leasing of hunting and fishing rights, provided that all such activity is conducted in accordance with state and federal regulations; however no leasing of waterfowl hunting will be allowed. Grantor retains the right to hunt waterfowl for himself and his guest only.

3.4 Impoundments. The right to repair, replace, or maintain existing or historic wetland impoundments, said impoundments being recognized by both Grantor and Grantee as beneficial to waterfowl, and other wetland dependent plants and animals, all subject to state and federal rules and regulations. The impoundments shall be managed primarily for waterfowl. To the greatest extent feasible and practical, the waterfowl management program shall be carried out in a manner that is conducive to providing feeding and nesting habitat for shorebirds, wading birds, and bald eagles, and other wildlife or plant species. The right to install additional water control structures subject to the approval of Grantee and subject to existing state and federal Regulations and procedures. Within the existing impoundments mowing, disking, planting, internal ditching, and diking will be allowed subject to existing state and federal regulations and permit procedures.

3.5 Clearing. The right to maintain and cultivate the agricultural and wildlife food plots that exist on the Protected Property at the time of the execution of this document and the right to clear additional areas as needed with permission of the Grantee which shall not be unreasonably withheld. Within the existing natural pine and mixed pine hardwood stands, up to 15% may be cleared for wildlife food plots in individual units not to exceed 10 acres in size.

3.6 Farming Methods. The right to engage in agriculture, as defined under in the paragraph 2.7, and wildlife food planting currently existing in open lands and in any additional lands cleared on the Protected Property (as permitted under 3.5 preceding). The use of any agricultural chemicals and biocides in connection with such agricultural activity shall be in accordance with applicable federal, EPA, state, and local regulations.

3.7 Biocides. The right to use biocides in order to maintain and keep open the main or secondary navigational canals on the property. All such biocides must be used in accordance with all applicable local, state and federal laws and regulations.

3.8 Agriculture. The Grantor reserves the right to engage in aquaculture and mariculture or to enter lease arrangements regarding same provided that same is conducted in a manner not inconsistent with the aims and purposes of the conservation easement which meets all state and federal laws.

3.9 Minerals. Oil, gas, and all minerals are reserved by Grantor and not conveyed by this Conservation Easement; provided, however, the Grantor comply with state, federal, and local law and regulation; and provided further that Grantor reserves to himself, his heirs, and assigns all interest in minerals found or to be found in, on or under the Protected Property provided that there may not be at any time any extraction or removal of the minerals by any surface mining method, and provided further that there may not at any time be used any method of mining that is inconsistent with the particular conservation purposes of this conservation easement, i.e., the protection of a relatively natural habitat of fish, wildlife, or plants, so that any permitted method of mining may have only limited localized impact on the Protected Property shall not occur within and may not be irremediably destructive of significant conservation interests. For example, production facilities must be concealed or compatible with existing topography and landscape and any surface alterations must be reasonably restored to its original state. Additionally, any mining shall be conducted in the manner consistent with the regulations governing qualified conservation contributions as the same may be adopted and from time to time amended.

3.10 Signs. The right to post "no trespassing" signs, directional signs, signs indicating and identifying occupancy and signs advertising the sale of the Protected Property. Signs may not exceed 12 inches by 18 inches in size.

3.11 Docks and Related Structures. The right to construct one small private dock in the area subject to all requisite government permits, for use by the owner of the property and his(her) guests.

3.12 Timber Harvesting. The Grantor reserves the right to harvest and thin timber as permitted under the Forest Management Policy attached as Exhibit "B" hereto, as amended from time to time by mutual consent of the Grantor and the Grantee.

SECTION 4
GENERAL COVENANTS

4.1 Cost of Ownership. The Grantor, for himself and for his heirs, successors and assigns, agrees to pay any real estate taxes or assessments levied by competent authority on the Protected Property. The Grantee shall not be responsible for any costs or liability of any kind related to the ownership, operation, insurance upkeep or maintenance of the Protected Property except as expressly provided herein.

4.2 Public Access. No right of access to the general public to any portion of the Protected Property is conveyed by this Conservation Easement.

4.3 Subsequent Deeds. The Grantor agrees that the terms, conditions, restrictions, and purposes of this Conservation Easement will be inserted by it in any subsequent deed, or other legal instrument by which the Grantor divests itself of either the fee simple, or its possessory interest in all or portions of the Protected Property, and that the Grantor will notify the Grantee, its successors or assigns, of any such conveyance.

4.4 Notices/Approvals. Any notices or approval requests required in this Conservation Easement shall be sent by registered or certified mail, postage prepaid, to the following addresses below or to such address as may be hereafter specified by notice in writing. Grantee shall be responsible to provide Grantor with a single response to each notice or request for approval within 45 days of receipt of such notice or request.

4.5 Notice of Breach. In the event that a breach of the covenants by the Grantor or by a third party acting at the direction of or with the permission of the Grantor comes to the attention of the Grantee, the Grantee may at its discretion notify the Grantor in writing of such a breach. The Grantor shall then have thirty (30) days after receipt of such notice to undertake actions including restoration of the Protected Property that are reasonably calculated to correct swiftly the conditions constituting such a breach. If the Grantor fails to take such corrective action, the Grantee may at its discretion undertake such actions, including appropriate legal proceedings, as are reasonably necessary to effect such corrections; and the cost of such corrections, including the Grantee's expenses, court costs and legal fees shall be paid by the Grantor, provided it is determined by the Grantor or a third party acting at the direction of or with the permission of the Grantor, is responsible for the breach.

4.6 Severability. In the event any provision of this Conservation Easement is determined by the appropriate court to be void and unenforceable, all remaining terms shall remain valid and binding.

4.7 Perpetuity. The burdens of this Conservation Easement shall run with the Protected Property and shall be enforceable against the Grantor and all future owners and tenants in perpetuity. The benefits shall be in gross and assignable but only to an eligible donee as defined in IRS Section 1.170A-14(c)(1) as that section may be amended from time to time.

4.8 Assignment by Grantee. The benefits of this Easement shall be in gross and shall not be assignable by the Grantee, except (1) if as a condition of any assignment, the Grantee requires that the purpose of this Easement continues to be carried out, and (2) if the assignee, at the time of the assignment, qualifies under Section 170(h) of the Internal Revenue Code of 1986, as amended, and applicable regulations thereunder, and under South Carolina law as an eligible one to receive this Easement directly. In the event that Grantee ceases to exist or exist but no longer as a tax exempt non-profit organization, qualified under Section 501(c)(3) and 179(h)(3) of the Internal Revenue Code of 1986, as amended, then this Easement shall automatically become vested in one of the following tax exempt non-profit organizations, qualified under Section 501(c)(3) and 179(h)(3) of the Internal Revenue Code of 1986, as amended, in the order of priority as listed [here]: 1. Lowcountry Open Land Trust, a South Carolina non-profit Corporation. 2. A tax exempt non-profit organization designated by the then owner of the Protected Property which has experience in holding similar conservation easements.

4.9 Judicial Extinguishment. If a subsequent, unexpected change in the conditions of the Protected Property or the surrounding property, make impossible or impractical the continued use of the Protected Property for conservation purposes, the restrictions shall be extinguished by judicial proceeding and all the Grantee's proceeds, if any, from a subsequent sale or exchange of the Protected Property shall be used in a manner consistent with the conservation purposes of this Conservation Easement.

4.10 Eminent Domain. Whenever all or part of the Protected Property is taken in exercise of eminent domain by public, corporate or other authority so as to abrogate the restrictions imposed by this Conservation Easement, Grantor shall take in appropriate actions at the time of such taking to recover the full value of the taking and all incidental or direct damages resulting from the taking. The net proceeds (including, for purposes of this subparagraph, proceeds from any lawful sale of the property unencumbered by the restrictions hereunder) shall be distributed among the Grantor and the Grantee in shares in proportion to the fair market value of their interests in the Protected Property on the date of execution of this Conservation Easement. The Grantee shall use its share of the net proceeds in a manner consistent with the conservation purposes set forth herein.

4.11 Enforcement Rights. The Grantee, its successors or assigns, do not waive or forfeit the right to take action as may be necessary to insure compliance with this Conservation Easement and purposes of this grant by any prior failure to act. Nothing herein shall be construed to entitle the Grantee to institute any proceedings against Grantor for any changes to the Protected Property due to causes beyond the Grantor's control such as changes caused by fire, floods, storm or unauthorized wrongful acts of third persons. Grantor agrees to reimburse the Grantee for all costs and expenses, including reasonable attorneys fees, incurred by the Grantee in connection with a breach by the Grantor of the terms of this Conservation Easement. The rights hereby granted shall be in addition to, and not in limitation of, any other rights and remedies available to the Grantee for enforcement of this Conservation Easement.

4.12 Amendments. This Conservation Easement shall not be amended, modified or terminated except in writing in a document signed by Grantor and Grantee; provided, however, no amendment shall be allowed that would adversely affect the qualifications of this Conservation Easement as a charitable gift or the status of the Grantee under any applicable laws, including Section 170(h) of the Internal Revenue Code, as amended, or the laws of the State of South Carolina. Any such amendment shall be consistent with the purpose of this Conservation Easement, shall not affect its perpetual duration, shall not permit additional development other than development permitted by this Conservation Easement on its effective date, and shall not permit any impairment of the significant conservation values of the Protected Property. Any such amendment shall be recorded in the real estate records office of Charleston County, South Carolina. Nothing in this paragraph shall require Grantor or Grantee to agree to any amendment.

4.13 Warranty of Title. Grantor hereby warrants and represents that the Grantor is seized of the Protected Property in fee simple and has good right to grant and convey this Conservation Easement, that the Protected Property is free and clear of any and all encumbrances, except easements of record and prescriptive easements, if any, and that the Grantee and its successors and assigns shall have the use of and enjoy all of the benefits derived from and arising out of this Conservation Easement.

4.14 Habendum Clause. TO HAVE AND TO HOLD this Conservation Easement together with all and singular the appurtenances and privileges belonging or in any way pertaining thereto, either in law or in equity, either in possession or expectancy, for the proper use and benefit of the Grantee, its successors and assigns forever.

IN WITNESS WHEREOF, the Grantor has set his hand and seal the day and year first above written, and the Grantee has caused these presents to be signed in its name by its Chief Operating Officer, and its corporate seal to be affixed, attested by its Assistant Secretary the day and year first above written.

SIGNED, SEALED, AND DELIVERED IN THE PRESENCE OF:

GRANTOR

_____

_____

GRANTEE

Wetlands America Trust, Inc.
A non-profit corporation organized under the laws of the District of Columbia

By: _____

Its Chief Operating Officer

STATE OF SOUTH CAROLINA   )
)
COUNTY OF   )

PERSONALLY appeared before me the undersigned witness and made oath that (s)he saw the within named_____ sign, seal, and as his act and deed, deliver the within written Purchase Agreement, and that (s)he with the other witness above named witnessed the execution thereof.

Sworn to before me this

_____ Day of _____, 199X.

[SEAL]

Notary Public of South Carolina

Draft Wetland Regulations for Local Governments

Local governments may want to use one of three approaches for zoning wetlands or regulating wetlands through special zoning-related ordinances or codes:

(l) They can formally endorse the Section 404 program by resolution and help the U.S. Army Corps of Engineers and other federal agencies implement the program by participating in public hearings, helping with monitoring, helping with public education, and through other techniques.

2) They can adopt a simple restrictive wetland conservation ordinance for wetland areas as part of broader zoning or as an independent ordinance. Such conservation regulations allow for open space but prohibit most other activities in wetland areas.

(3) They can adopt a more complete, performance-oriented wetland zoning regulation or independent regulation that establishes performance standards for wetland uses. This regulation will more closely resemble the Section 404 program regulations and many state regulations.

See Chapters 3, 4, 5, 6, and 10 for more detailed discussion of basic issues and procedures in local regulation relevant to the implementation of these approaches.

(1) Adoption of the Corps of Engineers program by resolution

Endorsing the Section 404 program by resolution may be a good option for local governments that do not wish to adopt their own wetland regulatory program due to staff or budget limitations and because they want to avoid duplication and confusion for applicants. However, under this approach, the protection of wetlands will be subject to all of the limitations and exemptions of the Section 404 program, including possible future modifications.

After a local government adopts the Section 404 program by resolution, the local government then notifies the Corps District office that it has done so and that it wishes to assist the Corps in implementing the program. The local government could request a complete set of Section 404 statutes, regulations, regional permits, nationwide permits, and other policy guidance from the Corps District office and file these materials in the local zoning office or another site, so that landowners have access to Section 404 permitting requirements. A copy also would be provided to the local zoning and planning commission and zoning administrators.

The local government also should request that the Corps District office provide it with copies of public notices and hearings on such applications within the local jurisdiction. The local government could then provide comments to the Corps upon proposed permits with regard to:

• Compliance of the proposed permit with all local floodplain, sanitary waste disposal, coastal zone, zoning, subdivision control, and other regulations;

• Compliance with local master plans and other plans;

• The impact of the proposed activity upon neighboring lands, including community roads, sewers, and water supply;

• The impact of the proposed activity upon wetland functions and values, such as fishing, waterfowl, and recreation; and

• The adequacy of mitigation measures and compensation measures (restoration, creation, and enhancement).

In addition, the local government could:

• Map wetlands to help landowners identify wetland areas;

• Provide technical assistance to landowners in identifying more precise wetland boundaries, understanding Section 404 regulations, restoring, or creating wetlands;

• Provide publications and conduct other education efforts concerning the importance of wetlands; and

• Carry out other measures. See the draft ordinance provisions for *(1) Endorsement of the Section 404 Program by Resolution.*

(2) Wetland conservancy zoning or other special regulation

The wetland conservancy regulatory provisions below are intended for use in a community that wishes to ensure adequate protection of wetland areas as part of broader zoning or as an independent special regulation. This ordinance may be adopted pursuant to interim zoning authority, home rule power, or special wetland regulatory authority, which is available in some states. This simple set of ordinance provisions work in the following way:

(1) Wetland areas are defined or mapped through use of wetland maps, such as National Wetlands Inventory maps, written definition criteria, elevations, distances from streams or lakes, topographic maps, soil maps, or other available data. Communities will need to choose the techniques appropriate to their circumstances.

(2) Limited open space uses without severe impact upon wetlands are permitted as of right, and other uses are prohibited unless permitted as variances.

(3) The local governing body is authorized to issue variances. However, the applicant must meet a variety of conditions for a variance, including a showing that no practical use is possible for his or her entire property without a variance and that mitigation measures and compensatory measures will be undertaken to compensate for loss of wetland functions and values.

(3) Performance-standard wetland zoning or other special regulations

The third approach may be adopted pursuant to zoning enabling authority, special wetland regulatory enabling statutes, or home rule powers. It is intended for use as a free-standing ordinance, as an overlay zoning ordinance, or as part of comprehensive zoning regulations.

The draft provisions set forth below provide the following regulatory framework:

(1) Wetland areas are mapped. The ordinance also provides a procedure for locating zoning boundary lines with more precision in case of boundary disputes.

(2) Limited open space uses without severe impact upon wetlands are permitted as of right; all other uses are permitted only as "special permit" uses.

(3) A special wetland regulatory board or the zoning board of adjustment is delegated power to issue special permits. Quite detailed criteria and procedures are provided for evaluation of permit applications. A landowner must show compliance with these criteria.

(4) The ordinance contains special provisions pertaining to existing uses, amendments, judicial review, special assessments, and other matters.

The draft regulation provisions that follow should be used in combination with monitoring of violations, mapping, public education, wetland and watershed planning, assistance to landowners, tax incentives for landowners, and selected acquisition efforts undertaken in cooperation with landowners.

DRAFT ORDINANCE PROVISIONS

(1) ENDORSEMENT OF THE SECTION 404 PROGRAM BY RESOLUTION

(1) The community of [community name] endorses the Section 404 program, including all attendant regulations, policies, and amendments. It is the intent of the community to help the U.S. Army Corps of Engineers and other federal agencies administer and enforce this program by requesting notices of individual permit applications within the community of [community name] and from the Army Corps of Engineers and by providing comments to the Corps on such applications.

The community of [community name] will assist the Corps by [community must select options. See Chapters 4, 5, and 8 for more information]:

• Monitoring compliance with permitted activities and reporting any violations to the Corps when discovered;

• Mapping wetlands;

• Providing public education;

• Providing assistance to landowners;

• Participating in efforts to conduct wetlands and watershed planning;

• Participating in efforts to provide tax incentives to landowners when they conduct wetland protection efforts;

• Participating in acquisition efforts conducted with landowner cooperation.

(2) WETLAND CONSERVANCY ZONE PROVISIONS

Section 1: Findings of Fact

The wetlands of [local unit of government] are indispensable and fragile natural resources subject to flood, erosion, soil bearing-capacity limitations, and other hazards. They serve multiple functions for wildlife, pollution control, storage and passage of flood waters, aquifer recharge, erosion control, education, scientific study, open space, and recreation. Many wetlands also are flood and erosion areas. Activities in such areas may increase flooding and water pollution, and cause other nuisances on other lands as well as be subject to flood and erosion damages.

Threats are posed to wetland resources due to uncontrolled use of land and waters. Destruction or damage to wetlands threatens public safety and the general welfare. It is therefore necessary for [local unit of government] to discourage further activities in wetland areas where those activities may be located at upland sites, to ensure that protection is provided for wetland functions and values, and to prevent nuisances and nuisance-like uses. It is the goal of [local unit of government] to achieve no net loss of wetland functions and values and acreage and to encourage restoration of lost wetland functions and values and wetland acreage.

Section 2: Lands to Which the Ordinance Applies

This ordinance shall apply to all lands within the jurisdiction of [local unit of government]: [options: choose one or more of the following]

• Which are mapped wetlands on National Wetlands Inventory maps [specify numbers, series, etc.];

• Which are mapped as wetlands on U.S. Geological Survey topographic maps [specific series and dates];

• Consisting of soil types designated as poorly drained, very poorly drained, alluvial, and floodplain by the Natural Resources Conservation Service or the U.S. Department of Agriculture Cooperative Soils Survey on soil maps [describe series, dates];

• Within ___ feet horizontal distance of the mean water level of the following bodies of water: [list];

• Within ___ feet vertical elevation of the mean water level of the following bodies of water: [list]

Section 3: Permitted and Prohibited Activities.

The following activities shall be permitted as of right within designated wetland areas to the extent they are not prohibited by any other ordinance, state statute, or federal statute or regulation and provided they do not require structures, grading, filling, dredging, or draining:

(1) Agricultural uses such as general farming, pasture, wild crop harvesting, haying;

(2) Outdoor recreational activities, including hunting, birdwatching, hiking, boating, trapping, fishing, horseback riding, swimming, skeet and trap shooting, shooting preserves, and ecotourism;

(3) The taking of shellfish, fish, and wildlife, consistent with the laws of the state of [add state];

(4) Commercial shellfishing and trapping;

(5) Forestry, providing wetland hydrology is not disturbed;

(6) Wildlife preservation and refuges; and

(7) Education and scientific research and nature trails;

In addition, the following structural uses are permitted, providing they do not involve grading, fill, dredging, or draining: catwalks, piers, boathouses, boat shelters, fences, duck blinds, wildlife management shelters, footbridges, observation decks and shelters, and other similar water-related structures, provided that such structures are constructed on piling so as to permit the unobstructed flow of waters and preserve the natural contour of the wetland.

All other uses and activities involving structures, grading, filling, dredging, vegetation removal, and disturbance of wetland water supply and flora and fauna are prohibited except as they may be permitted as variances.

All uses and activities that were lawful before the passage of this ordinance but which do not conform with the provisions of the ordinance, may be continued but may not be expanded, changed, enlarged, or altered.

Section 4: Variances

Uses and activities other than those permitted as of right in Section 3 may be authorized in special circumstances through issuance of a variance by the zoning board of adjustment if the applicant can demonstrate all of the following conditions:

(1) All other required federal, state, and local permits have been obtained;

(2) No practical use is possible for the entire parcel of land owned by the applicant and alternative locations outside of the wetland are not practical;

(3) The activity will not threaten public safety or cause nuisances, increase flooding on other lands, or violate pollution control standards or other federal, state, or local regulations. In addition, the activity must be reasonably protected against flooding, erosion, and other hazards;

(4) No net loss of wetland functions and values and no net loss of wetland acreage will be achieved though compensatory wetland restoration, creation, enhancement, or other approaches.

For a variance, the burden shall be upon the applicant to show compliance with these conditions. The [local unit of government] may require information concerning each of these conditions from the applicant. A public hearing shall be held before a decision is made on the application. The [local unit of government] shall attach conditions to the variance to minimize the impact of any proposed activity and achieve no net loss of functions and values and wetland acreage.

(3) DRAFT PERFORMANCE STANDARD WETLAND PROTECTION ORDINANCE

Section 1: Findings of Fact and Purpose

Findings of Fact

The wetlands of [local unit of government] are indispensable but fragile natural resources subject to flood, erosion, soil bearing-capacity limitations, and other hazards. In their natural state they serve multiple functions for wildlife, pollution control, storage and passage of flood waters, aquifer recharge, erosion control, education, scientific study, open space, and recreation.

Threats are posed to wetland resources due to uncontrolled use of land and waters. Destruction or damage to wetlands threatens public safety and the general welfare.

Due to this combination of natural hazards and natural functions and values, it is necessary for [local unit of government] to control activities in wetland areas.

Purposes

It is the policy of [local unit of government] that wetland activities should not threaten public safety or cause nuisances:

(1) By blocking flood flows, destroying flood storage areas, or destroying storm barriers, thereby resulting in increased flood heights or velocities on other lands;

(2) By increasing water pollution through location of domestic waste disposal systems in wet soils, unauthorized application of pesticides and algaecides, disposal of solid wastes at inappropriate sites, creation of unstabilized fills, or the destruction of wetland vegetation serving pollution and sediment control functions;

(3) By increasing erosion.

It also is the policy of [local unit of government] that wetland activities should not destroy natural wetland functions and values or destroy wetland acreage:

(1) By destroying natural flood storage and flood conveyance capacity;

(2) By destroying natural pollution prevention and pollution treatment capabilities;

(3) By decreasing breeding, nesting, and feeding areas for any forms of waterfowl and shorebirds;

(4) By threatening rare or endangered species;

(5) By interfering with the sources of and exchange of nutrients needed by fish and other forms of wildlife;

(6) By decreasing habitat for fish and other forms of wildlife;

(7) By decreasing recharge for groundwater aquifers;

(8) By destroying sites needed for education and scientific research;

(9) By interfering with public rights in navigable waters and the recreation opportunities of wetlands for hunting, fishing, boating, hiking, birdwatching, photography, camping, and other uses; or

(10) By destroying aesthetic and property values.

Section 2: Lands to Which This Ordinance Applies

Wetland District

This ordinance shall apply to all lands within the jurisdiction of [local unit of government] shown on the Official Zoning Map as being located within the boundaries of the Wetland District. The Official Zoning Map, together with all explanatory matter thereon and attached thereto, is hereby adopted by reference and declared to be a part of this ordinance. The Official Zoning Map shall be on file in the office of the [city clerk, town clerk, etc.]

Rules for Interpretation of District Boundaries

The boundaries of the Wetland District ordinarily shall be determined by scaling distances on the Official Zoning Map. Where interpretation is needed as to the exact location of the district boundaries due to ambiguity or discrepancy between mapped boundaries and field conditions, the Zoning Administrator shall determine the exact location through field investigation to apply the wetland definition criteria contained in the following section. The Administrator may consult with biologists, hydrologists, soil scientists, or other experts as needed in this determination. The person contesting the location of the district boundary may present his case to the Zoning Board of Adjustment and submit his own technical evidence, if dissatisfied with the determination of the Zoning Administrator.

Section 3: Definitions

Words or phrases used in this ordinance shall be interpreted as defined below, and where ambiguity exists, words or phrases shall be interpreted so as to give this ordinance its most reasonable application in carrying out the regulatory goals:

"Filling" means the placing of any soil, sand, gravel, shells, structures, solid waste, or other material that raises, either temporarily or permanently, the elevation of an area.

"Regulated activity" means any dredging, draining, filling, bulkheading, polluting, mining, drilling, excavating, or engaging in construction of any kind, or in any activity that will kill or materially damage wetland flora or fauna.

"Wetland" means [definition to be provided by the locality.]

Section 4: Permit Requirements, Penalties

Permit Requirements, Compliance

No regulated activity shall be conducted in a Wetland District without a permit from the Zoning Administrator and compliance with the terms of this ordinance and other applicable regulations. All activities that are not permitted as of right or as Special Permit uses shall be prohibited.

Penalties

Any person who commits, takes part in, or assists in any violation of any provision of this ordinance is guilty of a misdemeanor and may be fined not more than _____ dollars for each offense and subject to imprisonment not exceeding _____ months or both. Each violation of this act shall be a separate offense, and, in the case of continuing violation, each day's continuance thereof shall be deemed to be a separate and distinct offense.

The governing body shall have jurisdiction to enjoin a violation or threatened violation of this ordinance. All costs, fees, and expenses in connection with such action shall be assessed as damages against the violator.

In the event of a violation, the governing body shall have the power to order complete restoration of the wetland area involved by the person or agent responsible for the violation.

If such responsible person or agent does not complete such restoration within a reasonable time following the order, the authorized local government shall have the authority to restore the affected wetlands to the prior condition wherever possible and the person or agent responsible for the original violation shall be held liable to the [local unit of government] for the cost of restoration.

Abrogation and Greater Restrictions

It is not intended that this ordinance repeal, abrogate, or impair any existing regulations, easements, covenants, or deed restrictions. However, where this ordinance imposes greater restrictions, the provisions of this ordinance shall prevail.

Interpretation

The provisions of this ordinance shall be held to be minimum requirements in their interpretation and application and shall be liberally construed to serve the goals of the ordinance.

Section 5: Permitted and Special Permit Uses in the Wetland District

Permitted Uses

The following uses shall be permitted as of right within the Wetland District to the extent that they are not prohibited by any other ordinance and provided they do not require structures, grading, filling, draining, or dredging except as authorized by Special Permit:

(1) Agricultural uses such as general farming, pasture, wild crop harvesting, haying;

(2) Outdoor recreational activities, including hunting, birdwatching, hiking, boating, trapping, fishing, horseback riding, swimming, skeet and trap shooting, shooting preserves, and ecotourism;

(3) The taking of shellfish, fish, and wildlife, consistent with the laws of the state of [add state];

(4) Commercial shellfishing and trapping;

(5) Forestry, providing wetland hydrology is not disturbed;

(6) Wildlife preservation and refuges; and

(7) Education and scientific research and nature trails.

In addition, the following structural uses are permitted, providing they do not involve grading, filling, dredging, or draining: catwalks, piers, boathouses, boat shelters, fences, duck blinds, wildlife management shelters, footbridges, observation decks and shelters, and other similar water-related structures, provided that such structures are constructed on piling so as to permit the unobstructed flow of waters and preserve the natural contour of the wetland.

All other uses and activities involving structures, grading, filling, dredging, vegetation removal, and disturbance of wetland water supply and flora and fauna are prohibited except as they may be permitted as special permits and variances.

All uses and activities that were lawful before the passage of this ordinance but which do not conform with the provisions of the ordinance, may be continued but may not be expanded, changed, enlarged, or altered.

Special Permit Uses
Regulated activities other than those specified above may be permitted upon application to the [conservation commission, board of adjustment, etc.] and issuance of a Special Permit.

Section 6: Standards and Procedures for Special Permit Uses

Special Permits
Activities subject to a Special Permit shall not be conducted without prior issuance of such Permit from the [conservation commission, board of adjustment]. Application for a Special Permit shall be made in duplicate to the Zoning Administrator on forms furnished by him or her. Permits shall ordinarily be valid for a period of three years from the date of issue and shall expire at the end of that time unless a longer time period is specified by the [conservation commission, board of adjustment] upon issuance of the permit. An extension of an original permit may be granted upon written request to the Administrator by the original permit holder or his legal agent at least 90 days before the expiration date of the original permit. The request for renewal of a permit shall follow the same form and procedure as the original application except that the [conservation commission, board of adjustment] shall have the option of not holding a hearing if the original intent of the permit is not altered or extended in any significant way. The [conservation commission, board of adjustment] may require new hearings if, in its judgment, the original intent of the permit is altered or extended by the renewal, or if the applicant has failed to abide by the terms of the original permit in any way.

Permit Applications
Unless the [conservation commission, board of adjustment] waives one or more of the following information requirements, applications for a permit shall include:

(1) A description of the entire parcel of land owned by the applicant and the location of the wetland on the parcel;

(2) The purposes of the project and an explanation why the proposed activity cannot be located at other sites, including an explanation of how the proposed activity is dependent upon wetlands or water-related resources;

(3) A site plan for the proposed activity, including a rough map at a scale of 1 inch equals 50 feet showing the location, width, depth, and length of all existing and proposed structures, roads, sewage treatment, and installation facilities, drainage facilities, utility installations within 200 feet of the proposed activity;

(4) The boundaries of the wetland or wetlands which may be affected by the proposed activity;

(5) The sites and specifications for all proposed draining, filling, grading, dredging, and vegetation removal that may affect the wetland or wetlands, including the amount and procedures;

(6) Elevations of the site and adjacent lands within 200 feet of the site at contour intervals of no greater than .5 feet;

(7) A general description of the vegetative cover of the regulated area; and

(8) A description of measures that will be taken to reduce the impact of the proposed activity on the wetland or wetlands and measures proposed to compensate for any loss of wetland functions and values on acreage.

The [conservation commission, board of adjustment] may require additional information as needed, such as study of flood, erosion, or other hazards at the site and the effect of any protective measures that might be taken to reduce such hazards; and other information deemed necessary to evaluate the proposed use in terms of the goals and standards of this act.

Upon receipt of the completed application, the [conservation commission, board of adjustment] shall notify the individuals and agencies, including federal and state agencies having jurisdiction over or an interest in the subject matter, to provide such individuals and agencies with an opportunity to raise objections.

The [conservation commission, board of adjustment] shall establish a mailing list of all interested persons and agencies who wish to be notified of such applications.

Public Hearing
No sooner than 30 days and not later than 60 days after receipt of the permit application and after notice of the application has been published by the applicant in one newspaper having general circulation in the area, the [conservation commission, board of adjustment] may hold a public hearing on the application unless the [conservation commission, board of adjustment] finds that the activity is so minor as not to affect the wetland functions and values or acreage or have impact upon adjacent properties or the public at large.

All hearings shall be open to the public. A record of the hearing shall be made.

Any party may present evidence and testimony at the hearing. At the hearing, the applicant shall have the burden of demonstrating that the proposed activity will be in accord with the goals and policies of this ordinance and the standards set forth below.

Standards for Special Permits
The [conservation commission, board of adjustment] shall evaluate applications for Special Permits consistent with the following considerations and standards:

(1) The goals and purposes of the ordinance;

(2) The impact of the proposed activity and reasonably anticipated similar activities upon flood flows, flood storage, storm barriers, and water quality;

(3) Threats to the proposed activity from flooding, erosion, hurricane winds, soil limitations, and other hazards and possible losses to the applicant and subsequent purchasers of the land;

(4) The impact of the use and existing and reasonably anticipated similar uses upon neighboring land uses;

(5) The adequacy of water supply and waste disposal for the proposed activity;

(6) Consistency with federal, state, county, and local comprehensive land use plans and regulations;

(7) Alternatives to the proposed activity and alternative sites for the activity on the applicant's properties or other properties;

(8) Whether all reasonable and practical measures have been taken to minimize the impacts of the activities;

(9) The impact of the activity upon wetland functions and values and acreage set forth in the purpose of this ordinance, including the impact of the activity upon the:

(a) infilling of the wetland or other modification of natural topographic contours;

(b) disturbance or destruction of natural flora and fauna;

(c) influx of sediments or other materials causing increased water turbidity;

(d) removal or disturbance of wetland soils;

(e) reductions in wetland water supply;

(f) interference with wetland water circulation;

(g) damaging reduction or increases in wetland nutrients;

(h) influx of toxic chemicals;

(i) damaging thermal changes in the wetland water supply; and

(j) destruction of natural aesthetic values;

(10) Economic impact on applicant and whether economic uses are possible for the applicant's property.

Preference will be given to activities that must have a shoreline or wetland location in order to function and that will have as little impact as possible upon the wetland area. The regulated activity must, to the extent feasible, be confined to the portion of a lot outside of a wetland. All reasonable measures must be taken to minimize impact upon the wetland.

The [conservation commission, board of adjustment] shall deny a permit if the proposed activity may threaten public health and safety, result in fraud, cause nuisances, impair public rights to the enjoyment and use of public waters, threaten a rare or endangered plant or animal species, violate pollution control standards, or violate other federal, state, or local regulations. In determining the impact of the activity upon public health and safety, rare and endangered species, water quality and additional wetland functions listed in the purposes of this ordinance and below, the [conservation commission, board of adjustment] shall consider existing wetland destruction and the cumulative effect of reasonably anticipated future uses similar to the one proposed.

In evaluating the proposed activity, the [conservation commission, board of adjustment] may consult with expert persons or agencies.

Acting on the Application
The [conservation commission, board of adjustment] shall act on the application within [30 days, etc.] of the public hearing, except that where additional information is required by the [conservation commission, board of adjustment], it may extend this period by [15 days, etc.]. In acting on the application, the [conservation commission, board of adjustment] shall in writing deny, permit, or conditionally permit the proposed activity.

Conditions Attached to Special Permits
The [conservation commission, board of adjustment] may attach such conditions to the granting of a Special Use Permit or Variance as it deems necessary to carry out the purposes of the ordinance including, but not limited to, the prevention of all nuisances and the achievement of no net loss of wetland functions and values and net wetland acreage. Such conditions may include but shall not be limited to:

(1) Compensation for loss of wetland functions and values and acreage through on-site or off-site wetland restoration, creation, or enhancement;

(2) Limitations on minimum lot size for any activity;

(3) Limitation on the total portion of any lot or the portion of the wetland on the lot that may be graded, filled, or otherwise modified. This limitation may

be linked to an overall protection policy for the particular wetland (e.g., no more than 5 percent filling for this and all future development);

(4) Setbacks for structures, fill, deposit of spoil, and other activities from the wetlands;

(5) Requirements that structures be elevated on piles or otherwise protected against natural hazards;

(6) Modification of waste disposal and water supply facilities;

(7) Imposition of operational controls, sureties, and deed restrictions concerning future use and subdivision of lands, such as flood warnings, preservation of undeveloped areas in open space use, and limitation of vegetation removal;

(8) Erosion control measures;

(9) Modifications in project design to ensure continued water supply to the wetland and circulation of waters; and/or

(10) Restoration, enhancement, or creation of wetland areas to compensate for lost functions and values or acreage.

The [conservation commission, board of adjustment] may suspend or revoke a permit if it finds that the applicant has not complied with the conditions or limitations set forth in the permit, or has exceeded the scope of the work set forth in the application. The [conservation commission, board of adjustment] shall cause notice of its denial, issuance, conditional issuance, revocation, or suspension of a permit to be published in a daily newspaper having a broad circulation in the area wherein the wetland lies.

The [conservation commission, board of adjustment] may require a bond in an amount and with surety and conditions sufficient to secure compliance with the conditions and limitations set forth in the permit. The particular amount and the conditions of the bond shall be consistent with the purposes of this ordinance. In the event of a breach of any condition of any such bond, the [conservation commission, board of adjustment] may institute an action in [Superior Court, etc.] upon such bond and prosecute the same to judgment and execution.

Section 7: Restoration, Enhancement, or Creation of Wetland Areas to Compensate for Loss of Wetland Functions and Values or Acreage
The [conservation commission, board of adjustment] may require the restoration, enhancement, or creation of wetland areas to compensate for loss of wetland functions and values subject to the following conditions:

(1) Ordinarily restoration, enhancement, or creation may be allowed to compensate for damage or destruction only after the permit applicant has demonstrated that activity cannot be located on upland sites and that all practical measures have been undertaken to reduce impacts;

(2) On-site and in-kind restoration shall be preferred;

(3) Where on-site and in-kind compensation for all functions and values and acreage is not possible, compensation for as many functions and values and as much acreage as possible should be provided on-site;

(4) Restoration, enhancement, or creation shall not be allowed if it will result in on-site flooding or other problems at other properties at the original wetland site;

(5) Restoration shall be preferred over enhancement and creation;

(6) The restored, enhanced, or created wetland shall be designed to reproduce natural hydrology and to produce a functioning system over time;

(7) Acreage ratios for restoration, enhancement, or creation shall reflect the time it will take to become fully functioning, the risk of failure of the project in reproducing functions and values, and other factors;

(8) The project applicant shall provide maintenance of the restored, enhanced, or created wetland to ensure long-term functioning of the wetland.

Section 8: Non-conforming Activities

A regulated activity that was lawful before the passage of the ordinance but which is not in conformity with the provisions of this ordinance may be continued subject to the following:

(1) No such activity shall be expanded, changed, enlarged, or altered in a way that increases its nonconformity without a Special Permit;

(2) No structural alteration or addition to any nonconforming structure over the life of the structure shall exceed 50 percent of its value at the time of its becoming a non-conforming activity unless the structure is permanently changed to a conforming use;

(3) If a non-conforming activity is discontinued for 12 consecutive months, any resumption of the activity shall conform to this ordinance;

(4) If any non-conforming use or activity is destroyed by man's activities or an act of God, it shall not be resumed except in conformity with the provisions of this ordinance; and

(5) Activities or adjuncts thereof that are or become nuisances shall not be entitled to continue as nonconforming activities.

Section 9: Judicial Review

Any decision of the [conservation commission, board of adjustment] denying, approving, or conditionally approving a Special Permit shall be judicially reviewable in the [Superior Court, etc.]. The applicant, his agent, adjacent landowners, any agency, and any member of the public may challenge the decision of the [conservation commission, board of adjustment] as being unconstitutional or inconsistent with the goals and standards of this ordinance.

Based upon these proceedings and a decision of the court, the [conservation commission, board of adjustment] may, within the time specified by the court, elect to:

(1) Institute negotiated purchase or condemnation proceedings to acquire an easement or fee interest in applicant's land; or

(2) Approve the permit application with lesser restrictions or conditions.

Section 10: Amendments

These regulations and the official wetland map may from time to time be amended in accordance with procedures and requirements of the general statutes and as new information concerning soils, hydrology, flooding, or botanical species peculiar to wetlands become available.

Any person may submit in writing in a form prescribed by the [conservation commission, board of adjustment] a request for a change in the regulations or the boundaries of a wetland area. The request shall be considered at a public hearing held in accordance with the provisions of the general statutes not less than 90 days after receipt of the written request unless winter conditions prevent investigation of wetland areas. If winter conditions make such investigation impossible, such public hearing shall be held not later than 180 days after receipt of the written application.

Section 11: Tax Assessment Relief

Assessors and boards of assessors shall consider wetland regulations in determining the fair market value of land. Any owner of an undeveloped wetland who has dedicated an easement or entered into a perpetual conservation restriction with [conservation commission, board of adjustment] or a nonprofit organization to permanently control some or all regulated activities in the wetland shall be assessed consistent with those restrictions. Such landowner shall also be exempted from special assessment on the controlled wetland to defray the cost of municipal improvements such as sanitary sewers, storm sewers, and water mains.

Educational Materials on Wetlands: Some Sources

EPA Wetlands Hotline
800/832-7828
(Offers an Information Resource Guide with hundreds of sources, educational materials, and ordering information. A good place to start your search for materials.)

Adirondack Park Visitor Interpretive
Center/Adirondack Teacher Center
P.O. Box 3000, Paul Smiths, NY 12970.
Phone: 518/327-3000 or 518/327-5012
(Wetlands environmental curriculum for middle school children)

Bullfrog Films, Inc.
P.O. Box 149, Oley, PA 19547.
Phone: 610/779-8226
(Videos on estuaries, "the wasting of a wetland," and natural wastewater treatment)

Centers for Nature Education
P.O. Box 133, Marcellus, NY 13108.
Phone: 315/673-1350
(A curriculum guide for wetland education, grades K–8)

Ducks Unlimited
One Waterfowl Way, Memphis, TN 38120.
Phone: 901/758-3825
(Puddler Magazine for children)

Educational Images, Ltd.
P.O. Box 3456, West Side Station,
Elmira, NY 14905. Phone: 607/732-1090
(Videos including "Salt Marshes," "Freshwater and Salt Marsh," "Bog Ecology," and "Florida Bay and the Everglades," film strips, slides, cd-rom)

Elkhorn Slough National Estuarine
Research Reserve
1700 Elkhorn Rd., Watsonville, CA 95076.
Phone: 408/728-2822
(Environmental education curriculum manual)

Environmental Concern
P.O. Box P, St. Michaels, MD 21663.
Phone: 410/745-9620
(Activity guide and restoration/action guide called WOW — the Wonder of Wetlands)

Environmental Media Center
P.O. Box 1016, Chapel Hill, NC 27514.
Phone: 800/368-3382
(A World in Our Backyard: A Wetlands Education and Stewardship Program, wetland videos)

Izaak Walton League of America
707 Conservation Lane, Gaithersburg, MD 20878.
Phone: 301/548-0150
(Wetlands kit includes fact sheets, publications list, activities, and a poster)

National Audubon Society
325 Route 4, Sharon, CT 06069.
Phone: 860/364-0520
(Information guide, booklets, and posters on rivers, salt marshes, and freshwater marshes)

National Geographic Society
Educational Services, P.O. Box 98019,
Washington, DC 20090. Phone: 800/368-2728
(Videos on swamp and tidal flat ecosystems)

National Institute for Urban Wildlife
P.O. Box 3015, Shepards Town, WV 25443.
Phone: 304/876-6146
(Teacher's materials on estuaries and tidal marshes, freshwater marshes, and wetlands conservation and use, poster on wetlands)

National Project WET
201 Culbertson Hall, Montana State University,
Bozeman, MT 59717-0570.
Phone: 406/994- 5392
(Project WET: A Curriculum and Activity Guide)

National Science Teachers Association
1840 Wilson Blvd., Arlington, VA 22201.
Phone: 800/722-6782 or 703/243-7100
(Board game on energy flow in a wetland, posters on wetlands and "who lives in mud")

National Wildlife Federation
1400 16th St., NW, Washington, DC 20036.
Phone: 202/797-6800
(The Ranger Rick Naturescope Environmental Education Series contains a wetlands unit for preschool to grade 7)

Padilla Bay National Estuarine Research Reserve
1043 Bay View — Edison Road, Mt.
Vernon, WA 98273-9605. Phone: 360/428-1558
(Estuary guide for three levels: K–3, 4–8, 9–12)

San Francisco Bay National Wildlife Refuge
P.O. Box 524, Newark, CA 94560-0524.
Phone: 510/792-0222
(Salt Marsh Manual: An Educator's Guide)

South Carolina Sea Grant Consortium
287 Meeting St., Charleston, SC 29401.
Phone: 803/727-2078
(Sea Sampler: Aquatic Activities for Field and Classroom for elementary and secondary students)

Terrene Institute
4 Herbert St., Alexandria, VA 22305.
Phone: 703/548-5473
(Posters, buttons, stickers, guides, models, and games on wetlands)

U.S. Fish and Wildlife Service
Publications Unit, 1849 C St., NW, Room 130
WEBB, Washington, DC 20240. 703/358-1711
OR: Superintendent of Documents, Government
Printing Office, Washington, DC 20402.
202/512-1800
(Teacher's Kit, including posters, worksheets and more)

University of Maryland
Sea Grant Program, 0112 Skinner Hall,
College Park, MD 20742. Phone: 301/405-6371
(Marine science education workbooks, curriculum/activity materials on decision making and the Chesapeake Bay)

University of New Hampshire
Sea Grant College Program, Kingman Farm,
Durham, NH 03824-3512. Phone: 603/749-1565
(Curriculum/activity materials on coastal issues)

Washington State Department of Ecology
Cashier's Office, P.O. Box 5128,
Lacey, WA 98509-5128. Phone: 360/407-7472
(Curriculum/activity materials entitled "Discover Wetlands," posters and videos)

The Wetlands Institute
1075 Stone Harbor Boulevard,
Stone Harbor, NJ 08247. Phone: 609/368-1211.
(Coastal activity book and teacher's guide, grades 3–4 and 5–6)

APPENDIX F

Selected Bibliography

Association of State Wetland Managers, *Guidebook for Creating Wetland Interpretation Sites Including Wetlands and Ecotourism* (1994).

Association of State Wetland Managers, *National Symposium: Improving Wetland Public Outreach, Training, Education, and Interpretation* (1994).

Association of State Wetland Managers, *State Wetland Regulation: Status of Programs and Emerging Trends* (1994).

The Conservation Foundation, *Protecting America's Wetlands: An Action Agenda* (1988).

L. Cowardin et al., *Classification of Wetlands and Deepwater Habitats of the United States* (U.S. Fish and Wildlife Service, 1979). FWS/OBS-79-31.

T. Dahl, *Wetlands Losses in the United States 1780s to 1980s* (U.S. Fish and Wildlife Service, 1990).

P. Dugan, *Wetlands in Danger: A World Conservation Atlas* (Oxford University Press, 1993).

Environmental Concern, *WOW — the Wonder of Wetlands* (1995).

Environmental Law Institute, *Wetland Mitigation Banking* (1993).

J. Goldman-Carter, *A Citizens' Guide to Protecting Wetlands* (National Wildlife Federation, 1989).

J. Kusler and M. Kentula (eds.), *Wetland Creation and Restoration: The Status of the Science* (Island Press, 1990).

Land Trust Alliance, *1995 National Directory of Land Trusts* and other Land Trust Alliance publications.

J. Lyons and S. Jordan, *Walking the Wetlands* (John Wiley and Sons, 1989).

W. Mitsch and J. Gosselink, *Wetlands*, second edition (Von Nostrand Reinhold, 1993).

National Research Council, *Restoration of Aquatic Ecosystems* (National Academy Press, 1992).

National Research Council, *Wetlands: Characteristics and Boundaries* (National Academy Press, 1995).

W. Niering, *Wetlands: The Audubon Society Nature Guides* (Alfred A. Knopf, 1985).

W. Niering, *Wetlands of North America* (Thomasson-Grant, 1991).

M. Strand, *Wetlands Deskbook* (Environmental Law Institute, 1996).

U.S. Environmental Protection Agency, *Wetland Fact Sheets* (Office of Wetlands, Oceans, and Watersheds, 1995). EPA 843-F-95-x001.

U.S. Fish and Wildlife Service, National Wetlands Inventory maps on cd–rom (updates ongoing).

S. Wilson and T. Moritz, *The Sierra Club Wetlands Reader* (Sierra Club Books, 1996).

World Wildlife Fund, *Statewide Wetland Strategies: A Guide to Protecting and Managing the Resource* (Island Press, 1992).

Glossary

Adjacent wetlands: Wetlands that border, are contiguous to, or neighbor another body of water and have a hydrological connection to that body of water.

Alluvium: Alluvium, or alluvial soil, is soil composed primarily of eroded material, such as sand, silt, or clay, that has been deposited on land or on the bottom of water bodies by rivers and streams overflowing their banks. For example, an alluvial river swamp is a depressional area along the floodplain of a river or creek that is continuously or almost continuously flooded.

Bedrock: The solid rock that underlies loose material such as soil, sand, clay, or gravel.

Biochemical Oxygen Demand (BOD): The demand for dissolved oxygen needed for decomposition of organic matter in water. If the amount of oxygen dissolved in water is high and the organic matter present is low, the BOD is low, and vice versa.

Brackish: The mixture of fresh water and saltwater typically found in estuarine waters.

Breakwater: A structure, usually constructed of rock or concrete, to protect a shore area, harbor, or basin from waves.

Buffer: An area adjacent to a river, stream, wetland, or other water body that serves to lessen the impact of wave action, storms, floods, the input of excessive nutrients, or other impacts.

Conservation easement: A legal agreement between a landowner and a conservation organization or government agency, whereby the landowner retains title to the property but agrees to refrain from certain activities, or to allow the holder of the easement to perform acts on the property. The holder of the easement gains the right to seek enforcement of the agreement.

Covenant: A contract between a landowner and another party stating that the landowner will use or refrain from using his or her land in an agreed-upon manner.

Cumulative impact: The sum total of the impacts caused by separate activities.

Deed restriction: A legal mechanism by which a private landowner inserts clauses in a property deed that restrict the future use of the land.

Delineation: Determination of the boundaries of a wetland.

Dike: A bank or structure (usually earthen) constructed to control or confine water.

Drainage: The act of reducing or eliminating water from an area by artificial means, such as pumping or constructing a ditch or channel, that facilitates the movement of water away from a specific area or lowers groundwater or surface water levels.

Easement: See "Conservation easement."

Emergent vegetation: Rooted herbaceous plants that are temporarily or permanently submerged in water and have parts extending above the water surface.

Enhancement: To alter an existing wetland to add, or increase, particular wetland values and functions to levels not present under previous conditions.

Environmental impact statement (EIS): Written reports prepared to assess the environmental impacts of and alternatives to actions that may significantly affect the environment. The EIS is required by the National Environmental Policy Act.

Estuary: A tidal habitat that is semi-enclosed by land but has open, partially obstructed, or sporadic access to the ocean and in which ocean water is at least occasionally mixed with freshwater runoff from the land.

Fen: A peat-accumulating wetland that receives some drainage from surrounding mineral soil and usually supports marshlike vegetation.

Fill material: In a wetland context, the term "fill material" refers to material used for the primary purpose of replacing a wetland or aquatic area with dry land or of changing the bottom elevation of a waterbody.

Floodplain: That portion of the land bordering a river, stream, lake, or ocean that is periodically inundated with floodwater.

Floodway: That portion of the flood-prone zone along a river or stream that is needed to convey a 100-year flood with only a specified (usually one foot) rise of water level above the height of the unconstricted flood.

Functions: Normal or characteristic natural processes that take place in wetland ecosystems, or simply the things that wetlands do. Some examples: surface water storage, cycling of elements, maintenance of plant communities.

General permit: A permit issued by the U.S. Army Corps of Engineers, pursuant to the Section 404 program, on a regional basis for categories of activities that are substantially similar in nature, are deemed to cause only minimal adverse environmental effects when performed separately, and are deemed to have only minimal cumulative adverse effects on the environment.

Glacial moraine: See "Moraine."

Gradient: A rate of inclination; a slope.

Grading: The act of leveling or smoothing to a desired horizontal gradient.

Groin: A shore protection structure usually built perpendicular to the shoreline to trap sand and other material moving along the shoreline, thus retarding erosion of the shore.

Groundwater: Water that normally is located below the ground surface.

Growing season: The portion of the year when the soil temperature at 19.7 inches below the soil surface is higher than biological zero (5 degrees C). For ease of determination, the U.S. Department of Interior has stated that this period can be approximated by the number of frost-free days.

Headwaters: For regulatory (Section 404) purposes, the point on a non-tidal stream above which the average annual flow is less than five cubic feet per second.

Hydric soil: A soil that is saturated, flooded, or ponded long enough during the growing season to develop anaerobic conditions that favor the growth and regeneration of hydrophytic vegetation.

Hydrologic regime: The sum total of water that occurs in an area on average during a given period.

Hydrology: The science dealing with the properties, distribution, and circulation of water.

Hydrophyte: Any plant growing in water or on a substrate that is at least periodically deficient in oxygen as a result of excessive water; plants typically found in wetland habitats.

Hydrophytic vegetation: The sum total of macrophytic plant life growing in water or on a substrate that is at least periodically deficient in oxygen as a result of excessive water content.

Inundation: A condition in which water from any source temporarily or permanently covers a land surface.

Kettlehole wetland: A wetland formed in depressions left by the melting of blocks of glacial ice that remained after a glacier receded.

Lacustrine: Often used to describe wetlands in or adjacent to lakes or ponds.

Land trust: Land trusts are usually local, state, or regional nonprofit organizations that are involved in conserving land. Land trusts generally focus their efforts on protecting specific natural, historic, scenic, or recreational features in a specific state or geographic region, such as a watershed.

Levee: A natural or man-made feature of the landscape that restricts movement of water into or through an area, usually floodwaters.

Littoral zone: The shoreward zone of a lake or wetland. The area where water is shallow enough to allow the dominance of emergent vegetation.

Marsh: A frequently or continually inundated wetland characterized by emergent herbaceous vegetation adapted to saturated soil conditions.

Mineral soil: Soils low in organic matter, commonly containing less than 20 percent organic matter. Mineral soils usually have a soil profile made up of distinct horizons, or layers.

Minimize: To limit impacts by limiting the degree or magnitude of the activity affecting wetlands.

Mitigation: Mitigation includes avoiding impacts, minimizing impacts, rectifying impacts, reducing impacts over time, and compensating for impacts. Compensatory mitigation covers creation, restoration, or enhancement of adverse impacts to wetlands.

Mitigation banking: An off-site wetland area used to mitigate for a number of independent wetland development conversions. Under mitigation banking, a developer need not produce the compensatory wetland values but instead can purchase them from another entity that has produced and banked them for this purpose.

Moraine: A landform comprised of debris deposited by glaciers.

Nationwide permit: Pursuant to the Section 404 program, general permits promulgated by the U.S. Army Corps of Engineers headquarters for nationwide application for categories of activities that are substantially similar in nature, have been deemed to cause only minimal adverse environmental effects when performed separately, and have been deemed to have only minimal cumulative adverse effects on the environment.

Niche (ecological): The resources utilized and required by each plant or animal species within a biological community.

Nonpoint source pollution: A diffuse form of pollution that is carried to waterbodies, particularly during rain events. Nonpoint source pollution is typically associated with land use activities such as agriculture, construction, and forestry.

100-year flood: A flood with a 1 percent probability of occurrence in any year. A way of expressing flood magnitudes according to their estimated return interval.

Organic soil: Soils whose properties are dominated by organic materials; commonly contain more than 50 percent organic matter by volume and at least 20 percent by weight.

Outwash: Sediment deposited by streams flowing away from a melting glacier.

Overlays: Overlays are zones that are a type of resource protection zoning superimposed on traditional zoning to protect certain values, while still allowing some form of the underlying use. Overlay zones may also include set-aside requirements specifying, for example, the percentage of land that must be set aside before calculating the subdividable and developable remainder.

Peat: An organic soil composed primarily of the remains of plants in various stages of decomposition that accumulates in wetlands as a result of anaerobic conditions created by standing water or poorly drained conditions.

Performance standards: Standards that are written into zoning ordinances that identify the performance criteria that must be met by any development in the zone.

Periodicity: Used to define detectable regular or irregular saturated soil conditions or inundation, resulting from ponding of groundwater, precipitation, overland flow, stream flooding, or tidal influences that occur(s) with hours, days, weeks, months, or even years between events.

Playa: Term used in the southwestern United States for marsh-like ponds similar to potholes.

Pothole: Shallow, marsh-like pond or depressional wetland, particularly as found in the Dakotas and central Canadian provinces.

Practicable: Available and capable of being done after taking into consideration cost, existing technology, and logistics in light of overall project purposes.

Prior converted wetland: Wetlands that were drained, dredged, filled, leveled, or otherwise manipulated, including the removal of woody vegetation, before December 23, 1985, to make production of an agricultural commodity possible, and an agricultural commodity was planted or produced at least once before December 23, 1985.

Programmatic permit: Pursuant to the Section 404 program, general permits based on an existing state, tribal, local, or federal agency program other than the Section 404 program where the major objective is to maintain environmental protection and to avoid duplication.

Regulatory guidance letter: Regulatory guidance letters (RGLs) are letters issued by the Office of the Chief of Engineers. They provide guidance to the U.S. Army Corps of Engineers' District and Division Offices on policy issues relating to permitting programs. RGLs are not regulations; they are used only as a means of interpreting or clarifying current regulations or policy.

Restoration: An activity returning a wetland from a disturbed or altered condition to a previous condition.

Riparian zones or wetlands: Vegetated corridors or wetlands along rivers or streams that are occasionally flooded by those bodies of water but which are otherwise dry for varying portions of the growing season.

Riverine wetland: Wetlands found in the floodplains of rivers. Riverine marshes often border the forests or occupy pockets within them, sometimes in abandoned oxbows.

Saturated: Saturated soil conditions exist when all easily drained voids (pores) between soil particles in the root zone are temporarily or permanently filled with water to the soil surface at pressures greater than atmospheric.

Seawalls: An embankment to prevent erosion of a shoreline.

Sedimentation: The process of nutrients and sediments entering waterbodies and wetlands.

Seeps: A wetland often found at the base of steep slopes where the groundwater surface intersects with the land surface; a spring.

Seich: A wave that oscillates in lakes, bays, or gulfs from a few minutes to a few hours as a result of seismic or atmospheric disturbances.

Shrub: Woody vegetation less than 3.0 inches in diameter but greater than 3.2 feet in height. Includes multi-stemmed, bushy shrubs and small trees and saplings.

Spring: A wetland often found at the base of steep slopes where the groundwater surface intersects with the land surface; a seep.

Subsidence: To sink or settle. Land can subside when groundwater withdrawals exceed replenishment rates and water no longer exists under the subsurface to support the soil above or when tectonic plates shift due to differential deposition of sediment.

Substrate: The base or substance on which species can grow.

Swamp: A wetland dominated by trees or shrubs.

"Takings:" The unconstitutional denial of an individual's right to use his or her property. Refers to the Fifth Amendment to the U.S. Constitution and similar provisions in other constitutions, which prohibit governments from "taking" private property for public use unless they pay just compensation.

Tectonic: Relating to, causing, or resulting from structural deformation of the earth's crust.

Tidal waters: Ocean or sea waters whose levels periodically fluctuate due to the action of lunar and solar forces upon the rotating earth. These waters also are characterized by salinity.

Till: Glacial debris made up of an unconsolidated mixture of clay, sand, pebbles, cobbles, and boulders.

Topography: The configuration of a surface, including its relief and the position of its natural and man-made features.

Transferable development rights: The transfer of development rights from one parcel to another pursuant to state or local legislation. Transferable development rights allow the holder to develop the property to which the rights are transferred more intensively than the local zoning would otherwise allow.

Upland: Any area that does not qualify as a wetland because the associated hydrologic regime is not sufficiently wet to permit the development of vegetation, soils, and/or hydrologic characteristics associated with wetlands.

Values: Those aspects of wetlands that are deemed worthy, desirable, or useful to humans. Wetland values emanate from their functions. Perceived wetland values arise from their functional ecological process but are determined by human perceptions, the location of a particular wetland, the human population pressures on it, and the extent of the resource. See also "Functions."

Velocity: Velocity is the rate at which water flows. It is expressed as distance per unit of time (meters per second).

Vernal pool: Shallow, intermittently flooded wet meadow, generally dry for most of the summer and fall.

Water regime: See "Hydrologic regime."

Watershed: The region drained by or contributing water to a stream, lake, or other body of water.

About the Authors

Jon Kusler is the director of a consulting firm and the Executive Director of the Association of State Wetland Managers. He has a law degree, a Master's degree in water resources management, and an interdisciplinary Ph.D. in land and water management from the University of Wisconsin. Jon has worked with wetland, floodplain, lake, and other water management issues for more than 30 years. He was a co-founder of the Association of State Floodplain Managers, a co-founder of the Association of State Wetland Managers, an advisor to the National Wetland Policy Forum, and a member of the National Research Council's board concerning the restoration of aquatic ecosystems. The recipient of the Gilbert White Award in Floodplain Management and the Environmental Law Institute/U.S. Environmental Protection Agency Lifetime Achievement Award in Wetland Protection, Jon has authored more than 70 books, reports, and articles concerning wetlands and floodplain and sensitive lands management. He lives in the foothills of the Catskill Mountains in New York with his wife and two children.

Teresa Opheim is the Editor of the *National Wetlands Newsletter*, published by the Environmental Law Institute in Washington, D.C. She has journalism and law degrees from the University of Iowa. She has served as Senior Editor for *The Environmental Forum*, published by the Environmental Law Institute, and as an editor for the *EPA Journal, Investor's Environmental Report*, and other consumer and alumni magazines. She has written articles for several national publications, including *Country Living*, the *Utne Reader*, and *E* Magazine. Teresa lives in central Iowa with her husband and child.

Appendix I

The Environmental Law Institute

For a quarter century, the Environmental Law Institute has played a pivotal role in shaping the fields of environmental law, policy, and management, domestically and abroad. Today, ELI is an internationally recognized, independent research and education center.

Through its information services, training courses and seminars, research programs, and policy recommendations, the Institute activates a broad constituency of environmental professionals in government, industry, the private bar, public interest groups, and academia. Central to ELI's mission is convening this diverse constituency to work cooperatively in developing effective solutions to pressing environmental problems.

The Institute is governed by a board of directors who represent a balanced mix of leaders within the environmental profession. Support for the Institute comes from individuals, foundations, government, corporations, law firms, and other sources.

Environmental Law Institute®
1616 P St., NW, Suite 200
Washington, DC 20036
Telephone: 202/939-3800
Fax: 202/939-3868
E–mail: law@eli.org
Visit our Web site:www.eli.org